Carola Grindea was Piano Professor at the Guildhall School of Music and Drama from 1968-1990 where she started her research into the physical and psychological problems of musicians. In 1978 she founded the European Piano Teachers' Association and in 1980 launched the *Piano Journal*, from which these interviews are taken. Her research led to the founding of the International Society for the Study of Tension in Performance, whose journal she edits, and she is a director of the ISSTIP International Institute of Performing Arts Medicine and of the UK Performing Arts Clinic at LCMM. Her books and videos on piano teaching and music education are distributed worldwide.

For her pioneering work in the field of music education and music medicine she was awarded the Fellowship of the Guildhall School Of Music And Drama, and she was a finalist in the 2001 European Women of Achievement Award. In 2004 she was awarded the Romanian Order of Cultural Merit.

Great Pianists
and Pedagogues
in conversation with
Carola Grindea

Kahn & Averill
London

ACKNOWLEDGEMENTS

I want to express my gratitiude to Manus Carey for having patiently read all the interviews and the introduction and for his valuable suggestions; and to Simon Stern for being such a perfectionist in his setting of the text.

First published in 2007 by
Kahn & Averill
9 Harrington Road, London SW17 3ES.

British Library Cataloguing in Publication Data
A catalogue record for this book is available from the British Library.

ISBN [13] 978-187108287-6

Book design by Simon Stern
Printed in Great Britain by
Halstan & Co Ltd, Amersham, Bucks.

Contents

Introduction

These interviews with the great pianists of our time appeared originally in the *Piano Journal* published by EPTA (the European Piano Teachers
Association) in the series *Who's Who of Great Pianists*, and were conducted throughout the 1980s and 1990s. Founded in 1980 and still going
strong today, *Piano Journal* has a strong pedagogical slant, intended as it is
for a readership made up largely of piano teachers and other musicians,
mostly EPTA members eager to learn more about their profession. The
interviewed pianists provide fascinating and often illuminating comments about their experiences of the teaching profession, initially as
students themselves, and, later, as teachers for the next up-and-coming
generation. This method of verbally handing down musical ideas and
traditions from generation to generation of piano pedagogues is central
to the world of piano performance, and many of these ideas might have
been lost were it not for their preservation within the various texts on
keyboard teaching and performance published over the past few centuries. The thoughts expressed in these interviews contain many ideas
worthy of publication, concerning areas such as different pedagogical
and performance styles and attitudes to competitions.

Apart from the pedagogical element, one theme which is prevalent
throughout these interviews is the pianists' discussion of what has become known as the 'peak experience' or 'flow', those indefinable occasions when mind and body are one, and when the music seems to flow
effortlessly through their instrument. These moments, accompanied by
a loss of any fear, inhibition or insecurity, have been described as ones
of the 'highest happiness and fulfilment, when the performer experiences an ecstatic, non-voluntary state of total integration and internal
peace'. (A. Maslow, *Towards a Psychology of Being*, Princeton, N.J. Van
Nostrand, 1962). These can be extraordinary moments, for performer
and audience alike, when the performance is transcended, gaining new
dimensions, and when the performer experiences a magical state of ex-

hilarating lightness of body, totally free of any tension, while his mind remains alert, aware of the music 'flowing' through his whole being into the space around him and beyond.

Since this phenomenon is a subjective experience of a non-voluntary nature which occurs at the height of a performance – be it in music, theatre, dance, sport, or in moments of intense creativity such as writing and painting – it would be difficult to obtain a scientific study unless one uses highly sophisticated devices. At present it can only be studied through a systematic analysis of personal statements or self-assessments. Throughout these interviews, however, it is of interest to note that the description of these experiences and of their state of body and mind at those moments are very similar. There is a feeling of transcendence of the self and an altered perception of space and time. Most comments refer to a 'high level of mental awareness' or mention feelings of being 'not only the re-creator of the composer's intentions but also the creator of my own performance' or being 'aware of the inspiration flowing from within and from without ...' The following are some of these pianists' reactions to the peak experience:

> ...an extraordinary state of consciousness ...aware of being in tune with the universe...I feel like a vehicle through which the outside forces are moving to sustain my desire to serve the music which flows through my whole being towards the expectant audience. (John Lill).

> ... I experience a tremendous awareness...120% awake, ready to undertake any task...Everything seemed so right, the music just flowed and my body was totally in harmony with everything else. This 'body feeling' when performing gives me a familiar sensation that my piano is not only 'my instrument' it is part of my whole being...this affinity creates in me an extra sensation of being safe yet very alert. (Aldo Ciccolini).

> ...Such moments are very mysterious, they are truly spiritual phenomena ...perhaps this is what one calls inspiration, but there is much more to it. I find these experiences so powerful, so intense that I would be even afraid to analyse them ... (Andras Schiff).

> ...When I reach such a state I become even more aware of the space around me and although 'my space' does not expand I have the sensation that it never ends...I have the strange sensation that I am at the piano but I am also somewhere else in the hall, I am everywhere...I hear the sound of the piano going round the hall,

reflecting against the walls and coming back, enveloping me...At such moments I identify myself with the audience which receives my music and we become one single unit. (Aldo Ciccolini)

Most interviewees talk about 'being inspired' by the greatness of the music they were interpreting, 'creating and re-creating it' and, invariably, about the 'uniqueness' and the 'intensity' of those magic moments which stand out in the memory and, sometimes, create an uncanny emotional response only when describing them.

...for me it is the music that matters and if I am involved in the performance with all my being, the music helps me to find the way to achieve this. 'It plays', and it feels as if 'I am no longer playing it' although my mind is very alert and 'I am still in charge of my performance' (Barry Douglas)

...whenever I perform I give so much of my whole being, I feel the music so intensely that afterwards I am utterly drained, yet I emerge exhilarated from and by such an experience...(Moura Lympany)

...only the music and its challenge matter, demanding complete subservience of the player to the composer's intentions and to the spirit of the work...when I play I experience a wonderful sensation as if the music is 'sounding through my whole being', with no barriers and is communicated to the audience...(Edith Picht-Axenfeld)

When asked whether these experiences brought happiness and satisfaction or were disturbing and whether the players would like these to be part of every performance, the answers varied. Many spoke of the unforgettable state of utter fulfilment, a total integration of the being, with their instrument and the music. Some experienced inner peace, others immense joy and excitement, yet each one pointed out the transient nature of the experience, not knowing when and why it was happening, nor when it vanished. Only two artists admitted that, although they found these experiences enriching and very satisfying, they would not want them to occur every time they appear in public.

...I would not want to feel that the moment I start playing, the magic moment will be there. I like to know that I am responsible for what I intend to do and what I am doing...(Andras Schiff)

...I never understood how and when this happens and I do not wish to go through such experience every time I appear in public...I want to know that I am in full control, that I take my decisions as to the different sounds I intend to choose for every piece I perform...I detach myself emotionally and I am immersed only in the aural experience. The aural sensations are very much part of my music making, so much so, that I sometimes find myself being carried away from my 'homework', and hearing myself playing as I did not intend...(Aldo Ciccolini)

One pianist who has plenty to say on the subject of 'peak experience', having conducted an in-depth study of it herself, is Nancy Lee-Harper. For her it 'involves a very high state of awareness in which total concentration is present. When performing, we are not only in touch with ourselves but also with an infinite source of energy or life-force. I think that anyone can achieve this experience. It may take a lifetime for one person or it may happen more often than not with another'. Elsewhere she refers to:

...the excitement of the moment and the thrill of communicating with the audience. The Peak Experience (P.E.) far transcends the nervous condition present during performance, even though nerves can destroy everything if we let them. One of the interesting things – and perhaps unique, as there probably have been no cross-cultural studies done on this subject so far – is that P.E. is not exclusive to any race or culture. There are no boundaries, no borders. It is part of the human experience. Having interviewed Portuguese as well as Brazilian pianists about their experiences while performing, I am led to believe that anyone can experience it. The results were all very similar indeed. I believe P.E. is a birthright common to our human condition in general.

Throughout these interviews there are numerous other references to the 'peak experience' and to the pianists' different approaches to their preparation for performance, in order to allow these moments to come through (further discussion of this state of mind or oneness can be found in my article 'The phenomenon of Peak Experience' in the Piano Journal no.65, 2001).

At the time of publication of the first journal, Louis Kentner was the President of EPTA UK, and it seemed only fitting that he should be the inaugural interviewee. There followed many fascinating conversations with the great names of the piano world at that time, mostly active performers, but also some notable pedagogical figures, including Fanny Waterman and Peter Feuchtwanger. The interviews are presented in chronological order, as they originally took place. Although a few of the older generation have now passed away, many of these pianists are still active today in the concert hall. Some were interviewed at the beginning of their careers and as a result may well have changed direction or, as one might expect, may have changed their views on matters musical, pedagogical or otherwise. Such is the transience of musical performance that ideas are constantly reviewed and renewed!

CAROLA GRINDEA
2006

Louis Kentner

The Piano Journal *is now a reality and we wish to inaugurate our series on
'Who's Who among pianists' with a short talk from Louis Kentner, the President
of EPTA UK. We all know Louis Kentner the artist, but our readers will be interested to hear Kentner the teacher, guiding and inspiring the highly gifted children
at the Yehudi Menuhin School.*

I feel very honoured to be President, and must congratulate EPTA for
this laudable initiative in launching the *Piano Journal*, the first publication in Europe to serve our profession.

As to my work as teacher, I find it very difficult to talk about. I don't
think one can really teach anything that is not 'there'. One can only
bring out certain qualities in a student or guide him to reach an understanding of how to approach music, how to learn to listen, and above
all how to be able to express on the keyboard what he hears in his
mind. My main object in teaching is to able to help the pupils to find
what I call some 'short cuts', whether these are of a technical or interpretative nature, so that they will not go through the same traumatic
experiences as I did.

For instance, learning to play a perfect legato is the most difficult
thing in piano playing. Scientists will tell us that legato playing is not
possible on an instrument like the piano, yet we can do it, and even
very beautifully. We succeed in creating the illusion of a perfect legato
only through listening very intently and trying to reproduce that continuity of sounds which we hear in our imagination. With my pupils,
particularly the very young ones, I do not use words to explain how
to do it, I simply demonstrate and make them listen again and again
to what I call a satisfying legato and let them attempt to do it. In this
way they develop their inner hearing, which in turn will influence
the quality of sounds which they produce. To use words would take
too long, and, besides, it is not easy to convey clearly how it is done.

1

Many pedagogues have tried to explain in writing these physiological processes but I have yet to meet the student who has learnt to do a fine legato only from reading a text! In fact we musicians have to listen intently and use our aural faculties all the time, and the sooner the pupil learns how to listen, the faster he will develop. I must say that I believe in demonstrating at lessons as the simplest way to get the pupil to hear and see how most passages are played.

Another point I should like to talk about is the teaching of pedalling as I find that even with advanced players or professional pianists, this aspect of training has been neglected. When I mentioned some 'short cuts' I meant that I help pupils learn when and how to use the pedals by emphasising constant listening to one's playing, and I insist that they should mark the pedalling in their score and adhere to this. We all know how much some wrong pedalling can mar an otherwise good performance.

I am also interested in problems caused by unnecessary tension. I myself have never suffered from it. On the contrary, I can say that I found very early the measure – or balance – between tension and relaxation. Teaching pupils how to achieve this is not always easy or simple, and it takes time and a great deal of concentration. In my book on the piano I give some suggestions, particularly on the importance of the freedom of breathing.

In general, I find my work with the talented children at the Menuhin School interesting and rewarding. They are not only very responsive, but always well prepared by their coaches so that at our 'Open Classes' we can concentrate on achieving the best possible results in our music-making. I hope that I can pass on to them my experiences of a life-long study of music. I feel this very strongly as I, myself, did not have a great piano teacher and had to find solutions to the very many problems I encountered, the hard way. Fortunately, I had a great teacher for composition, Leo Weiner, who could play the piano, but not like a 'pianist'. I worked with him a large part of my piano repertoire and his advice was invaluable. When, at the age of seventeen, I decided that I wanted to study all the Beethoven Sonatas, I learnt one sonata every week. Leo Weiner would listen to me, and to this day I am grateful for the way he revealed Beethoven's ideas to me, approaching them as a composer inside the music. I worked with great tenacity but, in spite of this, I did not succeed in learning them in 32 weeks! But, by the end of the year, I finished op. 111, and this made me very happy.

Murray Perahia

*In a recent interview on BBC television, you said that you did not intend to become
a solo performer, but wanted to be a chamber music player. Was it after winning
the Leeds International Piano Competition that your career took a different turn?*

It is not quite so. There was never a question of a choice. Most of my life
was in music, and I simply could not see myself doing anything else
but being a musician.

I had the fortune to go to Marlboro – the Music Festival founded by
Rudolf Serkin – where I became involved with many outstanding musicians doing chamber music. Afterwards they invited me to play with
them in many concerts all over the United States.

It was my agent's idea that I should try for a European piano competition and that if I could win, this would boost my career in America.
That is how I found myself taking part in the Leeds competition and I
have not looked back ever since.

*We all remember that magical evening when you played the slow movement of
Chopin's E Minor Concerto on the television. Could you tell us something about
your training as a pianist?*

My training was not intended to make a prodigy pianist out of me. My
teacher did not encourage me to give recitals when I was very young,
and I had my first public appearance when I was seventeen. I remember
this concert vividly. I realised then that this was a great challenge, and
that I was an adult taking full responsibility. Until then I had been playing as my teacher wanted me to, but on that evening I played as I really
wanted, and at the time I thought it was a good concert.

Afterwards I decided to take some time off to think about my work
and about the directions it was going to take. Though I had always valued my teachers' ideas, it was only when I got away from him that I

3

started to think clearly about my ideals. Though one never really reaches these ideals and goes on searching, I knew somehow where I had to look. I knew that in interpreting the masterpieces of piano literature, I had to find for myself what a particular work was about and what the composer was trying to say. Every work is in itself first a statement, saying something very subtly. There are ideas which are then developed, there is always a special mood; to catch that from the harmonies, the melodies, from what I think and feel about that particular work, and make it my own – these were the processes I had to go through. It is a continuous search, and what is so wonderful about it is that I have not yet solved all the problems. Each work poses a challenge, and I encounter all kinds of difficulties. I love meeting with difficulties. Sometimes they are of a technical nature, but these do not worry me. My main concern is to hear in my mind what the piece should sound like. I have to work very intently – at times trying to hear the various sounds that the piece evokes, and then I work even harder to transfer those sounds onto the keyboard.

I start with imagining a picture of a sound or of different sounds, and how they relate to each other, emerging from the atmosphere determined by the mood of that work. I am then striving towards getting a conception of it, so that it does not sound fragmented, but appears as a whole. It must make organic sense, and this takes time. I must feel that I am totally living with that piece and then, and only then, the technical problems solve themselves. The playing seems easy, and I am aware of the continuous flow of the music.

I did give, and still give, a great deal of thought to my technique. In fact I spent one summer just going through all Chopin Etudes op.10 in the Cortot edition, doing all the combination of exercises he suggests. They created a lot of tension, but I believe that he purposely puts the pianist under a lot of strain so that in the end he can conquer the difficulties. Or, perhaps I misunderstood him. I have a small hand, and some of the Etudes gave me certain problems. It was particularly the Etude No.3 in A minor, which created a lot of tension in my right hand when stretching the hand to play the chords while playing the chromatic scale with the 3rd, 4th and 5th fingers. But a small hand should not be an excuse for not making the Etude sound the great music which it is.

I also think that Czerny studies are the best preparation for all Beethoven's so-called technical passages and I usually turn to them when I play Beethoven Sonatas or Concertos. After all, he was Beethoven's pupil, and he knew how these should be played. All of us have learnt so much from Mr. Czerny. Take for instance Horowitz. What an interesting and exciting pianist! It is interesting that he does not move one through the warmth of his playing, but more through the tremendous tension which he creates. Though he looks so tense when one watches him, one knows that he is in complete command. He wants a certain quality of sound for each note and he knows how to obtain it.

Another pianist whom I admire is Radu Lupu who, from the point of view of pianistic tension, has the most remarkable technique I've ever known. He seems to achieve the perfect balance between tension and release, and his technique seems to be an organic part of his music making. I do regret that I have never heard Cortot except on records. His playing was what I was searching for. I loved the sound he produced and the atmosphere he created. In a way, Dinu Lipatti, who studied with him, had similar quality but I believe he was a purer artist. One feels that Cortot had a profound influence on his playing, particularly in the conception of the works. For instance, if one compares Lipatti's performance of the Chopin Waltzes with that of Cortot, though in many ways different, they show a certain similarity in their approach.

Of course, we should not judge Lipatti by these records. Everyone knows the tragic events that surrounded his last recordings. There was a short respite in his illness through the treatment with cortisone, and the recording engineers were rushed to Geneva to catch, so to speak, his last breath at the piano. He was working sometimes for five or six hours at a stretch and he was physically exhausted.

You are now one of the finest young pianists of your generation and you have to spend much of your life travelling from one place to another to give concerts. How are you able to cope with such a strenuous existence?

This is a very serious problem. I know for myself that I need to have periods of rest from playing and from travelling. Fortunately, my agents are very understanding, and they arrange my concerts so that I can have some time away from the public. Continuous concertising is not good for me, and I believe it is not good for any artist. There must be times when one needs to stop and think about what one is doing, to study new repertoire or, occasionally, just take a rest. An artist cannot stand still, he must keep on moving to renew his ideas about the works in his repertoire. I could not play the same concerto again and again if I could not have some time to rethink its interpretation.

It is true that every performance is a new experience. One never plays in the same way. There is a different hall, another audience, and I find myself in a completely different mood or frame of mind. Besides, we pianists have to play on whatever instrument we find, as we cannot take our own around with us like Horowitz or Michelangeli.

You are now often appearing as pianist and conductor and I understand that you are preparing all Mozart's piano concertos with the English Chamber Orchestra. How do you find this extension of your work, being pianist and conductor at the same time?

I find this very satisfying, especially as I conceive the Mozart concertos as chamber music. Many of them have as much exchange between orchestra and the solo instrument as, perhaps, the piano quartets. In fact, Mozart's piano quartets have a bigger piano part than some of the concertos.

There is another aspect of which I am aware all the time. When working with other musicians, there is that atmosphere of give and take which is so stimulating. This is a very important atmosphere for me – it keeps my mind continuously refreshed and I feel that I don't stagnate.

As to the response of the orchestra – in my case, the English Chamber Orchestra – I think we get along very well. Basically this is because they are also very fine musicians, and we are making real chamber music. At moments, things get a bit difficult when I try to work on every phrase. An orchestra like this one probably finds that I don't really have much of a conducting technique. I am not a conductor, and I could probably get through rehearsals much faster if I knew exactly how to get results from them. As it is, I have to talk a lot, I have to explain what I really want from them, and this sounds like a lesson which musicians of that calibre cannot take. They are used to working with conductors who talk very little, and just do it.

My concern is that I cannot always emphasise certain points because I do not know how to obtain them and I get frustrated at some of the rehearsals, feeling a sense of loss. But then, something always happens during the performance. The players, all soloists, rise to the occasion, they respond to the great music, and you are grateful that they didn't let you down. An ensemble like the English Chamber Orchestra could actually play by itself...

What is your attitude to teaching? You were on the staff of the Mannes School of Music in New York, and you have given masterclasses which were a great inspiration to those taking part.

When I started to teach at Mannes School, I found that I was not really prepared to be a teacher. Apart from this, I was away travelling and playing a great deal, and I considered that it was not fair to my students to carry on if I could not give them regular lessons. Students must have continuity in their work, and I decided to leave the School. On the other hand, I love to do coaching, or what one calls these days 'masterclasses'. There is nothing I love more than discussing a work with a pianist and helping him to realise its interpretation. But helping a pianist to learn 'how to do it' is a completely different thing. Perhaps one day I will be ready to do this as well, but first I must be convinced that I, myself, know how to teach.

Piano Journal VOL 1 NO 2 1980

The Menuhins

Three dedicated pianists – each one a highly individual artist – have shared a common heritage of inspiration and artistic beliefs with Yehudi Menuhin, Hephzibah and Yaltah are his sisters, Jeremy his son.

'Perhaps one reason why I cannot play the piano is because I have been fortunate in having so many pianists in my family!

This continues, today, with my son, Jeremy.

I even have a brother-in-law, Louis Kentner, who is a pianist and who is the President of the British branch of EPTA.

No doubt the ability to play the piano represents musically a far greater intellectual capacity than does the ability to play the violin. I compare violinists with tenors as coming from a background of illiterate, itinerant gypsies, with the ability to read music but pianists have always been literate and the proximity of such delightful and gifted pianists must account for some of my musicianship.'

Yehudi Menuhin

Jeremy

Unlike the other Menuhins who were rigidly brought up to be performers you were not even encouraged to become a musician. You had to fight for it. When did you realise that all you wanted to do with your life was to be a pianist?

Without wishing to appear antagonistic about my upbringing, what really happened to me was that I experienced no encouragement about my music until I was nearly fifteen. Even then I was pining to be a musician. Not a pianist. I had no idea what I was going to be and I had no dexterity but I knew that my greatest desire was to be allowed to study music seriously. It was Nadia Boulanger who told my parents: 'Either he becomes a musician now or you can forget about it'. My parents listened to her and I was allowed a trial period in Paris. It was wonderful to be with Nadia Boulanger who taught me a great deal about music. I came back to England and as soon as I was able to play a few pieces adequately I found myself performing them in big concerts. I was even engaged to play on television with Louis Kentner (Bartok's Sonata for Two Pianos and Percussion). Soon afterwards, my father arranged for me to appear with him in some concerts. Of course, I was happy to perform, but at that time, I had no criteria and could not judge whether I was ready for the career. Gradually, I began to feel unhappy and I began to wonder if it would not have been better to start in a smaller way, by playing on my own in less important concerts. Playing with my father was a great responsibility for which I was not ready; perhaps he did not realise how damaging this might be for a young artist. It was even more distressing when people around us were trying to be nice and not make me feel totally inadequate.

You see, my musical identity was inextricably linked with that of my father and I had to get away from it all to find some answers for myself, to develop in whatever direction my talent would take me.

There is a point I should like to make. A lot of people might think that for me to achieve success in my career was the easiest thing in the world. Little did they know how hard I have struggled for it, and how much I had to fight for my music. I started to play the piano quite early and when I was six I was composing and parents were quite proud of me. But no one was really encouraging me to do some serious work. I do understand that my father wanted to protect me from having to live through the same painful experiences which marred his own childhood. However wonderful music may have been for my father and his sisters, it has also been a source of great pain. As a result, I was sent to various boarding schools to grow up with other children but these institutions did not enhance my musicianship.

Well, parents never seem to do the right thing no matter how hard they try. Yehudi's mother made the children unhappy because she was striving to reach perfection whatever the price. In your case you are dissatisfied because no one forced you to practice hard as a child. Moreover you were allowed to choose your career at an age when you knew what you wanted. You must admit that after your studies in Paris you received more encouragement than you really wanted.

This is exactly what happened. I found myself faced with a different kind of struggle, that of finding my independence as a musician. I could not afford to live permanently in someone else's shadow. This created a lot of tension and my playing suffered. I wanted to find out what was happening with me and started to think a great deal about my music and particularly about my piano playing. I found that tensions would build up mainly in the diaphragm area and this affected the freedom of breathing as if there were lack of blood in that part, lack of life in a way. I realised that before one can talk about tone production, problems of sound or interpretation, one must acknowledge the importance of rhythm. There is no such thing as an intellectual process called rhythm. It must be related to inner body rhythms, such as breathing or whatever rhythms we have within ourselves. I have been reading a fascinating book on this subject: *Gravity and Levity* by a Dr. McLashen. He is not a musician and does not talk about music, but what he says is very relevant to any activity. There is a remarkable chapter on rhythm in which he maintains that the secret of everything lies in the rhythm. I also believe that if a musician cannot feel this awareness of rhythm the spiritual cannot be attained.

This is the one supreme quality which I am looking for in an artist. A dazzling technical prowess or even an interesting interpretation does not satisfy me unless the performer has that spiritual quality which is immediately communicated. I must add here that I owe a great deal to that fine artist and pianist, Mindru Katz. Meeting him was a determining factor in my development as a pianist. I cannot define exactly how it happened, or how it happened. It was in Israel, after a concert, that Mindru came into the artists' room and said a few polite words. I was very unhappy at that time and I just told him that I was ready to hear something less pleasant. 'Well, if you want my honest opinion – he answered – if you go on playing like this you will find yourself with cramp by the age of thirty.'

Next day I knocked at the door of his studio and we started to work. For me, this was a great experience and I felt as though I had only then begun to play the piano. It was not so much his 'method' or his way of teaching, though I have learnt from him some vital concepts.

I only had about ten lessons with him, but those lessons were crucial. He helped me to acquire a keyboard mastery and taught me to play in a way as to feel free.

At first I was reluctant to bring myself to do what he wanted me. Perhaps I did not want to hear that what I was doing was wrong and, for some reason, refused to go through any changes. I knew he was right, yet I was resisting. I can only say that, to begin with, it was an emotional

blockage and, somehow, unconsciously I did not want to be free.
One day he said to me: 'I told you everything you need to know. Now
it is up to you.'

When I came back to England I began to work, slowly, trying to put
into practice the concepts I had learnt. It took me over two years to realise what he was trying to convey to me and now I am very grateful for
what he taught me. I know that I am working in the right direction.

As to the works I would like to perform, I choose programmes which
I would like to listen to if I were an audience. I don't find programmes
devoted to one composer satisfying, unless played by a very great artist. I heard Richter in a whole Debussy recital and I could have listened
to him all day! For one of my recitals I chose two composers, Schubert
and Debussy, but I play many works of Mozart and I love Brahms. With
Schumann I haven't much affinity but, perhaps, one day I shall discover
that I can play his music. There is still so much that I haven't attempted
to play yet.

Yaltah

*You must have been very young when you started to play the piano. Do you remem-
ber anything about your first years on the piano?*

I was about three when I began to play and I remember my first teacher
very clearly. She was a warm-hearted person and held me on her knees
most of the time. I cannot remember anything about the music but her
comforting presence is still with me in my memory. It was very amusing to hear her say, many years later, that I was her best pupil. We both
laughed when I asked her if that was the best she could do.

When I was four I was taken to Paris because Yehudi and Hephzibah
began to study there. Marcel Ciampi, the piano professor, accepted
Hephzibah but would not hear of giving lessons to a four-year-old
girl. Only when I rushed to the piano and began to play Schumann's
Kinderszenen did he agree to teach me as well. With him the lessons were
quite different. He was demanding, but could not help feeling paternal
towards me. I am grateful that he stimulated my interest in practicing,
making all the technical exercises like games, and I had to play them
in all keys, up and down the keyboard. But he also insisted that they
should be played musically, with all shades of lovely tone. Technique
was never separated from music and this was so important. In this way
you don't find yourself burdened with inspiration and no road to con-
nect it to.

Mother was undoubtedly a formidable person, but she did not sit with me or the others during practice. She just told us to do it and it was done. Yet I never felt that she was part of the real love of music which was sustaining me all along. She was more externally interested in our distinguishing ourselves in performances. Her attitude was probably that of her generation. She was worried in case Yehudi's tremendous successes, and later on Hephzibah's, might go to our heads. So she did everything she could to make sure we weren't in any way 'wordly'. She certainly had a special technique of making you doubt whether you had really achieved anything when the teacher was satisfied with your progress. Little did she realise that I was only a small child and did not have the self-confidence that needs to be discouraged. While my teachers were so kind and encouraging, my mother made a point of criticising everything.

In spite of the fact that all the attention was focussed on Yehudi and Hephzibah, I never felt left out, because the two of them were so en-closing, so loving. They made me feel that the three of us were *one* and whichever one was hurt, the three of us suffered. We never talked about it because mother did not believe in discussing one's emotions. It wasn't done. It would have been a sign of weakness and this would not have been admissible for a Menuhin. You had to be above fear, above illness. If you had fever, you practised. If you had surgery, you still walked and did your practicing and your lessons. This attitude helped create a bond between the three of us, and we would carry on with a high head and a light heart.

Many people thought that I was lonely and might have resented when Hephzibah started playing with Yehudi. It was not so. First of all, in a family of great talents one does not think of oneself as an individual. I was so much part of the atmosphere and I could not help becoming in-volved, especially during the days of concerts when vibrations were so high in the hotel rooms and you could feel the tensions in your parents. Concert days were not like ordinary days. They were like weddings and everything had to be special, sort of sacred.

Then there were the days of rehearsals. I felt privileged that I could listen to those two great masters, George Enescu and Marcel Ciampi, guiding the two young artists so protectively, yet giving them so much insight into the music. I usually was sent next door to do my practicing but I much preferred to sit quietly and listen to what was being said and I am sure I absorbed and learnt much more like that.

All I remember is that the two of them lived with music all the time and I also wanted to have music. When Yehudi and Hephzibah were practising, I also practised. But there was no question of having a career in music. My mother decided to marry me off at the age of sixteen, and this was a disastrous experience, so I came home to Washington, where my parents were then living. It was 1938, during those agitated days just before the war. I missed Yehudi and Hephzibah desperately. My only solace was my music, so I gave many concerts which were just a continuation of the life which had been so brutally interrupted. I was not interested in managers or success: I only wanted music to continue. And I started my life as a pianist, playing with all kinds of musicians and playing solo work or concertos. By that time I married again and I had to bring up my two sons but music continued to be part of my life.

It was only after meeting Joel Rice, my present husband, that my life and my playing took a different turn. I arrived in London to play with Hephzibah the two piano concertos in E flat by Mozart, with Yehudi conducting. I was thrilled that the three of us were going to make music together. I stayed at a place in Kensington, with Madame who let rooms with pianos to musicians. The first person to open the door was this dedicated, fire-like young man who was having lessons with Myra Hess and who never left his piano. We began to play duets, on one piano, on two pianos, and we both felt that, working together, each was like an extension of the other's personality. Not that we are alike. He has a beautiful large hand producing a fat tone. In those days, I was shy and hardly dared make myself heard. I had to play with so many violinists, cellists, bassoonists, who would say: 'The lid can stay down, can't it?' To have a pianist next to me sharing the piano, wanting true equality in the sense that there is always dialogue, I found what I was searching for. The next ten years of playing together were years of intense joy, of great development for both of us.

We did some teaching and it was while working at the Yehudi Menuhin School with those highly gifted children that Joel decided that he wanted to understand better his own mind and that of his pupils, so he switched to psychology. This is a long and slow process and I now find myself playing alone again. I feel, though, that I have learnt so much through our playing and working together that this helps me get through my work. Perhaps this has also helped sustain me in the past few months, when I had to stand in for Hephzibah who was unable to fulfill her engagements. I had to play the Schumann concerto, the Emperor, and several recitals. As to teaching, I have only one pupil, a very dedicated and talented one and that is…ME!

How did you find playing with the other Menuhins? You were one of the soloists in the triple concerto by Mozart, together with Hephzibah and Jeremy and Yehudi conducting during the celebrations of his 60th birthday.

It was rather strenuous for me because we don't meet often enough to work together. Besides, I am hopelessly emotional and, for me, music is almost a mystical, intuitive experience. For them it is combined with tremendous objectivity and self-control. When Jeremy joined us it was different because both my sister and I were like two aunts, wanting the little one to do well. It must have been a terrifying experience for him but I must say that Yehudi was absolutely splendid. Once on the platform there was nothing else but the music, and we, the soloists, responded in the same way.

Hephzibah

Hephzibah, you have so much to tell us about your life, your rich musical experiences, your piano playing. How do you feel about your long and very successful career?

As I grow older I think a great deal about my playing, about piano playing in general. I feel that to play an instrument, one must first of all be able to communicate one's thoughts. One is the same person with or without the instrument and what matters is the spiritual quality of the music. An instrument is only an extension of one's personality.

Looking back I consider myself very fortunate. I have had a life of enormous positive experiences in so many ways. And now, I am trying to convert them into something even more positive, that is, being able to share these experiences with others so that they in turn may achieve something. We live basically off the great thoughts of the creators who are no longer with us, but who live so intensely within us. The masters whose works we interpret are not only teaching and stimulating us, but help us to pass their message on to others and this is our privilege. This is in fact what I have learnt and am learning all the time, especially now that I am ill. I am learning to live with illness and conquer it and this has had an enormous effect on me; not only on my playing but on my whole being, and sometimes I find myself going through most extraordinary experiences.

Recently, I had to record Vaughan William's Sonata for Violin and Piano with my brother and I went through my usual sort of pattern whenever I am learning a new work. At first I feel repelled as if something is going to enter into me and I don't like it. Then, slowly it begins to grow inside me, I go to sleep, and when I wake up in the morning it is singing; it's got a life of its own. Yet I am still aware of a foreign body I am nursing.

After several rehearsals, Yehudi and I gave a performance in Cambridge for the Fitzwilliam Museum and the very next day we had to record it. I woke up that morning with a strange feeling and I realised I had fallen in love with the work. We recorded it in one day and I remember being in such a wonderful state that everything was easy; there were no more difficult leaps, no fear of anything going wrong and suddenly I knew what the work was about, I knew what it had to sound like. It was one of those great and beautiful musical experiences which transcend everything that one has learned to master.

My childhood was a strange one. My parents did not allow us to go to school like other children and we lived in a completely circumscribed world, totally unaware of anything outside ourselves. It was like another womb... Having been myself a mother I think that now I can understand my mother better. Music and practising had to come first and she imposed a rigid discipline but, I am sure,she did her absolute best. I do think that, after spending many years over the hurts of our childhood, we should be grateful to our parents for the good they have meant.

As a child, it was only natural that I wanted to do what Yehudi was doing. He was kind and loving and he spent many hours teaching me notation. Then I was taken to Judith Blockley, my first piano teacher, and on my fifth birthday, I remember playing some Bach and a few other pieces in a pupil's concert. That evening I went to bed very happy and I thought that I did not need to practise any more. When father came to get me up next morning I said: 'But I've finished. I played yesterday in the concert!' I often think of his answer: 'Oh, my poor child, you don't know what a long way you have got ahead of you!'

Soon afterwards we went to Paris where Yehudi had started to work with Georges Enescu and his friend, Marcel Ciampi, had agreed to give me lessons. He was a fabulous teacher who knew how to inspire a young child to enjoy the technical exercises as part of music making.

The most important event in my musical life came when I was allowed to play with Yehudi. In spite of his successes he was very modest and with him I always felt very safe. Of course, he was the leader and I followed him. It was not only that. There were the days of rehearsals before a concert, when Enescu and Ciampi, the two great masters, were giving us such encouragement, such valuable advice and inspiration. They instilled in us a feeling of humility that you, the performer, are only a vehicle for something very great and mysterious. The two of us felt that we were involved with something outside of ourselves which we were serving and there was magic. I couldn't really explain this. You must experience it, together with the experience of the listener which comes into it as part of your own. Music must have a spiritual quality and this can be communicated only when you are being 'carried' by the music instead of 'carrying' it. At times I thought of my brother as so much a person of spirit that if he would stand there, on the platform, without the violin and just think, his music he would create the same magic as when he plays.

One day, much later, Yehudi gave me the greatest lesson of my life. We were playing Bartok's Violin and Piano Sonata No. 1 in a remote American town, at an Army base, for a rather unmusical audience. Right from the start there was something that made Yehudi unhappy. His playing was somehow erratic and he was not doing what I was expecting him to do. I tried to listen very hard, not to lose him, and the more he hurried the more closely I hung on to him...like a leech. On top of it, the piano was terrible, and I was most unhappy. When the ordeal was over, I asked him what was the matter and he snapped: 'You were the matter! Do you have to repeat everything I say? Can't you think for yourself and take the lead sometimes?'

This incident made me re-think my whole attitude. It was really an invitation to adulthood, to stop being the little girl following him, knowing that if he holds my hand, I can't go wrong. How boring this must have been for him! Afterwards I knew that I had a job to do, which was more than following him, but listening and answering and asking questions from time to time. It has been very rewarding indeed and this has brought back that complete trust and ease when making music together.

In the same way, when giving a recital, or playing with an orchestra, I think of the work, as a whole, for quite some time. I don't practice much, just listen to it in my mind. If there are any difficulties in a particular passage, I look to see where the difficulty lies and I practice it so it becomes easy. Sometimes I think how a different fingering might sound and I am pleasantly surprised to find myself playing with a new fingering during a concert, for the first time. Perhaps I am able to do this because of the very profound changes that have occurred in my life in recent years and I have now a different sense of proportion, a different sense of values. To me, now, the notes matter much less than the message. I must confess that, occasionally, if there is a note that cannot be played without upsetting the line or if a passage demands a kind of artificial pedalling, I cheat. As long as the message is there I say to myself: 'Well, I don't think HE would have minded really...'

All the same, I think a great deal about my playing. I have only a very small piano now and when I work, I like to play very quietly to myself, without disturbing the others. Piano playing should not mean attacking the keys. One should play into the keys, caressing them, coaxing them and they will respond beautifully. As to the music I am playing, I think about it so intensely that I feel that there is continuous communication from my mind, through my shoulders and arms and into the instrument. There are no barriers and no frontiers, only an absolute and instantaneous flow of the lines into the keys.

As regards teaching the piano I often think how important it is for a teacher to consider his work as a mission – that is, to give his best to bring out the student, rather than to impose his own personality. I also think of a good teacher as a perpetual learner, alert and with a curious mind, striving to fulfil himself to the greatest possible extent. That is why it is so important that a teacher should also perform, whether it is making music with others in the home, playing Duets or in Chamber Music, or appearing before an audience. I have not done any piano teaching myself though I have worked with many youngsters at the 'Centre for Human Rights and Responsibilities' in which my husband and I are deeply involved. I have become aware of the fact that there are problems in people's lives that music itself will not solve. That is why I consider it a great privilege to be able to make music, whether on my own, or with other artists. At the same time I feel grateful for its healing quality...

I am so grateful that I had the privilege to talk to all four Menuhins and record these interviews, testimonials of their profound and intense experiences as unique musicians and performers, particularly in their constant quest for reaching higher realms of spirituality. These interviews are also a memorial to their artistry and greatness as human beings. Jeremy is the only one alive and carrying further the name of Menuhin, having developed as an artist and pianist as he has been striving to achieve.

Piano Journal VOL 1 NO 3 1980

Radu Lupu

You have often said that you did not think of yourself as a solo performer until you had won the International Piano Competition in Leeds in 1965. Could you tell us about the beginning of your training in Romania and afterwards in Russia? As a young pupil you studied with Florica Musicescu, the well known Romanian piano professor at the Bucharest Music Academy.

I cannot say that I was really a pupil of Florica Muzicescu like Dinu Lipatti or Mindru Katz, who studied with her from early childhood until they left the country to settle abroad. I was taken to Bucharest when I was about eight and studied with her only for a few months. All I remember is that she was a formidable person, and I was quite afraid of her. Had I stayed longer, perhaps I might have learnt to appreciate and even love her like all her other pupils.

As it was, my parents lived in Brasov, and I continued to have lessons with a local teacher. I was too young to judge whether she was a good teacher or not. She did not really teach me to play the piano, but to these days I am grateful to her, because she helped me to become a musician. She took me to concerts, she stimulated me to listen to music and to learn as much as it was possible in a town where there was not much music. I did not really think of becoming a pianist, all I wanted to do at that time was to be a composer.

When I was sixteen I was sent to Russia, and was accepted at the Central Music School in Moscow. My first study was composition, but I had to learn to play the piano, and had a very good teacher, Galima Eghiazarowa. Two years later I became a student at Moscow Conservatoire, where I stayed for five years, and at that time I decided to change my studies from composition to piano.

My teacher was Henry Neuhaus, but only for about one year, and afterwards, I studied with his son, Stanislav. I must say that the most important thing I have learnt from the Henry Neuhaus was to listen to the

18

piano sound. I have learnt to produce the physical, beautiful tone and play legato mostly by watching his very expressive hands, which moved so beautifully when illustrating a point. At that time, he could not play any more and he tried to explain what he wanted me to do by using his hands, like a conductor. Had he tried to explain through words I might not have achieved the same results.

You were the winner at the Van Cliburn Competition as early as 1961 when you were only 19. How is it that you did not think of embarking on a career as a pianist at that time?

I knew that I still had a long way to go. I had a great deal more to learn as a musician. In fact, I did not become really interested in the piano as an instrument until some time after the Leeds competition. I don't want to give the wrong impression – that I never thought about how one should play the piano. You see, as a youngster, I played more by intuition than by knowledge, and I was more influenced by conductors and orchestral playing than by pianists. I did not really understand the piano as an instrument and while at Moscow Conservatoire I took up the piano more as a sort of medium to express myself through a wide range of sound. What helped me most in my playing was that I always dreamt of being a conductor, and I tried to conduct, for myself, every single work I was playing. By striving to express everything through some sort of movement of the wrist I realised that I was applying the same movements when playing the piano. I have never studied conducting, but thinking so much about the orchestra, its texture and colour, made me search for the same texture and colours when using the keyboard. After all, this instrument is capable of everything.

During all those years as a student, I was going through a very difficult time. I found myself having certain technical problems not having been trained to be a pianist from an early age. I have a limited stretch between the third and fourth fingers on my right hand and this creates a strain when I have to play certain chords. I have to turn the hand in a particular way to reach those chords. Yet I knew that I had to try to get the best results. I also knew that there were many problems I had to solve over the years. Playing in public every two or three months was not the answer. Something important was missing in my development and I decided that I had to do something about it, though I did not know exactly what. I started to study many books on piano technique and listen to my friends' and colleagues' criticisms in a more objective way, but I was still very depressed.

I believe that a positive change in my whole outlook came about when I began to think about my own playing in a different way, allowing myself to be guided by the intellect rather than by my intuition. What helped me most of all, in the end, was studying Schoenberg's *Fundamentals of Musical Composition.* Until then, I was not relating my knowledge of composition to my playing, but afterwards I realised that if I approached the work as a composer, from inside the music, my musical intentions would find the right expression, and the technical problems somehow would solve themselves.

What do you think of your development as a pianist now, after fifteen years of searching?

I think that I have changed very much, both in my outlook and, I hope, in my playing. When I look back I realise that I was a sort of self-indulgent person, playing more by intuition, by feeling. I never worked, for instance, on slow movements. I was convinced that to play them beautifully it was only a matter of inspiration. It so happened that when I was in front of an audience I did get this inspiration. It was only later on that I began to think of the importance of each phrase, how to construct it and how to structure a whole movement. At first I found this kind of work almost traumatic. While until then I had hardly given any thought to these essential problems, from then onwards I found myself thinking too much, and studying too much. All I knew was that now I have to rely on my mind, on my intellect, as well as my intuition. Without intuition there cannot be a balanced performance, but the mind must be in control all the time. Otherwise nothing works as it should.

For instance, I am now preparing myself for an important series of recitals, playing all Schubert's sonatas at the Queen Elizabeth Hall in London. Since my first appearance in that hall, in 1965, after the Leeds competition, when I played the A Minor Sonata op.143 D.784, I believe that I have gone through some changes both as regards the reading of the scores, and my own conception.

First of all, in those days I did not think about the edition I was using, for the simple reason that I considered myself fortunate to possess any edition. Neither in Russia, nor in Rumania could one easily find Urtext editions at that time and only later I realised how inaccurately I played that particular sonata, mainly as regards phrasing. I believe that phrasing is of tremendous importance, but sometimes even one sharp or one flat can make a great difference to the mood of the piece. I find myself going now to the other extreme, working from three or four editions of these sonatas at the same time. The result is that I keep on finding slight variants, and then I have to think for myself which one I should use. Nothing seems to be really conclusive, so occasionally I follow the correspondence between various scholars (Brendel versus Konrad Wolff, for example), or try to use my logic, or perhaps I rely once again on my intuition. One example is bar 7 in the *Scherzo* of the A Major Sonata Op. posth. D.959, when one note appears differently in each of the three otherwise authoritative editions: a G, a B, and an A.

I also work now in a different way than before. Once I decide which edition I am using, I start preparing the score, not only in my mind, but actually noting down everything that I believe to be relevant about how I should play every single phrase, or even single notes, a kind of 'enacting' each moment of the performance. I cannot allow myself to rely on inspiration so that on a good day everything sounds right and on a bad day I am not able to recapture that mood. I prepare a score in its minutest detail before beginning to play that piece. In the end, I must have two scores, one heavily marked, unrecognisable, so that even I get lost in the jungle of my own notes, and another one with only a few vital points marked on it.

We should like to hear how an artist like you can cope with the tensions created by this strenuous life, having to travel and perform in different places, sometimes under quite difficult conditions, and how these affect your own playing.

I believe that being a practising musician is something very serious. There must be dedication and, surely, true artists have some special qualities, otherwise they would not survive. Of course, I am affected by playing in different places, by my mood on a particular day, by my physical state, or by a very long journey before a concert. I also find that the piano, the orchestra, or the conductor I am playing with influence my performance. Yet one knows that every performance is the product of many years of work and preparation, and every artist will rely on those valuable years and experiences. This is what being professional means.

I also consider myself very fortunate to be able to choose my programmes so that I only play the works I love most and with which I feel great affinity. I am not one of those artists who can perform all the styles equally well and if I am to remain true to myself I must play only those composers which suit me, or to put it better, I must play the works which like me best. I feel a great responsibility towards my audience, and I never allow myself to present pieces that are beyond my capabilities either as regards the musical conception or the execution. For each performance I prepare myself mentally, going through every moment of the piece in my mind, sometimes repeating again and again certain phrases which I consider 'key phrases' until I go on the platform. I am what one would call a 'nervous' player. Not one suffering from anxiety; on the contrary, all those nervous impulses create some extraordinary sensations in my arms, my hands and the tips of my fingers, and I am ready to begin. At such moments, I am aware of only one thing – that I am doing my utmost to do justice to the works I play so that I can offer to my audience an interpretation as near as possible to my ideals.

I can only add that talking to you about your life, your attitude to your work has been a real eye opener. The respect and the integrity with which you approach the works you are studying in their minutest details are a great lesson, indeed, for all of us.

Piano Journal VOL 2 NO 5 1981

Fanny Waterman

You hold a special position in piano pedagogy in England, having been responsible for a number of prodigies as well as some fine artists who have won prizes in international competitions. You have never been associated with a music college and one could describe you, perhaps, as a 'solo performer' rather than a 'chamber music player' among pedagogues.

Well, I think that I have got the best of all worlds. I teach at home where I have the freedom to go on for as long as I want or for as long as is needed. I don't have to follow a bell that says that end of the lesson is here and I can stop when I feel that my pupil would benefit if we talk about his problems over a cup of coffee, or we look at some books and listen to a record. Another factor intervenes: how I choose my pupils. I don't choose the pupils, I choose the parents to make sure that I am going to have the right co-operation. While the hour lesson is vitally important, what goes on during the six days before the next lesson is also vitally important. It is no good having a child who learns an instrument if the mother is not there to supervise his practicing. I write down the details for the daily practice and the parents must see that the work is done.

I consider teaching as the greatest profession and a piano teacher, especially, has a very special trust and a great responsibility because of the one to one relationship. The teacher is expected to be a good musician, a good psychologist and to know the craft, how it has to be done and how to express this clearly to the pupil. When a pupil comes into my studio, I see immediately whether he is confident or depressed, or if he is bogged down with the work for his examinations. I cannot help getting involved with his work, his life, his well-being. The way I begin the lesson will often depend on his need at that moment. Of course, I gradually steer the lesson so that I am able to 'charge his musical batteries'. A pupil must leave the lesson feeling refreshed in spirit and eager to start the week's work anew. Boredom is the enemy of progress and I cannot allow a pupil to experience this during his practice.

In my work I consider the three aspects of musical training which I believe to be of paramount importance – learning to be a craftsman, learning to be a musician and, lastly, becoming an artist.

Learning the craft means to master every technical problem of piano playing such as: to play a scale at speed with each note of equal brilliance or pearly delicacy; to play trills dynamically controlled to suit the mood of the music; tone production and pedalling with their infinite problems on how to make the piano sing; wrist staccato, powerful octaves, skips, perfect co-ordination between the hands; balancing of parts when more than one melody is playing at once; double thirds and sixths and many other problems too numerous to mention now.

This work should occupy only a fraction of a pupil's working day as craftsmanship, or technique, cannot be treated in a vacuum. There is no dividing line between technique and the next stages of the work – musicianship and artistry. With regard to the teaching of musicianship I believe that right from the beginning every pupil must learn how to shape and colour a phrase, how to join several phrases together rhythmically so that a large section is fused together and finally how to build together large sections of the movement to give it rhythmic unity and to make one architectural whole.

The teacher must help the young musician to do this by developing a strong rhythmic sense, forcing him to play metronomically in time with even the shortest and most unimportant note in its 'timespot'. When this rhythmic understanding is secure one learns to use rubato where speeds fluctuate, almost imperceptibly in classical music and more markedly with later composers. This involves the fascinating study of style, and here a knowledge of the composer's lives and times, what instruments were used and sounded like, is helpful. Again, every pupil must be able to produce every nuance of tone from ppp to fff and in between each one of these dynamics there are so many different musical shadings demanding a very large musical palette.

How can a pianist equipped with technical virtuosity and musical sensitivity blossom as an artist? The third and vital step is impossible to teach. Artistry is one quality which, I believe, is innate and therefore cannot be taught, only stimulated. I advise my students to develop a wide appreciation of the Arts in general, listen to many live great performances and not one model gramophone record, to take part in chamber music, listen to singing of lieder and opera, symphonies, operas etc.

24

In your teaching you work with complete beginners as well as with professional and concert artists, many of them having studied with you from their very first lesson. Most of our readers know your 'tutors' (which you have written in collaboration with Marion Harewood for Faber music) but I am sure that they would be interested in what the format of your lessons are.

Young beginners can only concentrate for a short time so their lessons last approximately half an hour while the normal lesson for school children is about an hour. With these I do some technical work, some pieces, sight-reading and aural tests.

To begin with I believe that in order to acquire dexterity of passage-work, scales and arpeggios must be mastered. We start with the first note of the scale – even on one single note we can play from the softest to the loudest sound. After one note we learn to play two connected notes with the same power and evenness, in a see-saw movement, transferring the weight from one finger to another, starting very slowly and increasing the speed and grading the tone from *ppp* to *fff*. I make sure that the arm is relaxed and the child does not use the arm or wrist. After two notes, exercises with three, four and five notes follow and I insist that all fingers should be bent and placed in the middle of each key. The weakest finger, the fourth, receives special attention and the pupils play scales up and down the keyboard using three and four, then four alone, as legato as possible, with a loose arm and raised knuckles. For the thumb passage I give special exercises and also I ask the pupil to play with the thumb alone, in all scales, including chromatics. This is very good for octave work when the same exercise is used for the little finger.

During the lesson the pupil will be tested on the weeks work with marks given for each item and a percentage for the whole lesson. He receives stars and prizes when he deserves them as I am a great believer in incentives. But I do tell my pupils not to pay too much attention to my marks, but to my remarks!

Advanced students are encouraged to listen to each other's lessons which last between one or two hours. Though I insist that technical work should absorb every pianist from his first lesson to his last performance, I rarely do exercises, scales or studies with these students. They should be able to adapt their knowledge of how to practice their technique when studying the passagework in their pieces thus spending more time increasing their repertoire.

At the lesson the student brings a piece of his own choice, though I may make a suggestion as to what he should learn next to build up a balanced repertoire. He performs the whole piece or movement without interruption, from memory. Whatever mishaps may occur, he must continue to play – he must learn to cover up mistakes in performance. Afterwards, the real work begins, in the greatest detail and the pupil must be able to start from any beat of the bar, from memory, separate hands only, until each part is clearly expressed. The very opening of a phrase may take practically a whole lesson (for instance the tone and rhythm of the first page of the Appassionata Sonata). I often tell my pupils: 'Well, Beethoven left you a legacy, the thirty-two sonatas; Chopin left you his sonatas and so on. You must take this very seriously because you are the beneficiary of a will; you receive these works but you act as the executor and you are entrusted with carrying out the composer's instructions'. This is not easy because although the composers write down how they want their music to be played there are many ways of doing it. How soft is soft? Soft can be a very full sound as in the works of Brahms who loved the dark, rich kind of sound of the viola, or it may mean an ethereal sound. What is important is that an artist should have a very wide musical palette and that he realises that there is meaning to music. Every phrase can be compared to the line of a poem, and if he does not breathe and does not punctuate musically the meaning is lost.

Yet, it is one thing to play in your home or in the teacher's studio and a completely different experience to perform in public. Things happen on the platform which never happen in one's drawing room. I strongly believe that the responsibility of a teacher when he takes on a pupil is that he or she must be psychologically prepared to take on not just the music lessons but that student's well-being and his career. Pupils should be encouraged to perform from very early stages because 'the only way to learn the job is to do it'.

You certainly fulfil your responsibilities towards your pupils, seeing to their needs so to speak from their musical cradle to their mature life as artists. You have also realised your greatest ideal by being the founder and Chairman of one of the most important International Piano Competitions which has brought tremendous prestige to the musical life in the U.K. as well as internationally, and this must give you immense satisfaction.

In which way do you think that the Leeds competition differs from other similar events?

First of all we believe that the most important aspect of the Leeds competition is the way the competitors are judged. The jury does not give marks as we all agree that a performance of a masterpiece cannot be 'measured' by marks. Each member of the jury is asked to listen to all the participants in the preliminary stage, make notes, think about them and choose, in their minds, sixteen players whom they would like to hear again not only in the next stages of the competition but as young artists on various international platforms. Then they must nominate the first sixteen candidates to appear in the next stage (which actually has twenty players). It is very interesting to note that, although no one discusses his/her choice with the others almost invariably the first sixteen candidates are the same on everybody's list! After a further vote, twenty players appear in the following tests out of which eight are selected to go further. Every candidate in the finals is judged on his or her overall performances, as recitalist, chamber music player, and, in the final appearance (of the chosen six), as soloist in a concerto with orchestra. This, the jury considers to be a fair judgement as to the qualities of those young artists who are to be launched in their career. It is a well-known fact that not only the first prize-winner, but most of the six finalists find themselves in great demand and their career almost blossoms overnight. The jury's responsibility is to make sure that the artists of their choice will be able to stand up to the strain of the profession.

Thankyou for your illuminating talk about your approach to teaching, the care you take of each pupil's piano playing as well as his/her well being.
I only wish that more teachers would learn from this interview, particularly how to get the child to develop his fingers and hand in such a healthy way — watching that their arms are relaxed. I find your idea of the child playing first with one finger, with those infinite gradation of tone from ppp to fff, then using two adjacent fingers, learning to transfer the weight from one finger to another, in a perfect legato. Gradually you introduce a whole octave of a scale in this way, which teaches the pupil to listen carefully to the sound he/she is producing.
I do think that your books (Faber and Faber) are still the best for their clarity and ideal structuring to achieve constant progress and I hope teachers realise their importance.

Vladimir Ashkenazy

As you may well imagine, our readers are greatly interested to hear something about your training in Moscow, first as a child at the Music Schools and afterwards at the Moscow Conservatoire.

Well, my training is not different from that of any other pianist I know. I started to play quite early, when I was about 5 and all I remember is that I had to play scales and finger exercises at every lesson, and doing them regularly, at home, every day. I hardly remember the first few pieces which my teacher made me play, but the moment I started things like Schumann's *Album for the Young*, or Tchaikovsky's pieces for children I was thrilled. I could learn everything very fast and I must have been considered a talented child but the truth was that I loved the pieces and I enjoyed playing them. At the age of seven, I was accepted into one of those music schools where gifted children receive complete education. The discipline is quite strict, but most children take to it, and great was my joy when I was allowed to play with the school orchestra, when not yet eight years old. I played the *Finale* of the Haydn Concerto in D and everyone thought that I did very well.

Soon afterwards I was transferred to the Central Music School, the main music school in Moscow where the very gifted children are sent. My teacher was Anaida Sumbatian who made me work very thoroughly at my technique, practising scales, arpeggios, octaves, playing all sorts of studies to have the tools with which to perform the very demanding repertoire. The standard was very high indeed and like all the other children, I worked with great seriousness and involvement because all I wanted was to become a pianist. Besides, once in a Music School, every pupil was expected to do his utmost, there was healthy competition and listening to one another either at lessons or at the school concerts.

When I was eighteen, I was accepted at the Moscow Conservatoire in the class of professor Oborin. The training I received at the Central

28

Music School helped me adjust to the new life. I loved my work and although I still spent many hours perfecting my technique, I had many opportunities to perform both in recitals and with the orchestra. I found even greater stimulation first from my teacher and then from the colleagues who had the same dedication as I had. Some of them have made a name for themselves inside Russia and abroad, like Lazar Berman. While in the Conservatoire, I met my wife who was an Icelandic student who had been a pupil of Harold Craxton at the Royal Academy of Music in London. She was a prodigy pianist and was sent to the Moscow Conservatoire to continue her studies, and we soon got married.

Of course, it was after winning the first prize (which I shared with John Ogdon) in 1982, that my career took a definite turn. In 1963 I was sent on a concert tour to England which was very successful. My wife came with me and as she was longing to return to London to be near her parents (her father is himself a very fine musician in North London) we decided to remain in England. From then on I was engaged to play a great deal, in many countries, and of course I went to play also in Iceland and we soon made Reykjavik our home where we stayed for ten years. We both wanted to help develop the musical life in Iceland and we invited our friends, many of them great artists, to participate in the Reykjavik festival which, obviously, was attracting a great number of tourists who were also music lovers. I am very glad to hear that EPTA Iceland is an important organisation and that most piano teachers are members. In fact I found that the standard of teaching and playing is very serious.

Your work is taking you all over the world performing or conducting, one week you may be playing or giving Masterclasses in China, the next one in Japan, and so on. How do you cope with the strain of travelling from one end to the other of the globe, getting ready for rehearsals as soon as you leave the airport, sleeping in different hotel rooms and at the same time performing a varied repertoire – as you are one of the very few artists who excel as an interpreter of almost every composer, be it Beethoven, the great Romantics or the Russians and even some of the contemporary ones?

Indeed this is the plight of today's artists in the jet age. I work very hard not only at my music but at planning intelligently all my engagements. I must be careful not to become the victim of bad planning, otherwise it would be impossible to survive, because the demands are enormous and I must apply great control over my own enthusiasm.

This is not easy, and, here again, my wife is of tremendous help. We have now a residence in Switzerland, so that the world connections are easier for us both as she often accompanies me on my travels. She also helps me during rehearsals advising me on the acoustics of the hall or the balance of tone. Recently, I played the two Brahms Piano Concertos in one evening with André Previn conducting. This was the first time that I played both concertos, and of course it was a new experience. At the rehearsals my wife was listening intently and I relied on her comments. Previn's support was simply marvellous and I felt that there was great affinity between conductor, the orchestra and myself during the performance. Here I must say again that had it not been for a careful and intelligent planning I would not have been able to sustain such a 'marathon' evening.

Not long ago I heard your son, Vladimir Stefan Ashkenazy, in a concert at the Royal Festival Hall. What is it like having another pianist in the family? At the same time, what advice can you give to budding pianists?

I am very happy that he is so very serious about his work and that he is doing so well. He is still a student at the Royal Northern College of Music in Manchester. His professor is Sulamita Aronowsky whom I knew in Moscow when she was teaching at the Moscow Conservatoire. I consider her a very fine teacher; she is very good to him, which is so important to a young, sensitive musician, and he has grown into a good pianist under her guidance. Besides, it is his own choice to become a pianist and we hope to help him to develop in this direction. And I want to say to all young pianist what I tell my own son: 'If you find that your talent is not a great one, don't have too many ambitions. But, if you have talent, then work hard! There is no short cut. Only through real dedication and continuous work can one achieve something valuable in the world of music and particularly in piano playing'.

Vlado Perlemuter

You are one of the great artists of our time, and a very well-known pedagogue (the 'Great Vlado', as John Amis called you in one of his BBC Music Talks). You have been the European President of EPTA ever since its foundation and this has greatly contributed to the prestige of the organisation.

Although I have not been actively involved in EPTA's development, I have always followed its growth with great interest and I am delighted to know that I have been, to a certain extent, instrumental in the founding of EPTA West Germany by introducing Professor Karl-Heinz Kämmerling to you. It is good to know that there are now five European National Associations. And, of course, I find the *Piano Journal* a most stimulating and useful publication in bringing together pianists and teachers from many corners of the world. I particularly like the design of the cover, and Michael Garady's sensitive sketches.

I have read recently in the book Chopin Playing: From the Composer to the Present Day *by James Methuen-Campbell (Gollanz) that as a young boy you were a pupil of Moskowsky, the celebrated Polish pianist who had taken Paris by storm.*

My professor at the Bucharest Royal Academy of Music, Constanta Erbiceanu, went to study with him in Paris when she graduated from Leipzig. You are one of the very few artists who could still tell us something about this very interesting personality.

I was only twelve when I was taken to have lessons with Moskowsky, yet I remember vividly how he liked to sit on the left hand side of the student, intently watching the hands, and continuously marking the score. In particular, he made various notes on fingerings, trying out several possibilities, then putting down the one he decided upon. He seemed greatly preoccupied with the choice of fingering to suit each hand and he often made some rather unorthodox suggestions, but when I tried them they appeared quite natural, and even logical.

He was already an old man at that time. He had great disappointments during the First World War, as he was a German citizen, and was not well treated by the authorities. It was only thanks to some of the ladies in whose Salons he had played, and who remained friends with him, that he was allowed to be free. He was also to carry on with his profession, and he was quite busy teaching and giving concerts although his playing was not as great as in his younger days.

When I was studying with him he was working very intensely preparing some new editions of Beethoven piano sonatas and of a group of Chopin pieces.

I would recommend to pianists and students to look at them as they will find quite a few of these unusual ideas on fingerings, and these might give them an idea of the way he worked and how he placed his hands on the keyboard.

I believe he had a genius for fingering a score which was always very pianistic. It was that of *an artist* who belonged to what I call 'the natural school of piano playing', of a Rosenthal, a Godowsky, a Joseph Hoffmann, and is unlike the fingerings of Schnabel, for instance, in the Beethoven sonatas, which I find rather 'gauche'. To my mind, this is the fingering of a *musician* who is preoccupied not by what is more suitable to the player, but by the musical thought and expression in relation to his imagination and to his own hand.

When I was thirteen I was accepted into the class of Alfred Cortot at the Paris Conservatoire, and this was a crucial period in my development. Cortot devoted a great deal of his time to his students, in spite of his many concert tours, and it was also very stimulating to be in a class with outstanding young pianists like Yvonne Lefebure, Clara Haskil, and others. He gave us a real insight into the music of Chopin and the other great romantics and he introduced us to the works of the French composers. As to the 'pianistic technique' I loved working under his guidance. I am still faithful to the school of playing 'at the bottom of the keys', not on the surface. The touch needed to create all kinds of tones is the one which the French call *enfoncer dans les touches* – gently pressing the keys down to the 'key-bed'. By producing a wide range of sonorities, the performance gains in intensity, and one is able to communicate the musical intentions and the inner *élan*.

I do not agree with the school which encourages 'soft hands and fingers', as if they have no muscles. The playing loses its bite, and the result is rather a monotonous performance. It is easy to be supple, but this is not enough. One must find the right balance between being supple and having tension, between a supple arm, wrist, hand, and the support of the bridge formed by the knuckles of the hand, so that fingers can move freely. The fingers must be firm and supple at the same time.

This is what Lipatti also said: 'The pianist's fingers must be like steel covered in velvet gloves'. You are considered one of the great Chopin players of our time, but your name has often been linked with that of Ravel. You have played a great deal of his music, and I believe you have worked through all his piano pieces with him.

Indeed, I have played his music from a very early stage in my career, and recently I have completed a new set of recordings for Nimbus. I was fifteen when I finished the Paris Conservatoire with a Premier Prix, and I became intensely interested in the French music of the time – Debussy, Ravel, and Fauré.

In 1927 I went to meet Ravel because I had studied all the piano works which he had published until then. He was greatly surprised to meet a young pianist who had devoted so much time and so much interest to learn all those works, and thus began a close collaboration. He showed great appreciation of the way I prepared his piano works, and we went together through each piece, discussing the tempi (he thought that the Minuet of the Sonatina was played too fast), the rhythm and nuances, and I still have some old copies with his own markings and even with a few changes of the printed page.

In 1929 I gave two Recitals, all devoted to Ravel's music, and these were greeted as an important musical events in Paris. Ravel, who was present, was very pleased with the response of the audience and of the critics.

I cannot say that there was real friendship between us. He was over 50 at the time, already a celebrated composer, while I was a young pianist, at the beginning of my career. Besides, he was a very reserved and mysterious man who avoided a close relationship even with his best friends. The only exception was Hélène Jourdan-Morhange, a very fine musician herself, who was his permanent companion. Ravel's biographers describe this as a platonic and beautiful friendship which began through their great love of cats, and lasted until he died. He greatly valued her opinion, and played to her every single piece which he was writing, listening to her suggestions.

A few years ago Madame Jourdan-Morhange invited me to participate in a series of *Conversations* on Ravel's piano music over the Paris Radio.

The broadcasts had a simple format. Hélène Jourdan-Morhange would talk about a certain work (we presented them in chronological order), telling the listeners about Ravel's method of writing, describing many interesting and sometimes amusing details, and afterwards she would ask me what indications he gave with regard to the interpretation of that particular work. On the one hand, I was an artist able to pass on to the listeners what Ravel had told me, not so much about tempo or nuances, but especially about subtleties of touches demanded by the changes of moods, the specific sonorities, or the colours so characteristic of his music; on the other hand there was Madame Jourdan-Morhange, his closest friend and companion, who had profound knowledge of all his works. She had been there when they were created.

These 'Conversations' are now in book form and musicians must have found them of interest as it is in the fifth edition. Perhaps an English edition will also be published – I think it might be of some help to young pianists to know about Ravel's own indications, as I find that many seem to be getting further and further from the 'truth'. (*Ravel by Ravel*, Kahn & Averill)

You have always been in close contact with young pianists, first at the Paris Conservatoire, where you have been professor for many years, and also travelling to many countries giving recitals and masterclasses and you are very often a member of the jury at international piano competitions. Which are, in your opinion, the aspects of piano playing which strike you as most important or, perhaps, which are the qualities lacking in today's pianism?

It is true that I may be one day at an International Piano Competition in Tokyo, a few weeks later in Budapest, or soon afterwards in Texas. I must admit that I find these youngsters amazing, most of them play very well, technically, a great number of works. You all know how demanding these competitions are. But, when it comes to the interpretation of the truly great works, the general impression is that too many competitors are not ready for these. Occasionally one hears some fine performances, but as to new discoveries of young pianists with real 'star' qualities, well, these are rare. For instance, at the last Tokyo Competition, no first prize was awarded and two pianists tied for the second prize. And this seems to happen more and more often, partly because the juries feel too great a responsibility when launching young artists on their career, so to speak, over night.

It is true that these competitions place tremendous strain, physical and psychological, on the candidates, but it is also true that even if they don't win a prize (there are only a few, of course!) they have the chance to be heard by a discerning audience and sometimes by critics who like to listen to other tests, not only the finals.

Occasionally the audience, or sometimes even the critics, do not agree with the jury's decision, and this is a very healthy reaction. This means that other candidates, not only the winners, get some publicity, and this is of tremendous help in their career. Of course, I have some reservations. It is one thing to obtain a prize, or the approval of the audience, or that of the critics, and another thing to be able to carry the burden of the stress which seems to be the permanent companion of any successful performer as he tries to keep up with the demands of his career.

Piano Journal VOL 3 NO 7 1982

Russell Sherman

You are not only one of the most outstanding pianists on the American scene, but I understand you are also a keen sportsman, and have appeared in radio programmes devoted entirely to discussions on athletics, and its various problems. Is there any relationship between piano playing and athletics?

Indeed, I have just been re-engaged to be the guest speaker in *Sportscope*, a Boston Radio programme, and this pre-occupies me passionately, for some of the vital questions regarding athletic coaching are so similar to our own. I am reminded of the philosophy of a certain coach – I believe he was an Englishman – who once said: 'The object of baseball is to hit a round ball with a round bat – squarely'.

Does this not remind you of the philosophy of a pianist, Anton Rubinstein, who said: 'To play the piano, one has to hit the right note, at the right time, with the right finger'?

Most people think the most difficult accomplishment is to hit a pitched baseball, which spins at 90 miles per hour, from 60 feet away, and being able to gage the speed and the spin of the ball as it curves, and at the precise moment, to strike it. This requires, in fact, the greatest combination of connection, of resilience, of elasticity, of relaxation, of tension. And that is exactly what is needed in piano playing. I believe that to achieve a superb combination of all these factors, the relationship between the conscious field and the unconscious energy needs to be developed through continuous and disciplined study. The nature of the study must go full circle, from the most intuitive to the most consciously planned movements, to produce the one right stroke at the keyboard to obtain the tones we want. Or, to phrase it in a more practical way for our students, the unconscious can only flourish upon a very highly developed conscious framework and context, which is the result of highly disciplined and serious preparation. 'Luck is when opportunity meets preparation' is indeed a very apt saying.

And this brings me to another very important point. In piano playing, the correct movements in response to the musical thought, are of tremendous importance, but it is of even greater importance to inhibit unnecessary movements. I wish to emphasise that movements should be part of music-making, as a result of the musical intentions and not vice versa. I see many students who are trained to use certain motions, so that the 'pure motion', untrammelled and unqualified by any other criteria, including musical criteria, becomes a circular thing in itself. The motion is so predominant that it tends to swallow the music and reduce its intensity – the disparities, the contrasts, the dramatic tensions, and produce the same kind of texture from one composer to another. This type of playing may do very well for certain music which demands elegance or gracefulness, but there are moments, for instance, when some bass notes must initiate a flow of energy which is best served not by a rotating pencil that descends like a swallow on those notes, but rather from a deeply grooved preparation when the tone is springing up, out of the keys, with great speed and intensity, ready to make its motion from that energy. That action may be also related to sports, to those most effective moments in boxing, when the sportsman throws punches which are not like long, curvilinear patterns, but are rather extremely charged and concentrated movements, full of energy which is immediately released.

Such playing, whether one is a pianist or a sportsman, requires supreme co-ordination of all senses and, to allow such a co-ordination, there must be some sort of centre from which everything springs out. I believe that the spine is the area where such a centre is situated. We are talking here about that state of the body 'beyond relaxation' – a state of balance which brings with it an economy of motion, which can result only from the perfect communication between all the facets and factors of the mechanical apparatus. As this is the 'sole apparatus', everything has to be in an ideal feedback cybernetic state within each part of this apparatus, so that the task can be completed in the most economical and successful way. One must study consciously every moment of the performance during the preparation, but in the actual performance you have to trust your body. There is no way, in the performance, that you can repeat and 'categorise' all the preliminary blueprints that you have made in the thousand hours of practice, those hours of careful and disciplined study. I am convinced that most tensions, whether physical or nervous, result from inadequate preparation. If the performer knows his music thoroughly in its spiritual, interpretative, and technical aspects, he has a much better chance of being in control during the performance. Yet, there is never a one hundred per cent guarantee. And it would be folly to deny that in every one of us artists, there is at times an emptiness and a doubt, and, in my case, even a nausea which sometimes holds an accusing finger as if saying: 'Are you sure that this is really the message which you wish to communicate?' In spite of this, there is a tremendous urge to go on initiating and communicating the music to an audience, and this struggle must have a meaning. After all, it is of our own choice!

With regard to my own playing, I was what one calls a rather late starter. My parents were not musical; they did not have money at that time, and I did not have lessons until I was eight years old. As a boy I enjoyed my piano lessons, as much as kicking a ball. With the years, I was getting more and more involved in making music, and when I was eleven I was very fortunate to have Edward Steuermann as a teacher. He had only recently arrived in New York, and, as he had not yet become the well-known teacher from the Juilliard School, my parents could afford to pay for the lessons, so that I had three lessons every week. Working with him was a revelation. He made me go through masses of technical exercises and studies, just as he had been trained to do in Poland, but he also introduced me to the works of the great masters. By that time, my mother was determined that I should be a pianist. I was still getting great excitement from baseball and other sports, and, one day, when playing with my brother, his little finger of one hand was badly hit and broken. I shall never forget my mother saying: 'Thank God it wasn't Russell's hand!' In fact, it was not only my mother, I had also made up my mind that this is what I was going to be – a pianist. Thanks to Mr. Steuermann, I soon acquired a good technique, and I was an avid reader. I wanted to play everything that came my way. We all know that a teacher can open a door to a student, but the artist really develops much later when he is alone, and the responsibilities are his.

I thought a great deal about my own playing and my teaching, and, I must say that I am pleased that now I am able to choose my students. With my students I try to work in the way that Edward Steuermann taught me, giving them a good foundation. I don't think there should be any distinction between the virtuoso and the musician, one without the other cannot exist. As to those 'physically gifted', I call this kind of playing 'facility', not real piano technique, and there is no room at the top for such players. Technique means actually 'to serve', in other words, to serve the spiritual and the musical.

Like most of my colleagues, I am very concerned about the great number of cases of tendonitis among piano students. Though I am quite relieved that there is no tendonitis in my own class, this is nevertheless a problem which has to be studied by all of us. It is difficult not to think that there is a psychological component involved, and this may come from the student's relationship with the instrument. If there is a local injury, this will become exaggerated by the stress surrounding the attitude towards the piano as an essential bridge to some very quick, unattainable success. When a student needs to get somewhere very fast, he does it with a certain ambitiousness, even certain desperation, and he keeps on driving himself. Strangely enough, I find that tendonitis affects mostly those students who appear serene, even relaxed, but, perhaps this is only on the surface, that 'butterfly' appearance being only a shield to hide the inner anxiety. It would be interesting to find out more about the relationship between the student's personality and tendonitis.

I believe that this has a great deal to do with the processes of action and reaction in piano playing, and of tension and relaxation. If one relaxes too much in one area, it over-compensates in another, and that is the point where the affliction occurs. One should, in fact, think in terms of a superb co-ordination, which allows the right distribution of tension in all its variety. The co-ordination necessary in any performance, whether playing an instrument or a fine game of sport, could be described as a series of suspensions: the spine is suspending the shoulders, which are suspending the elbows, which are suspending the wrists, which are suspending the hands, which are suspending the fingers, which are suspending the finger-tips... It is this series of interlocking suspensions, together with a kind of fluctuating feedback principle, which involve the total 'being' at the moment of performance. As teacher and as performer I am constantly working towards this goal. And I believe that this should be the goal of every musician, teacher or performer.

Piano Journal VOL 3 NO 8 1982

Jorge Bolet

You are one of the great pianists of our time, in the true tradition of the Golden Age of piano playing. As you yourself remarked in your famous Wigmore Hall conversation with the music critic of The Guardian, Edward Greenfield: 'There are not many of us left...' At the same time you show great interest in teaching, in communicating your knowledge and experience to young people. Do you agree with some of your colleagues — Myra Hess was one of them — who think that 'by giving so much of oneself to students, there is not enough energy left for one's own work'?

I don't think that is a good argument or a realistic argument. I think you can communicate to a student everything that you know, or as much as you know, or as much as you want, and still have twice as much left for yourself. I teach purely out of a sense of my own duty and much responsibility to the young generation. I think that musicians like myself have received something from the great masters of the past. If we just keep that to ourselves and do not pass it on to the next generation, the tradition stops. Yet, in spite of our work, this tradition will naturally evolve and take, perhaps, different shapes and different channels — but still it must be maintained.

I agree that it must take different channels. When we look back into the nineteenth-century style of performance, we find that artists took great liberties with the scores. As long as the performance highlighted the artist's own virtuosity and search for effects, the composer's intentions and markings were almost ignored.

On the other hand, today's scholars demand an exaggerated purism in the interpretation of the score, using computers to find things about certain notes which the composer did not put into the autograph score, but meant to. In my own case, I am trying to maintain the traditions of the Golden Age of piano-playing, as we mentioned earlier. Indeed, I believe that there are not many pianists left to represent this tradition, like Horowitz, Cherkasski, and perhaps just one or two more. I think piano-playing today has made tremendous advances as far as mechanics are concerned, but as far as what I call making music, that is, taking a dead piece of music and making it live through your own personality and your own ideas, communicating it to the listener – I think that kind of piano playing is in a low state today.

We have such opportunities today, with the many recordings both by contemporary artists, and those which have been reissued from the Golden Age. Now, when people can hear these recordings, there should be no room for mediocrity. So where do you think the problem lies? Is it in the teaching, is it the young people who haven't understood the spirit of the music – what do you think it is?

Well, how many young pianists do you know who know anything about the playing of Gieseking, Backhaus, Ignatz Friedmann, or Rachmaninov – not to mention Hoffmann? I find that the students are often totally ignorant of that kind of piano playing, that kind of personal approach to what they play. I think that you will find that the bulk of the young pianists today, the competition contestants, have the kind of mentality that would hear a performance by one of the older pianists and say, 'well, of course, that's passé, that's what they used to do a hundred years ago'. For instance, I have a student in Philadelphia who was one of the three winners of the Chopin competition in Florida. Yet I don't think he is the kind of performer to stand up to the major competitions. He is the type of young pianist I admire. He has musicianship and dedication, but I would never advise him to embark on a 'competition circuit'. You see, I think a competition winner is someone who plays everything well – which is the worst thing I could say about anybody. They play everything well, but they don't play anything superbly.

You have been associated with the Curtis Institute all your life, and now you are directing the Piano Studies.

Well, the Curtis Institute in Philadelphia, where I teach, is a unique institution. We have only a hundred-and-fifty-six students. I had two openings for piano for next season, and we auditioned almost eighty-five young musicians. I myself have just six students...

Do you teach in a masterclass situation, or do you teach your students individually?

I hold what I call 'class' generally in the recital hall, so that the students get used to playing on a platform with people listening. I think good preparation is essential, which is why we at Curtis like to get our students as young as possible. In an audition, for example, if there are two students of equal talent, and one is eighteen and one is fourteen, then we always take the younger one. All the members of our piano faculty came to the school young – I myself was twelve when I came to Curtis to study with David Saperton, another one was only nine – so we're all great believers that the time to get the really great talents is when they're young. Of course, that raises its own problems. For instance, right now, I have a fourteen year old student who has been in school since she was ten, and has been studying with me since the beginning of this year. She's a truly extraordinary musician. Naturally, we are all very much against her doing many concert performances on a big scale because that would ruin her…she would have three or four years – and then, who knows? So now we have to walk a fine line, giving her enough performances to keep her interested and happy. We would like to keep her in the school for another four years, until she is eighteen. She will still be young enough, yet sufficiently mature to start her career.

To be able to 'serve' the music, and do justice to the great works of piano literature, one must have the right tools to express the musical intentions. What is the secret of your own unique tone?

There is really no secret. As a general rule, I don't play for my students. I don't sit down at the piano and play what they're playing. I might play something that they don't play at the time to try to illustrate a point. My teaching is really concerned with showing them what the possibilities are, and what they can do, and, especially, steering them away from the pitfalls that a certain approach may lead them into.

Of course, I try to teach them style – which is something I find lacking in young pianists today. They play everything the way they play a Beethoven sonata. Whatever score they take, they study it in exactly the same way. There is one thing I tell my students, and this might shock your readers! Let us say we are studying a really romantic work, the Chopin Preludes, for example. All right, they have learnt the work, they know the notes, they know exactly where all the *sforzandi* are, where the *crescendi* or *diminuendi* are written; they can play it perfectly! Then I say, 'All right – now take the score, and throw it in the dustbin. From hereon just use your imagination. Just think of, and try to do, everything that is interesting – in fact, use your imagination, use your head!'

This does not mean that I do not respect the score myself. You might have heard that I have acquired a very bad reputation as being someone who doesn't give a damn about what the composer wrote. But ask anyone who has studied with me and they will tell you I am always pointing to the score, to say look what's written, and look at the way it is written. And nobody studies a score more carefully than I do. I assure you, whatever changes or alterations I might make in a score have been the result of many years of thinking and probing. Of course, in the performance there is the question of the artist's *personality* and this is what I am trying to encourage in my students, so that each one is able to bring his own personality and not attempt to imitate me or other famous performers.

You talked about ideas on the training of young talents like some of the prodigies in your care at Curtis, so that the great tradition of the Golden Age of piano playing is carried on. Perhaps you can tell us something about your own training, as you yourself were a prodigy.

As you know, I was born in Cuba and I just played the piano from an early age. When I was about ten an American lady came to Havana and heard me in the house of a friend. She thought that I had an unusual talent which should be cultivated, and soon afterwards I heard that I was accepted at the Curtis Institute, where Joseph Hoffman was the Director. David Saperton was his assistant and he took me in his class. I was already twelve years old at that time, and I loved every moment of my lessons. He was very strict, but also very understanding, and his students were giving of their best. Saperton was the great Godovsky's son-in-law — Popsey, as he called him. There was no lesson in which he would not mention what Popsey would say about a certain work, or what Popsey would do about a certain passage. Such reverence is rarely encountered. After about two years of studies, Mr. Saperton decided that I was ready to go to New York and play for Godovsky, but not before giving me one hundred pieces of advice on how to behave. I was terrified. No sooner had I arrived at Godovsky's studio when he told me in a solemn loud voice: 'I never say the same thing twice, so you'd better listen to every word I say, and if what I say is not applied or not understood then there is no need for you to come again.' I think I was all ears that afternoon and did not dare to ask one question. But I must not have done badly on my second visit, because he did not send me off. I went again on other occasions and my teacher was very proud that Popsey showed interest in his young student. As to the actual teaching, this was intended to develop a virtuoso technique and, at the same time, an understanding of the different styles of each composer. This was instilled in me from an early age and, of course, this is what I am trying to do in my own teaching. Talking about composers, I like to quote what I believe Godovsky, or perhaps someone else, said about Mozart. When a great musician arrived in Heaven he had a vision... Jesus Christ was on God's right side and Mozart was on God's lap. Isn't this a marvellous way of putting it?

Wherever I go now, I find that pianists and students are suffering from physical and nervous tension. Lately, I have found many cases of tendinitis – if not, the more serious 'carpel-tunnel' syndrome. Are many students at Curtis affected?

Yes, I have had experiences with tendinitis. I believe that most of these cases can be traced to over-exertion during practising, whether in the wrong or even in the right way. One of my students – a very good pianist, who won some important prizes – got the idea that unless he could play the Chopin Study Op. 25 twelve times straight through without getting tired, then he couldn't play it at all. Well, that was pure insanity. He got tendinitis. If one over-exerts muscles and tendons one is bound to cause some injury. I always tell my students: 'Whenever you are practising and you feel that your muscles in the forearm are all tense, and even get hot, stop! Don't try to go on. When your muscles are relaxed then go ahead.' There is another thing that can contribute to the problem: a piano with stiff action. Many people think that a good practice piano would have a stiff action, but they would not dream of performing on such an instrument! I also think that no matter how fortissimo a passage should be played, one should not use too much energy – it isn't necessary to use an inordinate amount of strength if one plays at the bottom of the key, with the arm weight. Regardless of how high the dynamic level is, the sound must always be round, beautiful, compact, and the pianist must listen all the time. Actually I find some of the outstanding pianists using too much tension in their playing, there is never a moment of repose or simplicity in the way they project their music...No wonder that there are physical injuries as a result! Really the important thing is always to achieve the utmost with the least effort.

Piano Journal VOL 4 NO 10 1983

Joseph Bloch

You are well known as a performer and lecturer, and, like Maurice Hinson, you have also been greatly involved in the study of piano literature. For the past three decades or so, you have made this field known to generations and generations of piano students at the Juilliard School, where you have pioneered the course on Piano Repertoire.

Yes, I have been fortunate. When I started my career, I had what was at that time an unusual combination of training as a performer and as a musicologist, with a Masters Degree from Harvard. Today, that kind of background is a *sine qua non* for a professional musician. I have been able to use that training to happy advantage at the Juilliard, where you have the very talented and career-oriented students, as well as excellent facilities. Thus, I have had the privilege of influencing and shaping the tastes of many young pianists, while developing the piano literature courses. I have visited many music schools all over the world, and I have been surprised to find that if a piano literature course exists at all, it is usually for one year only and attendance is optional. At the Juilliard, all the piano students are required to take this course in their third and fourth years as undergraduates, and then during all their graduate years. Thus it is possible for a student to study piano literature with me, for five years in great depth. The undergraduate course presents a general, chronological survey over a two-year period; starting with the 17th century (since the music of that period is played on the piano), we go through a great deal of Bach, Mozart, Beethoven, the great Romantics, up to the present time. At the postgraduate level, we concentrate on either one composer, or on specific forms of composition, such as sonatas, variations, concertos etc. The choice of subjects changes from year to year. For instance, this year we are studying the piano music of Fauré, which is a sheer delight for me and my classes, especially since Fauré's piano music appears so seldom on recital programmes. Last year we did all Mozart concertos; we have in the past studied all Schumann's piano music; and of course there is the music of Bach which takes many years to study in depth. As you may well imagine, the course remains constantly interesting for me, and over the years I have learnt a great deal about piano literature myself. The course is designed to be practical, and there are no exams or long essays to write. I have succeeded in eliminating all this, and I created just one place where all the students, as well as their teachers, can gather and play for each other. When we study either a particular period or one composer, each student plays one piece, or as much as chooses to present to the class. Sometimes the students just sight-read through the music if, of course, they are equipped to do so. Otherwise each one prepares a certain work. It is not a masterclass in the accepted sense and we do not criticise the performance. We talk about the music, the various styles and the various periods. I try to encourage the students to prepare their pieces quickly, because I know that this is an important aspect of a pianists career, to be able to do things quickly and adequately. But there is no pressure on them to give a polished performance. At the same time, our class is a wonderful place to try out a programme before an exam, or recital, and that is the time when the other professors like to join us.

I think that what is most important is not only that you teach all the piano students, and bring them together, but also that you inspire them to aim for the highest standards. They have a chance to develop under your guidance and your influence. I know the admiration and gratitude they all felt towards you and many admit that your classes have been the highpoint of their time at the Juilliard.

Well I've been there a long time. I have a lot of experience and I am very happy to be at my students' disposal whenever they want to play. I have learned not to give a piano lesson when someone plays for my class, and if he does something that I disagree with, I do not say, 'Where did you learn that?' Instead, I might suggest three or four other ways of playing that particular passage. Winning the trust of my colleagues to encourage their students to play in my class has not been easy, but I have learnt that diplomacy pays. Instead of criticising the performance we discuss problems of interpretation. I try to bring contemporary information from treatises of the period so that we know what was the general performing practice of the time. To return to Bach, whenever one student brings any of his works, I emphasise the importance of knowing about the performing practices that led up to his time. It is important to know about the first treatise of Diruta, at the end of the 16th century, which gives useful information about ornamentation, about rhythmic 'inequalities'. Also they should know about the Italian treatises, keyboard performances, the Frescobaldi Prefaces, about French treatises like Couperin's or Rameau's and the French ornamentation and so on. This is the aim of my course. It is not just to present incidental information but to let students know that such things exist. I try to be as objective as possible, for instance, in the case of the controversial questions of *notes inégales*. My own feeling is that rhythmic inequality is a useful device that can add colour and variety to a performance. It is essentially a French device, but there is a certain amount of evidence that Bach himself employed it. In any case, I let my students make up their own minds. If they want to play exactly as the music is written, the way so many fine performers do, that is their decision. But they should make their decision after knowing the other possibilities.

You have managed to combine your work at the Juilliard with your career as a performer all these years. Though it is true that you have often given lecture recitals using your wide knowledge of the piano literature and presenting it at teachers' conventions, you have also given many recitals and played with quite a few orchestras.

Yes, of course I started my career hoping to become a well-known pianist. For this it was necessary – just as it is today – to give a debut recital in New York and to embark on recital tours, almost from coast to coast, to get the critics to know my work and write about it. But, when I joined the Juilliard School, I realised that I could not spend all my time travelling and performing. Besides I did not want to do only that. I became very interested in studying music that was rarely played, and introducing it to students and teachers. I also enjoyed making these lecture recitals into an artistic experience for myself and for my audience, as I was not allowed to forget for one moment that I had a very critical audience of students, week after week. My lectures had to be presented in such a way that they were constantly interested and stimulated to learn more. I became greatly interested in composers or some particular works, like Scriabin, or Clementi sonatas, or the Delius concerto, and many others. With Scriabin it was 'love at first sight' although I was never convinced that he was a great composer. An interesting composer, yes, but not great! I had the privilege of visiting the Scriabin museum – which is really his last apartment in Moscow – which is kept exactly as it was when he lived there. I was allowed the play the sonatas no.5 and no.10 on his piano and to look at his manuscripts. As to Clementi, I have been trying to find out why he is still *terra incognita*. He wrote not less than 123 sonatas, but he is greatly neglected as a composer. But he is not an unjustly neglected genius. While some of his sonatas are interesting, with some movements well-written and containing some beautiful music, there is never a third movement to match the previous two. It is true that not all 123 sonatas are available but I have looked through about 35 of them in the original Clementi edition (a complete edition is in preparation) and each one of these presents the same structural weaknesses, mainly in the development of thematic material. Of course, we pianists owe a great deal to him as he is the first 'real' piano composer. He understood the instrument and *Gradus ad Parnassum* is indeed his masterpiece, a great lesson for pianists, giving them everything they need to play the piano literature of that time. He is known to many generations of piano pupils who have been brought up on a diet of Czerny studies and Clementi sonatinas which are quite charming when well-played. Occasionally one hears one of the Clementi sonatas at the beginning of a recital, and, thanks to Horowitz's recording of the F sharp minor sonata, this appears more often. It is interesting to mention that Beethoven was a great admirer of Clementi's *Gradus ad Parnassum* and of some of the sonatas. According to Schindler (his biographer) Beethoven had very little music in his personal library, he did not have any Haydn or Mozart sonatas, but he did have some of Clementi's! And, of course, every student of his had to know very well C.P.E. Bach's *Essay on the True Art of Playing Keyboard Instruments*.

Where did you study and who were your teachers?

I studied in Chicago with Rudolf Ganz, a Swiss pianist, pupil of Busoni. He was my model for many years, a versatile musician, a superb pianist, though not interested in being a pianist as such, a conductor anxious to introduce new music to audiences, a composer and a truly great teacher. He was particularly a protagonist of new music, knew all the important composers and gave the first performance of pieces by Debussy and Ravel who actually dedicated his *Scarbo* to Ganz. It was thanks to Ganz that I came to know Alkan's music as all of his students had to play some of the pieces. He got me so interested in this strange musical personality that I wrote what I believe is the first thesis on Alkan, for my Masters degree at Harvard. Ganz liked to tell how Busoni, his teacher, introduced him to Alkan. Busoni was a true admirer of Alkan and when he was asked to conduct the Beethoven third piano concerto in Berlin around 1900 he invited Rudolf Ganz to be the soloist, on the condition that he played Alkan's cadenza. This is a monstrosity, which takes more time to play than the whole first movement of the concerto, and introduces even the theme from the fifth symphony in the climax... Of course, the critics just tore that cadenza – and poor Ganz – apart for doing it! Yet, he retained his interest in Alkan's music and I am grateful that I studied some of the virtuoso pieces like *Scherzo Diabolico*... They did me a lot of good.

As a teacher, Ganz was most inspiring and stimulating when discussing interpretation, but he had no time, and no inclination to teach technique. He passed on his students who did not posses a virtuoso technique – and I was one of those, as I came rather late to the piano – to his assistant, Mollie Margolies. She was a wonderfully understanding and patient teacher, dedicated to teaching and very devoted to Ganz. Thanks to her I developed my technique and she made me go through Chopin's Etudes, mastering them only because she knew how to teach them. Some of my most valuable technical experiences were passed on to me by Mollie who was very inventive with giving special exercises for each specific problem in the Etudes, not unlike Cortot's ideas later on. The most valuable hint was what she called 'doublings' – for instance in the *Double Thirds Etude*, every pair of notes is to be played twice, thus 'doubling the difficulty'. Take the group of first four 16ths and play the first two 16ths twice, and the other two, twice, and so on. Also, we had to do these in different keys, in different dynamics, and legato, staccato, etc... and it worked. Her philosophy was to expand the difficulty by multiplying the problems. When meeting, let us say, a one octave leap (as in the last page of Ravel's *Toccata*) she advised me to practise a *two* octave leap down in the bass and afterwards, the one octave leap seemed so easy!

Later on I went to New York to study with the then famous teacher, Olga Samaroff. She was a great lady, a sort of high Priestess of the Samaroff cult, who took great interest in her students, if they were any good. But, like Ganz, she had no interest in teaching technique as such. Her greatness came through her extraordinary personality and through the way she introduced her talented students to the public and built up their careers. Of course, she was a very stimulating teacher. She knew what she wanted and she knew how to get it. Nothing less than perfection was good enough for her! She did not hold masterclasses, instead she gave soirées when the girl students had to wear formal dresses with the hair done just as Madame had suggested, while the boys had to wear black tie. Famous people, conductors, critics, managers, potential patrons would be there and she would invite anyone who could be useful in furthering a young artist's career. It was an ordeal to appear on such evenings but those of us who survived them certainly succeeded later in the profession. What better training could one get to cope with the strain of performing?

Joseph Bloch, you have been a great friend of EPTA right from its beginning and this is greatly appreciated. Many of us remember your first lecture recital on Schumann's Kinderszenen at the first EPTA conference in Chichester, and now we are proud to have your video-tapes with the Satie Sports et Divertissements and the illustrated talk on Clementi, in the EPTA Centre's library. We are, of course, looking forward to many more such appearmances.

Indeed, I am very proud to be associated with a prestigious organisation such as EPTA, which has brought so many pianists and piano teachers together, not only from Europe but from far away places like Australia, Singapore, Japan, Canada, Israel, USA. As Maurice Hinson says: 'The EPTA pipe-line is constantly busy!'

Piano Journal VOL 4 NO 10 1983

Maurice Hinson

Your interests as a musician and pianist are so diverse that it would be very important to hear you talk about your work in its various aspects: as a scholar, as the editor of the American Liszt Society Journal, *as a performer and presenter of unusual piano repertoire and also as a pedagogue who has given a great deal of thought to the problems of teaching.*

Well, let me first say that everything I do is to help someone else. This is the basis of my philosophy. If I have been given any talent or any abilities it is my duty and responsibilities to pass some of this on to others. I have tried to make performers and teachers conscious of the great range of piano literature that exists as most of them are hardly aware of the treasures lying beneath the surface. This has been the direction of many of my efforts over the years, focussing my research specifically on this great body of literature and making it available to piano students and teachers. I started with research into solo piano repertoire, when I was studying at the University of Michigan, where I became greatly interested in various editions. This was back in the fifties when Urtext editions were just beginning to appear and this brought me to do some study in this area. A few years later, Irvin Freundlich, professor at the Juilliard School, asked me to collaborate in producing a new book on 'Music for Piano'. We decided that I should work from Haydn to contemporary music while he would concentrate on the repertoire from pre-Bach to Haydn. I duly finished my half during my first sabbatical when he called me to say that, as he had no time to do his part, I should complete the whole book, and, if I wished, he would edit it. That is how *Guide to the Pianists Repertoire* came into being. I had great encouragement and inspiration from Freundlich throughout the whole project. The profession seemed to receive it very well and the next thing I knew I was asked to work on *The Piano in Chamber Ensemble*, an annotated guide. Afterwards, another book followed, *Music for Piano* and *Orchestra*, which, basically, consists of the concerto repertoire. In the meantime I produced *The Piano Teachers Sourcebook* to help teachers to decide what to choose for their teaching, which can be done only if they know what has been written about the various methods and books on piano teaching. Lately I have been working on a new project researching 'music for more than one piano', which actually involves not only two-part literature, but also some oddities for three, four or even more pianos. I am looking at literature than tends to treat the instruments equally, not just as a reduction of an orchestral part. Of course, the work I am doing as editor of the American Liszt Society Journal has to do with my continuous interest in musicology. I am very interested in Liszt's contribution to the world of piano playing and there has been some original research into his music and his pianism which we are happy to publish in our bi-annual journal. I do have one assistant – I have always worked with only one assistant – usually one of my students in the doctoral programme at my college, the Southern Baptist Theological Seminary, in Louisville, Kentucky.

In my teaching, I believe that acquiring a 'working' technique is absolutely vital. One cannot play the great works of piano literature without having the technique to execute it. I strongly believe that there is no difference between art and technique but, to reinforce this, it is essential to have, so to speak, at ones finger-tips the ability to play scales, arpeggios, octaves etc., not as simple exercises with fingers moving up and down the keyboard, but as keys, listening to the sound and colour of each tone, each chord, to the way one produces a crescendo or a diminuendo, and so on. I spend a lot of my time in the lesson to make sure that all aspects of technique are mastered. Above all I try to make my students aware that in order to perform the music of the 19th century great romantics the hand is actually divided in two parts: the thumb and the second finger, or sometimes the third, forms one part, while the other fingers usually have to play a melodic line, thus forming the other part of hand. These are some the points I emphasise in my teaching. But, this is only through listening, listening and again listening, that one develops as an artist.

It is also true that I can be of great assistance to my students through the work of research that I have been doing along the years. It is not enough to know about the piano literature. It is important to know something about the composer, about the background of how the piece studied was written, when it was written, why it was written, to whom it was dedicated, and so on, if we are to understand the style of the composer and of that particular piece. You know very well that each piece represents its particular character and its specific style. There is another aspect of my teaching which I believe is an essential part of the teaching of my students. I am strong believer in developing the inner ear so that one hears every single nuance that is in the score. That is why I encourage them to study the score away from the keyboard, and then to think through it, still away from the keyboard. This is an ideal way of practising, and the students realise that one can do this better when one is not at the keyboard worrying about the finger technique! I have devised a silent keyboard which is on one side of my desk while I sit at the other side with the score, watching the student playing his programme silently, from memory. This is the best training I know which helps the student to gain the confidence that his memory will always serve him. The students preparing for graduation have to go through their programme on that silent keyboard, from memory, at least six weeks before the recital.

You are one of the few artists who excel both as a lecturer and a performer. What is your secret of being able to maintain this high standard of piano playing in spite of the many other time consuming activities?

Perhaps I can achieve more in one day than many of my colleagues because I am a very early riser. I am up at 4 am, when I do my writing and other studies at home, undisturbed in my studio. At 8 am I am in the college practising the piano until 10 am when I start teaching. The two hours I spend at the piano every day keep me in form, and I am always able to present at least two recital programmes. But, as we all know most artists go through much of their study of repertoire away from the keyboard, and I do the same whether reading a score or just going through some pieces in my mind.

Naturally I owe this disciplined and methodical way to my training from early childhood. My mother was an organist, one of my sisters played the violin, another sister was a piano teacher and there was always music in the house. We went to many concerts in our own town and in the neighbouring areas and I heard some of the greatest artists and orchestras of that time.

Although I did not start having formal piano lessons until I was 11 – rather late! – I always played the piano on my own, by ear or trying to learn what my sister or my mother played, or playing duets with them. But soon afterwards I had the opportunity to attend the summer courses at Sherwood Music School in Chicago and for a boy of 13, eager to learn, this first meeting with real musicians made a tremendous impression. Leo Podolski, a famous pianist and teacher (now in his nineties and still going strong!) gave me lessons that summer and I returned to the summer school until I was 15. At that time I wanted to have a change and attended the Juilliard Summer School. As I was at school all throughout the year, I could only study music thoroughly through the summer months and I was fortunate that at the Juilliard, the great Olga Samaroff accepted me into her class. I never expected such an honour, since most of her students were already well known young artists like Rosalyn Tureck, Eugen Liszt, Isabel Byman, Joseph Bloch. She spent a lot of time teaching me the essential technical skills always insisting on the correct hand position. But mainly she taught me the art of listening to the tone I was producing and of listening to my own playing with a critical ear. She was very demanding and this made me work even harder to get the right results. Perhaps it was through her influence that I became such a compulsive worker, never satisfied and striving towards higher achievements. She was very kind to me and understanding of my youth and limitations and when we were working at a Mozart sonata she would send me to the Metropolitan Museum to look at 18th century paintings and at the furniture collections; she gave me a fine biography of Mozart and insisted that I should go to hear the Marriage of Figaro. She also gave me a book of Moliere's plays to get me to understand Mozart's style! I try to instil the same interest in the arts and literature in my students. I think that so many times, we piano teachers and pianists do not look around us to know more about the other arts and that such knowledge should be part of us. I always remember Madame Samaroff telling me: 'Maurice, above all, you must exhaust the printed score!' When Madame Samaroff died a few months later I was in the midst of working for my debut recital in the New York Town Hall, so I went to the then-famous Edwin Hughes, who had been Leschetizky's assistant in Vienna for several years. Thus I was introduced to Leschetizky's teaching. My recital was well received by critics, though most of them wrote that 'this young man – I was only 16 – has talent but he needs to study more...' I then went to the University of Florida where I took my BA in music and afterwards spent one year in France where I became acquainted with the French composers whose works were hardly ever played in the States. Debussy and Ravel were already included in pianists' programmes, but Fauré, even today, is very seldom performed. For me it was a revelation to discover Fauré's piano music, and I think that his Theme and Variations is one of the great sets of variations ever written. At the University of Michigan, where I prepared my Doctorate, I worked with Joseph Brinkman, who had studied with Schnabel, and his influence on my development as a pianist and musician was very important at the time. I am convinced that Schnabel was a force, there is no question about it, and I don't think that the world of piano has been the same since... I remember one of the masterclasses which I attended when a student was going to play an English Suite by Bach. She asked what she should do about repeats. 'Just play them better the second time' came Schnabel's reply amidst great laughter...

To sum up my work, I am trying to be true to my philosophy – to give others as much as possible, through music, whether I teach, perform or write. And this gives me great satisfaction.

Piano Journal VOL 4 NO 10 1983

Kendall Taylor

Your long and distinguished career as a performer and teacher has been widely recognised, and your experiences in the service of music have now been summed up in one of the most important books for pianists and teachers alike: Principles of Piano Technique and Interpretation. I believe that it has already been translated into several different languages. Moreover, the great number of young pianists who have made a name in this overcrowded profession are a vivid and constant testimony to your achievements.

I am happy to hear this. Indeed, I have always found teaching and working with young pupils a great source of joy and inspiration. One learns so much, and I know I could not have written this book at an earlier stage. I needed that continuous study along the years, revising and rethinking, looking at the masterpieces of piano literature again and again, finding perhaps new angles and new approaches. There is never an end. And I can say that every pupil has given me some new ideas, as each one presented not only his own personality, but a different physique and it was fascinating to find how different hands cope with the same technical problems. On the other hand I should hate to be known as the teacher who has churned out pianists which one recognises immediately as 'Kendall Taylor's pupils'. No. I like to think that they have developed in their own direction and that they are themselves, with distinct personality in their playing. It is true that I have been privileged to get some of the most talented youngsters as students, not only from this country, but from many other parts of the world. My main concern is to give them a sound foundation of technique, and to make them think for themselves about the pianistic problems. Without such a foundation they cannot develop as artists – technique and interpretation are really one. But once they have acquired the tools, I encourage them to 'branch out', in their own specialised style according to their own personality. This I have also learnt from my own teacher, Herbert Fryer, who allowed – or better say 'stimulated' – each of his students to be first musicians, then pianists. Each one of us developed our own personal style. There was Cyril Smith, my contemporary and very great friend, and Lance Dossor, and, later on, Colin Horsley came into Fryer's class and, well, we are all so different. As to his teaching, he was mainly interested in the music, and getting us to expand our repertoire. Most of his students were dedicated young musicians determined to enter the profession as concert pianists. Fryer did not talk much about technique, and if a student did not have a serious technical foundation, he did not gain much. Or, perhaps, Fryer was not interested either. But for those who could play the piano – as was the case with Cyril Smith, who had a splendid mechanism – he could be a most inspiring teacher.

I was fortunate that I came from a musical home, and I started to play the piano very early. I did not have formal lessons, but my father was a professional cellist, and he encouraged me to play with him. Thus, my first contact with music was by learning to accompany him. I just kept going, and soon afterwards I found myself playing trios and other chamber music with my father's friends, and I became a very good sight-reader before I had any foundation of technique. It was decided that I should have piano lessons, and my first teacher was Vera Dawson, who had studied in Frankfurt and who believed in Czerny studies and plenty of technical exercises as a daily diet for a budding pianist. Being such a fluent sight-reader, I could polish off at least half a dozen of the *School of Velocity* or *Finger Dexterity* every week, so, when I got my scholarship at the Royal College of Music, I was immediately accepted in Herbert Fryer's class. At that time I was also very interested in composition and I joined Gustav Holst's class, and this was a turning point in my development as a musician. I think that he had the greatest influence on my whole life. He also introduced me to the works of other English composers, and I started to perform their piano music. Another important musician from whom I learnt a great deal was R.O. Morris, a fine scholar whose book on sixteenth-century counterpoint is still a standard textbook. Although I had to do a lot of teaching to support myself because my father died when I was only thirteen, I was working very hard to develop as a pianist, as this was what I wanted to be. It is true that I received a great deal of encouragement and support and I consider myself fortunate that I was able to play in public, giving recitals and as soloist in concertos, quite early in my career. I found myself in great demand during the last war, and, afterwards when travel was again possible, I think I visited most parts of the world, performing, teaching, lecturing, adjudicating. It was Barbirolli who first took me abroad. When he returned from America where he had been conducting the New York Philharmonic for about four years, he took over the Hallé Orchestra in Manchester, and I became a regular soloist with the Hallé. Playing with such a fine conductor was a wonderful experience. and we performed many concertos, from Mozart, Beethoven, the Romantics, to twentieth century and, of course, English composers were often included. Barbirolli asked me to be his soloist in Vienna, at a music festival, when I played the Prokofiev Concerto No. 3. This was my first appearance abroad, and afterwards, he took me to Yugoslavia, then to the Cannes Festival, in France, where the John Ireland Concerto was very well received. The British Council sent Barbirolli and myself to many parts of the world as 'ambassadors' of British music. I always included our composers in my recital programmes, and I am very happy and proud to have contributed to make them known.

I am soon going to Canada for a tour of concerts and masterclasses, and I shall perform the First Piano Concerto of Alan Rawsthorne again, which I think is a very fine work, perhaps the best among British concertos. He wrote a second one for the Festival of Britain in 1951, but, like most specially commissioned works, it lacks spontaneity, in spite of Rawthorne's superb craftsmanship. The First Concerto is a very original work, and I do hope that some of our young pianists will introduce it into their programmes. It has three movements: Capriccio, then a Chaconne, and the third movement is a Tarantella. When I played the concerto for the first time with the Vancouver Orchestra, in Canada, at one point during the rehearsal the whole orchestra burst out laughing, and I was rather surprised and actually embarrassed. What could I have done? The conductor then asked me if I was aware that the North American drinking song 'My God, how dry I am' was included in the Tarantella. Of course this was very amusing, but I had no idea that it appears towards the end of the concerto.

From Canada I am going to Yugoslavia, a country which means a great deal to me, as you know. I met my wife over there during one of my early tours, and I am happy to know that I have been instrumental for many of the artistic exchanges between our two countries. There are some outstanding pianists and composers in Yugoslavia and I do play some of their music.

You are giving a masterclass and recital at the next EPTA Conference, in July. Indeed, you have done much to bring Yugoslav and English pianists and teachers together. After all, this is what EPTA is about, giving piano teachers from many countries opportunities to meet and exchange ideas. Could you perhaps give us a brief outline on your approach to conducting a masterclass?

I shall conduct the EPTA masterclass in my usual manner. First, I emphasise some general principles of technique, as I do find that even the most talented youngsters, with real keyboard skill, need some elucidation, some understanding of how to use their arms, hands, and particularly the wrist, with complete freedom. Then I talk about the basic approach to interpretation with reference to the particular work we shall study. You see, music is essentially progressing in time, it is flowing before you all the time and you cannot stand back and see the whole work as when looking at a painting. Yet, when learning a piece of music, we must also try to get a perspective view of the entire work, and only afterwards begin studying it in detail. I believe that the rhythm is most important, it must be scanned first so that the student feels it strongly; and that he realises the length and direction of each phrase, how the short phrases flow into one another, and gradually the whole structure of the work is clearly defined. There should not be any excessive punctuation or breaks, but I advise the student to find a 'common denominator', a tempo that works for a whole movement. A fine interpretation demands a unified tempo, not a rigid, metronomical one. Sometimes it is so tempting to linger, as for instance, in that sublime opening of the Beethoven Concerto No. 4 in G, only to find afterwards that the orchestra must go on, and picks up another tempo! So, you have to think of it, turning it and shaping it in your mind, humming it while conducting the phrase, and making it as expressive and as moving as you can, but a 'common denominator', on which the whole work depends, must be established. I often ask the students to stop playing sometimes, and just think. What is the work about? Can you go silently through it in your mind? Or perhaps, if you are playing – let us say – a Beethoven sonata, imagine yourself conducting it, orchestrating the work in your mind, listening to the different timbres of each instrument. This would give tonal colour and, of course, a work comes to life through sensitive use of tonal subtleties. I am looking forward to the masterclass at EPTA, and I do hope that the young pianists who will play for me will gain something from our working together.

You have made a thorough study of the piano literature, performing a great many works and teaching them to generations of pianists. Do you find that your approach to these works has changed along the years?

Of course, one does not stand still, and I am grateful for this. When I was very young I wanted to play all the pieces demanding great virtuosity, as I was anxious to impress the audiences. I vividly remember my first recital in London, when I dared play the Liszt Sonata. You see, at that time, it was very rarely played, not like today when many young pianists include it in their programmes. Although I love hearing it – I believe that it is a truly great work – I do not wish to play it myself. I seem to be turning more and more towards late Beethoven works, Mozart; I still love playing the French Impressionists and, of course, Chopin's music is, for me, so satisfying. As for twentieth-century music, well, I am still rather 'conservative' in my tastes. I love playing Bartok, Hindemith, Messiaen, and some of our English composers like Norbert Fullton, John MacCabe, John Ireland – we have now a splendid batch. Recently, I was asked to play the First Concerto by Ginastera, which he wrote eight years after his Sonata, with the same kind of ideas. There is a fine Scherzo movement, with very inventive music, and I am quite interested in performing it.

Among your students you have quite a few youngsters who have been at the recently established music schools, like the Yehudi Menuhin, Cheatham, Purcell and St. Mary's. As you know, some of these talented pupils have already participated in important national and international competitions. What are your views on these competitions?

I am not against competitions in general. In spite of their negative aspects, there are many advantages, and many young pianists have the opportunity to play for very discriminating audiences. But, I believe that the age of participants should be raised to at least 19, so that the pressure of school work, with the taxing O- and A-level examinations, is over. Preparing for an important competition, then performing under the glaring light of television cameras, when many of them are, perhaps, appearing for the first time in a public concert, puts enormous pressure on these young talents, and the strain may damage their health. Then, there is added anxiety for the winners, who find themselves in great demand and not all are able to fulfil the engagements. They have not had the necessary time to go through a large repertoire, and this needs some maturing before being presented in public. There should be closer co-ordination between the organisers of such competitions, the directors of music of the specialised music schools, and perhaps headmasters and parents should also have a say. I, personally, am glad that this matter is now being taken up by a number of professional bodies like ESTA, and EPTA, and that, at the European Conference of EPTA Associations in Hamburg in October 1983, there will be a special symposium on the 'Pros and Cons' with regard to International Competitions for instrumentalists under 19 years of age.

Piano Journal VOL 4 NO 11 1983

Edith Picht-Axenfeld

You hold a very interesting place in the musical profession — pianist, harpsichordist, pedagogue, educationalist, and editor. Recently, you found the time to devote your energies to the running of EPTA West Germany, as one of its three Presidents. How do you combine these activities, at the same time coping with the strain of constant travel?

It is quite simple. You must love what you are doing. All my life I have been involved in making music and, really, I cannot remember much beyond sitting at the piano, playing or studying new works. It is only natural that I should want to share my experiences with others, with my students, with my audiences, and I am grateful that I have something to offer. I spend a great deal of time working at my instrument, or shall I say instruments, but I also believe in 'meditation', not in the accepted sense of the word, belonging to a specific mystical group, but being alone with myself; thus, my travels are not a waste of time and energies. On the contrary, I spend this time quietly, thinking, being in touch with myself and my music, listening in my mind to every sound of the works I am going to play at my next concert. When I reach the next destination, I get off the train, or the plane, and I feel that I am ready to begin. There is always continuity.

I have also practised the Alexander Technique for the past ten years or so, and I have found this discipline akin to my way of thinking. It has brought new dimensions to my awareness of a lightness of the body in spite of its weight, a totality of my whole being. When I play I experience a wonderful sensation, as if the music is 'sounding through my being' with no barriers, and is communicated to the audience. The music is allowed to 'happen', my whole body has an upward direction with my arms moving freely along the keyboard.

Your name has always been associated with Bach's music. Recently you have given no fewer than fourteen recitals, all devoted to his keyboard music. To achieve such a 'marathon' you must know this music, understand it, and love it profoundly.

Yes, this is true. I do not remember exactly when I began to play the piano; I must have been three, or perhaps four. I was the youngest of five children, and my brother and my elder sisters all played an instrument. I loved listening to them, and tried to pick up their tunes on the piano. When I was five my grandmother convinced my parents to allow me to have piano lessons. My teacher, Paula Roth Kastner, came from Vienna and, although she was quite strict, she knew how to guide me, and I loved every moment of my studying with her. Fortunately for my development, she had been brought up on a diet of Bach's music, and there was never a lesson without a Minuet or a little Prelude. Sometimes she would play for me some of the more difficult pieces, and she would often mention that when I was six I ran into my mother's room, excited, and with tears in my eyes, shouting: 'Oh, mama, I want to play Bach all my life!' And this I have done.

I stayed with the same teacher until I was eighteen, and I studied the great Classics – Haydn, Mozart, Beethoven – playing a great many sonatas and concertos. She did not encourage me to play Chopin or other Romantic composers. But there was always Bach. I found his music so satisfying, so natural to play, and very 'self-sustaining'. Thus, by the time I was thirteen or fourteen, I had played every single piece by Bach that I could lay my hands on. My teacher was quite impressed when one day I brought the Goldberg Variations to my lesson, which I had learnt on my own and memorised. She inspired in me this great love of Bach's music, and I shall always be grateful to her.

But I owe my deep understanding and my intense desire to learn more about Bach and about music in general to a young violinist and musicologist, Erich Doflein, who came to live in our house in Freiburg when I was about fourteen (he later married my violinist sister, and together they founded a well-known Violin School). Freiburg was an old, quiet town with a cultured and very musical population. There were frequent concerts with fine artists, and I remember being taken every year to hear the St. Matthew Passion, an important musical event in our town. Erich decided to start a series of courses, more like seminars, together with two of his friends, presenting regular musical Soirées, which included music from Bach to 'modern' composers. This was in the early Twenties, when the 'modern' composers were Schoenberg, Stravinsky, or Hindemith – whose works had recently been published. He simply said: 'Edith, you will play the illustrations for my talks' –

and I did. He began with the Two-Part Inventions and the Sinfonias, then the Suites and Partitas, and so on. Every week he would bring a pile of music which I had to prepare for the next seminar, sometimes producing 'new music' in manuscript if it was not yet published. It was hard work, but very stimulating. What greater opportunity for a young player, eager to learn, than being allowed to take part in this music making? I owe it to Erich's encouragement that I got acquainted with masterpieces of piano literature, and that I was able to develop as a performer. His humility and his devotion to these great composers taught me another lesson – he made me realise that a performer is there to serve the music. At about the same time I had another revelation, perhaps one of the most important experiences of my life. Erich came home one day, very excited – it was in 1928, I think. The orchestral arrangement by Graeser of The Art of Fugue had just been published, and its first performance was to take place in Basel Cathedral – a Swiss town not far from Freiburg. Of course, every aspiring musician and music lover was there, and I was among them. This was to be a crucial point in my musical development. Soon afterwards I got hold of the score and I began to study it, guided by Erich. I wanted to play this extraordinary music, but I did not find the piano sound satisfactory. It needed different timbres, I thought, and I decided to teach myself the harpsichord. Actually, my generation of harpsichordists were all self-taught. We had to find out everything about the instrument, its rules and how to use it, by ourselves. It was only later that a number of books appeared, and students could go to some well-known players to have lessons. Although I teach my students to play Bach on the piano, I, myself, have always played it on the harpsichord. As I have mentioned earlier, I recently presented a series of fourteen harpsichord evenings, all devoted to Bach's keyboard music. Why fourteen? I could perhaps have included three or four more programmes, but I stopped at this number quite unaware of its implication until one of my colleagues remarked on the importance of the number 14 in Bach's music. It is the symbol of his own name, and it is a known fact that numerical symbolism played a great role in his music. If one considers that every letter of the alphabet corresponds to a number: B-2, A-1, C-3, H-8, these add up to fourteen. It is interesting to note that the subject of the first Fugue in C in Book 1 of The Well-tempered Clavier has fourteen notes, as if Bach had inscribed his signature at the beginning of this work.

I might also have subconsciously decided that these recitals should 'not have an end', just as Bach himself had written on the last page of the Goldberg Variations manuscript: 'U.S.W. – Und so weiter (and so on)' – to the Infinite. These variations are among the few works published during Bach's life, and they represent an example of the rigid rules of proportion and numerical symbolism to which he subjected his composing. Friedrich Sound, a well-known German musicologist and theologian, has published a study on this aspect of Bach's music, and there are several other scholarly essays on the subject. The structure of the *Goldberg Variations* has often been compared to the window of a Gothic cathedral: they begin with the Aria, then the 30 variations grow, reaching a climax at the 15th variation, and end coming back to the same point – the Aria. When Christof Wolf discovered the manuscript in Strassbourg, he remarked that there was an extra page on which Bach showed how new canons and other endless combinations could be written on the famous Bass figure, ending with the inscription 'U.S.W.'

Did you decide to embark on a concert career, or did this emerge as an organic experience, through your continually living with music and, as you said earlier, always wanting to share it with your listeners?

Although I have played in public since I was thirteen or fourteen, my parents did not encourage me to launch on a concert career until I had a teacher's Diploma. They sent me to Switzerland when I was eighteen, and I was accepted as a pupil by the outstanding musician and pedagogue, Anna Hirzen-Lagenhahn. She lived in the mountains, in a small castle, surrounded by a circle of artists, poets and musicians, over which she presided. Every evening there were poetry recitals, concerts, and discussions. She was a most stimulating musician, and I stayed with her two years at first, but later on I returned again to work with her, but not on a regular basis. She had developed her 'own method', with special technical exercises which we all had to practice assiduously every day. She was very demanding, and only the best performances were good enough for her, but she was a woman of great vision when it came to the interpretation of the masters. From her I have learnt the importance of beginning my daily practice sitting still at the piano, with arms and hands in playing position, with eyes closed, listening intently to the sounds in the head, slowly beginning to feel the keys, their smooth ivory, their depth, and gradually allowing the music to flow through the body, through the instrument, reaching the listener and going beyond. This she called 'meditation'. Indeed, Schott's have recently issued Anna Hirzen-Lagenhahn's book on piano technique (*The Art of Piano Playing*), which I have edited, and I hope that one day it will be translated into English.

I was also very fortunate that I have been able to study with Rudolf Serkin before the Second World War. He was very young when I first heard him play in Freiburg with his father-in-law, the violinist, Adolf Busch. I was so impressed with his playing that I had only one desire, to be accepted by him as a student, and was thrilled when he agreed to give me lessons. The Busch-Serkin Duo left Germany when the Nazi regime came to power and they settled in Switzerland for some time, in Basel. It was very difficult for me to cross the frontier to go to Basel from Freiburg, as I had to get special permission every time, but I did manage to study with him until late in 1935. This young artist was not only a great performer but also a great teacher. Very intolerant. There was never the slightest mention about you, the player, only about the music and its challenge, demanding complete subservience to the composer's intentions, and to the spirit of the work. I brought the *Hammerklavier Sonata* one day to the lesson, and summed up my courage to tell him that I did get rather tired when playing the Fugue. He laughed and said: 'But, Edith, if there is still anything left of you after playing this Fugue, this means that you have not played it at all!'

Technique was hardly ever mentioned, and he expected you to solve your own problems by thinking musically. I wonder if he ever noticed that I was less than half his size!

With Serkin you studied mostly the great Classics, but you have also made a special study of Schoenberg's music and that of his pupils, Berg and Webern. Your London Recital (October 1982) showed great insight into the complexities of their works. It was an unforgettable experience, as if we heard these pieces for the first time.

Erich Doflein's influence on my development as a musician was decisive, and thanks to him I became acquainted with these works when they were first published, or sometimes, even in manuscript. But it was much later that I decided to study them thoroughly, during the centenary of Schoenberg's birth, in 1973. With my friend and colleague, Professor Budde from the Berlin University, we worked out a programme which included Schoenberg's complete piano works, and those of his pupils, Alban Berg and Anton Webern. We introduced this programme in many parts of Germany to very enthusiastic audiences – Professor Budde talking about the works while I was playing them. We thought that, through in-depth analysis of these complex compositions, students may understand how to perform them. It is a great honour for me to have been invited to present the same programme in Vienna, the birthplace of these great composers, and, during the summer of 1983, to give a series of courses and concerts on 'Twentieth-century Viennese Music' at the famous Mozarteum in Salzburg.

You have been a professor at Freiburg Hochschule für Musik since its foundation in 1947, working with piano and harpsichord students. Do you find teaching a rewarding experience?

I started to teach quite early on, and when my husband and I got married, we came to live in Hinterzarten, at the Birklehof School, where he was appointed Headmaster. These were the difficult war years, and I found solace in my working with young pupils in a boarding school, in charge of the music department. I had to conduct the choir, build an orchestra, teach class music, and give piano lessons, but also, I did a great deal of playing. We even managed to build a special Concert Hall, and there was music every evening. The Preludes and Fugues of Bach became our daily prayer and these, I am convinced, sustained us through those agonising times under the Nazi regime. We were a very close community, and this taught me the importance of bringing music to young children. I strongly believe that every child should be given the opportunity to learn about music and the great composers; it is so necessary for their development as human beings.

When Freiburg Hochschule was founded, after the war, I was invited to join it, and I have been teaching there ever since. We remained in the Old Birklehof House, and sadly, my husband died last year, but I am carrying on as, I am sure, he had wished me to do. Actually, I am now retired, but I have been asked to continue to teach a number of piano and harpsichord students at the Hochschule. I love working with them, they are all fine musicians and we make music together. We discuss the works in depth, and, if their technique is not well developed, I find the Langenhahn exercises most useful for strengthening the fingers and hand, and for acquiring dexterity. But many of my students come from Japan or other Far Eastern countries, and they have extraordinary physical ability; they are all very well taught with regard to technique. I try to stimulate them to become more aware of the profound ideas expressed in the music, about the importance of working away from the instrument, thinking about the music, the structure, its direction, and feeling it deeply. I sometimes use the Langenhahn approach to 'meditation', helping them to experience that stillness in the mind and in the body, so beneficial to all of us.

Piano Journal VOL 4 NO 12 1983

Shura Cherkassky

In a recent issue of the Piano Journal we published an interview with Jorge Bolet who talked, among other things, about piano playing today. He said that 'there were very few pianists of the stature of a Joseph Hoffman, a Godowsky, or the Lhevinnes left, but certainly Shura Churkassky is one of them.' What do you think of such a statement?

Well, it is not easy for me to answer such a question. What Bolet really meant was that he himself is hoping to keep up the tradition of the 'Golden Era' of piano playing and he does it splendidly. The two of us have been prodigy pupils at the Curtis Institute in Philadelphia and have been brought up in this particular tradition which demanded not only a virtuoso technique, but also great imagination, a sense of performance, knowing how to project the music; and the artist's personality was allowed to expand freely. While I believe that today's piano playing has reached a very high standard of technique and the teaching is of a high calibre, considering the number of very good young pianists, something of the originality of the artists mentioned by Bolet is perhaps lacking in these young performers. They are so concerned with giving performances true to the Urtext and they listen so conscientiously to recordings of artists whom they admire that their own personality becomes subdued. Yet, from time to time, one hears a young pianist who has something to say, a truly great artist such as Martha Argerich, Murray Perahia, and a few others.

I was accepted at the Curtis Institute when I was very young, and Joseph Hoffman, who was then Director, decided that I should study for a while with David Sapperton, his assistant. Sapperton was a marvellous teacher (he also taught Bolet) and he knew how to train a pianist's hand. Nothing was left to chance. He was also very demanding, insisting that we respect the written text. He was greatly concerned that his pupils should be equipped with the right tools, to be able to cope with the great works of piano literature. I learnt a great deal from him and I am grateful that he gave me a fine control of the keyboard. Soon afterwards I was considered 'ready' to have lessons with the Master himself. Working with Joseph Hoffman was completely different experience. He was not a teacher in the accepted sense, he did not really teach, he was only concerned with bringing out the essence of the music. The lessons were very inspiring. He would sit at one of the pianos while I was playing on the other, stopping me whenever he was not satisfied, talking about the particular work, the phrasing, the various touches and possibilities for producing the kind of tone he wanted, making me play again and again until the quality of sound or the tone quality was realised. He often sat down and played, hoping that, through the right illustrations, a pupil could learn to listen more intently. It was his way of playing *rubato* which was so difficult to sense, the kind of *rubato* which enhances a phrase, while the pulse is maintained and the music gains momentum. For a young student this was by far the best way of making me realise the beauty and meaning of these works. Hoffman's magnetic personality and his genius had us all spell-bound and, like all the other students, I was striving to achieve all the subtle shades of tones and nuances, and playing with the precision and clarity which he demanded. Once a student came into his class he had to cope with the master's way of making music. Indeed, he treated us all, no matter how young some of us were – and Curtis was swarming with prodigies – as adults and responsible musicians.

Working with Hoffman was a decisive experience in my life, and his influence was tremendous. Although he allowed my personality to develop – and he was convinced that this was so – my unbound admiration for the man and the artist made me try to imitate his playing in its minutest details. To play exactly like the master was my only ambition and I became almost like a puppet... Fortunately this period did not last too long. I had to find my way of studying and it was only after leaving Curtis that I really learnt how to work, practising and broadening my repertoire continuously and performing for all types of audiences. Travelling and giving concerts were important experiences which helped me to develop fully as an artist and to liberate myself from the strong influences of the college years.

I often meet young pianists who ask me how I practise. If they expect to get some special message or revelation they are in for a disappointment. They might even be very startled if they could hear me practise. I play very slowly, every movement is calculated and controlled and only I know why I do certain movements. I am constantly listening to sound I wish to produce and very often I practise without pedal, still very slowly to be more aware of the utmost control of the keys. Only afterwards I play the entire work. My greatest critic when preparing a programme is the tape-recorder, and I advise young performers to work with the tape-recorder. It teaches you to listen to your own playing in a detached way and there is no greater lesson than hearing yourself on tape. It is true that I do listen to records to know how other pianists interpret certain works, but I do not try to imitate them, on the contrary.

When I study a piece which I have played for some time I may find myself playing it quite differently than when I first performed it. I try to approach it as if I have never played it and work in my usual way – very slowly, very 'calculated' so that I always know what I am doing and why. When I perform Romantic works I may decide on a slight change of dynamics, or a *rubato* spontaneously. Actually, I don't think that I can play a piece twice exactly in the same way, and some critics have remarked that on a particular evening my playing was quite different than in previous recitals. Does it matter? I don't think so. What matters is that an artist should always give his best, that the performance is alive and communicated. Only then can the artist carry the audience along with him. I would not treat a composer like Beethoven or Bach or any other classical composer in the same way. I work with great care and I decide what my interpretation should be, and do not dare change the composer's markings. Trying to be original at all costs is not my goal and it should not be the goal of the true artist.

Some of the pianists I interviewed said that they avoided listening to their performances on tape or on television. How do you feel about your own performances?

Well, I don't know many artists who are always satisfied with their performances. I invariably say to myself that I could have done better in a certain passage, or that I would have preferred another way of expressing my thoughts in others and I was surprised to hear some exaggerated nuances. I am always very critical of my own playing and I think this is as it should be. An artist must strive to do better and better. If one stands still, one stops being a creative musician. Besides there are many ways to interpret a work and we are always searching for the 'truth' – whatever that may be. Perhaps, what I mean is that, as an interpreter, the artist must try to be true to himself and to the composer whose work he is interpreting. One of my exhilarating experiences when listening to my tapes is when I hear myself playing a particular work just as I wanted and as I imagined, and I am absolutely delighted, like a child, with the exquisite sounds which come out of the box. This is one of my rare moments, but then I know that I have achieved something. After all, the response of the audience is so important to us, it is our 'life-line'. I am happy to say that wherever I go – and I have travelled a great deal, in many parts of the world – I play to most enthusiastic audiences. Perhaps the most musical public I met was in Russia and I should love to be able to return there one day.

I am often asked if I have a favourite composer – as you know this is one of the typical questions one hears in the artist's room, after a concert. My answer is that I have no favourite composer and, the one I am playing at the moment is the one I love most at that moment. My repertoire is vast, after all I have been playing since I was a young boy and I was always interested in studying new works. Although I don't often perform contemporary composers, I do study many of them, I have even played Stockhausen, and I feel great affinity with Alban Berg whom I consider one of the important composers of the twentieth century. His sonata, op.1 is a very fine work indeed and I often include it in my programmes. I also love Messaien.

With my agents I have a very good relationship; they allow me all the freedom to choose the programmes I like. By now they know that they can trust my taste and my judgement. There is so much good music and I love playing many different composers and there is such a great variety of works which I am happy to share with my audience.

Have you ever thought of accepting a few students to teach? You have so much to offer and your advice would be invaluable.

I think that I would make a very bad teacher and the truth is that I never wanted to teach. We, performers, are rather self-centred, and, at least, I am like that. I am primarily concerned with my own playing, and I must have all my time for myself: practising, preparing many programmes, planning the concerts with my agents, meeting friends socially, and going to concerts. I love being with people, this is important for me. As I have to do a lot of travelling from one place to another, I must keep in good health so I treat my body with great care. I do exercises, have regular massage, and have relaxation sessions as these are just as important for a performer as for any sportsman and we must really learn from them how to take care of our physique.

Teaching requires a different personality, a musician who is devoted to his work, who is deeply interested in other people's problems, and loves being of assistance. One is a 'born teacher', but this does not mean that anyone can teach the piano well. There must be knowledge of repertoire, of the various styles, and, above all, of the piano technique, and how to help the pupils acquire it. If someone comes to me for advice on how to play certain passages which he finds difficult, all I can do is show him how I play them, but I could not teach him what to do or how to practice them. Only a real teacher would know how to help him. Or when a young pianist brings a work to me, as it sometimes happens, I listen carefully and with interest, but I can only say what I like or what I do not think is very good. I am afraid I am rather intolerant and I cannot help being honest and telling a young pianist the truth and this is not always so good. A real teacher, and one who is dedicated and, at the same time able to inspire students and fire their imagination, would know how to handle such a situation and be of use. *As to myself, I think that I can only teach myself. And I work very hard at it, all the time!*

Piano Journal VOL 5, NO 13 1984

Magda Tagliaferro

You are almost a legendary figure in the piano world, and it is no secret that you have reached a venerable age. You are now in your nineties, and still command the same great prestige as artist and pedagogue, being one of the first patrons of EPTA. Your two Wigmore Hall recitals in London, within less than a year, are still talked about as supreme examples of great pianism, and great lessons of style and conception. I am going to ask a question which by now must have become a sort of 'leitmotif' whenever you are being interviewed: What is the secret of your stamina, and of your having maintained this keyboard wizardry? Your playing shows such lack of effort, such elegance, and is aesthetically shaped throughout.

There is no secret, and I am saying this again and again. The answer is very simple; it is Love, with a capital 'L'. And this has always been my motto. I love everything I am doing, every moment of my life. It is not only the music and the instrument of which I am passionately fond of, but I love people, I love my audiences, my friends, my pupils, I love all the other arts, nature – perhaps I can say 'I live with love'. But this is not all. It is this intense living that gives me the curiosity to know more, to learn all the time, to find new ideas, new approaches to the repertoire – whether I am playing myself or I am introducing it to my students. As you know, the interpretation of masterpieces has no limits. My curiosity is insatiable and I believe this keeps me young and in touch with everything that goes on, in the world of music in particular.

I have always been a very thorough worker but, again, everything I am doing brings me great satisfaction: the pleasure in the work itself, the joy I hope I am giving to my audiences, but, above all, the satisfaction I get through my students' interesting response, or when they develop in their own direction stimulated by my teaching. I think that it is our responsibility as artists to pass on to the younger generations of musicians our knowledge and our experiences as performers.

My 'Courses on Interpretation' which I hold at regular intervals, bring together many young pianists eager to learn 'my technique' and, so to speak, from the 'horse's mouth', how to play the great works of the French composers. I call these classes *Les Couleurs dans l'Harmonie* – not easy to translate into English I am afraid. The nearest I can think would be 'The Colours in Harmony'. I do not treat these classes as conventional piano lessons; that is why I insist on this title. I am trying to stimulate young pianists to learn to listen intently to the sounds they produce, to experiment with searching the immense possibilities which the instrument offers, but everything is done through the music, through the musical phrases. In this way, they may develop a sensitive 'inner hearing', which in turn helps them to realise a richer palette of pianistic tones. Usually, my courses have specific themes, the students must prepare certain works which are then analysed in detail, a sort of 'History of Piano Repertoire'. But, in trying to 'teach' the interpretation, I insist on the 'musical contour', the design of each phrase. Just as in my own playing, I insist that the pianist should learn to hear in the mind, to follow in his imagination the phrase as it starts and moves along from note to note, listening intensely to the intervals of the design. If a phrase sings in the imagination, it will be played legato, or with the articulation demanded by its character. At the same time, while the phrase is designed in the mind, the arm will also design it, and there is total co-ordination between the musical thought and the movement, bringing the contour to its end at the right moment.

I began to play the piano when I was perhaps three or four years old. My father, a fine pianist himself, and a very good teacher, realised that I had great ability. He used to say that I was a 'born pianist', and he devoted at least two hours to practice with me every day. I do not remember much about the teaching; all I know is that I greatly enjoyed playing, learning many pieces, performing them, and he must have been patient and tolerant, yet stern enough to see that my practising was consistent and no time was wasted. In Brazil, at that time, music was not greatly developed, and the public was not yet educated enough to go to concerts to listen to music. These were more like social gatherings for the upper class. When I was 13, my father decided that my talent deserved to be further developed, so he took me to Paris to play to the young pianist who was making a great name at the time, Alfred Cortot. We were very thrilled when Cortot pronounced his judgement. He accepted me immediately in his class at the Paris Conservatoire and by the end of the year, I got my very coveted *Premier Prix* (the highest exam for performers) before my fourteenth birthday. But my studies with

Cortot did not end then; in fact, I studied with him, and we remained friends throughout his life. I owe to him a great deal of my knowledge of the instrument and its possibilities, an essential foundation for any pianist, but most of all, the continuous search for more and more beautiful sounds, the richness of tone colours as well as the fine conception of the masterpieces of piano literature. At the time when I began studying with him he was busy trying to work out his 'Rational Principles of Piano Technique' which have become the Bible of so many pianists all over the world.

I must add that, at our lessons, he was so interested in studying the great piano works with me that he did not expect me to go through all his exercises. Not only that he thought that my technique was serving me well enough, but he realised that it was enough to show me a certain movement of the arm or fingers to express certain musical ideas, that I could immediately do it, not by just copying him, but simply because I could hear the music in my head.

I think I was also trying very hard to imitate him, as everything he did had such exquisite beauty and even the most dramatic chords and passages had ample sonorities, always velvety. Needless to add that, for me, as for all his students, Cortot was the ideal pianist and artist. In turn, I have been trying to instil in my own students that continuous search for greater and greater beauty of sounds, always inspired by the music one plays.

Living in Paris at that time was a unique privilege for a young pianist, eager to study and be part of the musical life which offered a variety of trends and currents created by a group of young composers who brought French music to most unexpected hights. Fauré, his student Ravel, Satie, then Debussy, and all the young artists in their group performing their freshly produced compositions in public concerts or in salons, accepted me and encouraged me to join in. I played piano duets with Fauré and I gave many first performances of the new works of these important composers. I had also the opportunity to meet George Enescu, that phenomenal musician, who took me as his pianist on several tours. Playing his sonatas for violin and piano with him, are unforgettable musical experiences, and I cannot express my gratitude enough for having been able to develop as a pianist and artist during those most interesting and important years in Paris.

My repertoire is, obviously, very large. I have studied most of the works for piano by composers of various periods and styles, and it is so difficult for me to say which I like best. I think I love the ones I play at the time, but, as I have said before, I have an immense capacity to love, especially music and there is so much great music by many different composers. Of course, French music, like Spanish, is so much part of me and my development. Yet, I have great affinity with the Romantic composers, and I find Schumann's rhythmical structure very suited to my South American temperament, but it is the 'Romantic' Schumann which appeals to me so much. And, if I may say without false modesty, I think that my interpretation of Chopin's music is nearest to the 'truth', and sometimes I wonder what would Chopin say if he would return to this world and he could hear me. I just hope that he would say: 'Yes, this is it!' My great ambition is to come back to London and give a recital of Chopin's music only. I love the English audiences, they are so enthusiastic and so responsive. And they seem to love my playing which gives me enormous satisfaction: this makes me feel good. At my last Wigmore Hall Recital I played the monumental Schumann Sonata Op. 11 in F Sharp Minor and, although there is material for four major works and it lasts nearly forty-five minutes, I could feel the profound silence in the hall, the kind of silence which one can expect when the listeners are at one with the performer.

Although I still play a great deal not only in France, but also in the United States, England, and in other countries, I have always been involved with working with young pianists, and I think that there are many young pianists who are now performing and also teaching 'my technique'. It is true that, as my father mentioned when I was at the beginners stage, I was what is known as 'a natural', born to play to piano. I developed a virtuoso technique at any early age, but when I was launched as a performer I began to search for new ideas, first trying to analyse my playing in great detail, and then studying the way other artists played. I believe that it is this perpetual curiosity which has played such an important part in my life. I became very interested in the use of 'relaxation' in piano playing, and I think that this has brought a very valuable development for us pianists, and, in fact, for all performers. I developed a technique based on relaxation, not a flabby playing, but one which allows total freedom of movements of arms, hands, fingers. The body, the pianist's posture, all must be an integral part of performance, and the pianist must be aware of this complete freedom of movements. I make use of my arm, of the hand, constantly, as my playing is not at the surface of the keys, but has depth. The secret of a beautiful piano technique lies in the fact that one must practice slowly, carefully, but, in performance, one must forget everything and just allow the music to flow. I am still a believer in using finger articulation to develop agility, and strong fingers to support the arm weight without collapsing. The basis of my technique is what I call 'the arcade' of the hand; the bridge formed by the bolted hand and the finger knuckles, the point of resistance when the arm weight is transferred to the keys. The movements of my arms are in response to the musical phrase. I did say earlier that I teach and I insist on the importance of 'hearing' the design of a musical phrase in the mind, and the pianist's arm designs that same phrase at the same time. Not exaggerated gestures, but supple and elegant, as those of a race-horse. I think that pianists should watch horses galloping and learn from their exquisite movements how to use their arms and, particularly, how to use their elbows, freely, without any hindrance. The elbows must be allowed to bend or stretch when necessary, but these are directed towards the keyboard, not rotating outwardly as if swimming.

'The Touch'? *Le Touche?* – well, this is a very personal matter. Yes, the sensation of touch is first conceived in the imagination: one must hear the sound, and the gesture will be created in response. But, it is not the intellect, it is the feeling of the artist who will decide, ultimately, 'how to press the keys'. Most teachers and great pedagogues have talked about their way of teaching various touches – pianists have been concerned with these complex problems since the piano was invented. I also try to teach my students how to use the fingers, hands, arms, how to press the keys in order to obtain certain tones. Yet, ultimately, each pianist will produce 'his' tone. I think it is the intimacy between the player, the instrument, and the music which creates a particular tone. Perhaps this may be a too simple explanation of the mystery of a very beautiful 'touch' which places an artist in a very special category. It was always said about Cortot's tone that it had such an extraordinary quality that one could recognise it from among a hundred pianists, and this is what I mean by the touch being a 'very personal matter'.

There is a French saying: '*Le style c'est l'homme*'– I can say, 'the pianist is his tone.'

Piano Journal VOL 5 NO 14 1984

Reginald Gerig

Your book Famous Pianists and their Technique *is undoubtedly the most complete anthology covering the development of the schools of piano technique along the centuries. This important study, which has become the bible of pianists and piano teachers, must have taken you years of research in many libraries and in many countries. Readers of* Piano Journal *would be very interested to know how you have achieved this 'tour de force'.*

In a very real sense, I feel that I was preparing throughout most of my musical life to write my book *Famous Pianists and their Technique*. During about five of my most impressionable pre-college years, I was greatly privileged to study piano in my home-town, Fort Wayne, Indiana, with Edith Foster, a close friend and pupil of Joseph Lhevinne, an enthusiastic perfectionist, who imparted to her students Joseph's very natural and musical approach to piano technique and music making. No wonder that most of her pupils, while still in high-school, won prizes and gold medals in state-wide competitions.

Further studies at Wheaton College and Juilliard School widened my musical horizons and earned me several music degrees. My teachers at Juilliard were Sascha Gorodnitzky and Joseph Raeff, also Lhevinne pupils, and Carl Friedberg, one of the last of the romantics who in his youth had known and played for Clara Schumann and Brahms. I had, thus, the goods fortune to learn how technique could be developed naturally, receiving instruction from different personalities belonging to different schools.

My interest in books on piano playing started very early indeed. As a teenager I remember Joseph Lhevinne autographing my very first book, his *Basic Principles to Pianoforte Playing* – still a gem and classic in the field. Another vivid memory is that of browsing through the shelves of books in the small Schirmer's store at the old Juilliard School. The monumental classics by Otto Ortmann that I saw there back in 1946 captured my attention, although I did not fully realise their importance at the time. I purchased *The Physical Basis of Piano Touch and Tone* while passing over the more important *The Physiological Mechanics of Piano Technique*.

My teaching experience through the years at Nyack College, the Eastman School of Music and Wheaton College added background for undertaking the exhaustive research that a book such as *Famous Pianists and their Technique* entailed. The major part of the research and writing was done over about a five-year period in the mid-60s, thanks largely to the grants offered by the Wheaton College Alumni Association – who also honoured me with the '1984 Alumni of the Year Award' for distinguished service to Alma Mater.

I undertook the project with the strong feeling that there was a great need in the piano teaching field for such a study. Serious pianists and teachers needed a volume that would give them an overview of the rich heritage of piano technical thought that has been left in writing over a span of several centuries. Yet, not many were making use nor were they even aware of it.

One incentive to embark on my project came from observing at one point in my career, at first hand, the teaching of some of my colleagues, particularly the rather lopsided approach of one of them who taught a brand of Breithaupt-ian 'weight-technique' which she thought had come to her by 'special revelation'. And if you did not teach it or did not believe in it you were not worthy of calling yourself a piano teacher... History must have shown her that no one can hold a patent on 'technical truth'.

This brings to mind Francois Fetis' Méthode des Méthodes – a collection of the important piano methods up to 1832. In his preface he pointed out that each method has its own qualities in spite of every author's claim that 'his was the only true method'. We had to wait for Otto Ortmann, who, in his search for scientific truth, dissected and analysed the movements of pianists while playing, experimenting with 'home-made', yet highly sensitive apparatus at the Peabody Conservatory. Did your research on theorists and innovators such as Deppe, Briethaupt, Ortmann, and later on Schultz, have any bearing on your own teaching?

Undoubtedly. I have tried to communicate to my students something of the importance and meaning of the findings of these great thinkers. The scholarly studies of Ortmann and Schultz also take up a considerable amount of space in my book because I feel that what they have to say is very significant and ties together so much of the historical thought preceding them. Deppe, Briethaupt, the musical giant

Matthay, all come together in Ortmann's study and this forms a solid basis for my own teaching. The foundation premise of 'Famous Pianists and their Technique' is that a fine, valid technique that makes possible a musical performance is a natural one. A truly natural technique is characterised by personal individuality, ease of execution, intelligent adaptation to the demands and limitations of the instrument (the same is true for harpsichord and organ), and, most important of all, by an harmonious assent to the laws of nature which are relevant to piano playing – in the areas of physiology, physics and acoustics. The great pianists and theorists of the past and present all stress this naturalness in their own performance and their teaching. Ortmann articulately and accurately many of these laws of nature effecting piano technique, and showed, under scientific laboratory conditions, the results of obeying and disobeying them. An overriding concern of his was the all-pervasive problem of muscular co-ordination in piano playing – of tension and freedom in so many different performance situations. His numerous definitions of co-ordination and inco-ordination run through *The Physiological Mechanics of Piano Technique* like a scarlet thread. These definitions and the research that helped formulate them give valuable background material for today's further research in the area of performance tensions. Schultz's analysis of effective muscular co-ordination in high-velocity finger passage-work as presneted in the *Riddle of the Pianist's Finger* is also very thought-provoking.

In my own work with students, I found it of great value to provide them with a rationale and specific practical suggestions that will be meaningful and helpful to them, and it is not enough to tell a student to 'relax'. They must understand 'how' this can be done, and particularly, 'when', and I believe that all piano students should study the piano writings of these great thinkers.

You had many personal contacts with both Ortmann and Schultz while preparing the chapter of your book on their studies – what was their reaction to your summarising their writings?

My personal contacts with both Ortmann and Schultz date back to 1964 when I was doing much of the basic research for my project. As I studied their penetrating technical thought, its great importance became quite evident and this was also strengthened by the evaluation of some of the most eminent musicologists. Dr William Newman (from University of North Carolina, at Chapel Hill) stated that 'not until the writings of the Americans, Otto Ortmann and Arnold Schultz, has there been enough understanding of allied sciences like acoustics and anatomy to permit of scientific conclusions'. Also, it is significant that Ortmann and Schultz are the only American theorists on piano technique listed in the bibliography of 'Piano Playing' in the first edition of the Harvard Dictionary of Music.

Piano Journal VOL 5 NO 16 1985

Bernard Roberts

Your name has been associated with Beethoven's piano music for many years and you are now one of the outstanding interpreters of his works. You have given many recitals devoted entirely to Beethoven's music, and your series of the thirty-two Piano Sonatas has attracted large audiences. Moreover, the record company, Nimbus, issued the complete set of the sonatas in 1977, and I believe you are the first British pianist to have achieved this marathon. At what stage in your career did you decide to devote most of your artistic life to the study of Beethoven's works?

I don't think that I ever took a deliberate decision. I know that I always loved Beethoven's music, since I was a child. My parents were very musical, and we had a great deal of music in the house. My mother had studied at the Royal Manchester College of Music (today's Royal Northern College of Music), and she became a well-known piano teacher. I don't remember when I started to play the piano, as I enjoyed picking up tunes, and my mother thought that it would be better if she would give me proper lessons. As soon as I could read music I loved playing duets with her, and thus I was introduced to the then very popular arrangements of Beethoven's symphonies and other works. My mother's own teacher and great friend, Dora Gilson (who was already teaching at the Royal Manchester College), often came to the house, and I spent many happy hours listening to their music making. My father, an amateur organist, was music critic of the *Manchester Guardian* (today's *Guardian*), and wrote articles for music journals, among them *Music and Letters*. I still have some copies of this old journal with his articles.

My progress must have been quite obvious, and my parents decided that I should also have lessons with Dora Gilson. She had been a pupil of the celebrated Egon Petri, one of the famous students of Busoni, and was a warm stimulating teacher who knew how to treat a youngster like me. I stayed with her until I was sixteen, and these were, indeed, very important years for my musical development. She gave me a thorough foundation without ever trying to impose a rigid method. She often remarked that just as she had what one might call a 'natural hand-position', I also showed the same ability. Or, perhaps, my mother had taken care of this, and made sure that I used my hands and fingers in a correct and natural way. Of course, Dora made me play scales, arpeggios, plenty of Czerny and other etudes, but never as exercises, mechanically played. She insisted on beautiful sound and a real performance, no matter what I was playing. It is true that Czerny studies can be absolutely charming when well-played. But these 'technical' exercises and studies were only a small part of our lessons, as we went through all kinds of music. I was an avid reader, and tried to play everything that I could lay hands on; it was always Beethoven's music which fascinated me.

I was fortunate to have grown up in an enlightened town like Manchester, where music played an important role in the cultural life of the community. The Hallé Orchestra Concert Series was the highlight of the musical season, and my parents took me regularly to hear the symphonic concerts and the great soloists who visited our part of the country. The Mancunians have always been proud of their cultural tradition, and they greatly supported the Arts. In the past they had links with the old German towns and universities, and other seats of learning. They brought to Manchester the great conductor Hans Richter to take charge of the Hallé Orchestra, the pianist Egon Petri to teach at the RMC, and many famous artists were invited to participate in the weekly concerts. By the time I was old enough to be taken to concerts, these artists of the past were only a legend, but they had left their mark. Through my parents, who came to Manchester at the turn of the century and through my teacher, who remained on the staff of the RMC for fifty years, I received almost unconsciously the feeling of what the town must have been like at that time.

When I was sixteen, I won a scholarship at the Royal College of Music in London, to study with Eric Harrison. He was not much older than me – he was only thirty-one – and we developed a wonderful relationship. He had a decisive influence on my whole outlook; he was not only a teacher, but my mentor and friend, and I found him tremendously inspiring. At his best, he was an electrifying performer with a stupendous command of the keyboard. Piano technique was part of the baggage of any performer, and he made sure that his students also had the right tools.

*His famous exercises to build a virtuoso technique with just 'one hour a day' prac-
tice are well-known. Did he use his students as guinea-pigs to perfect them?*

He had not published them when I was his student, but I think that he
did base them on the results he obtained while teaching us. Actually, he
believed in practising specific exercises essential for developing certain
aspects of piano technique, rather than working at length at many studies. Thus, I learnt from him how to divide my practising time, spending only a small part of it trying to perfect those concentrated exercises
which, in turn, allowed me to go through the great works of the piano
repertoire. Yet it was always Beethoven's music which took precedence
over other composers, and I was immersed in studying it and reading
all the books I could find about his life and his works. I became very
excited when I read that, in his youth, Beethoven had close links with
the newly founded universities in Bonn and Cologne, where the wave
of liberalism and ideas of freedom were predominant. The climate was
not yet ready; these were dangerous times, and I was particularly interested to find that the young fighters for freedom were looking towards
the town of Manchester where such ideas had found resonance.

*You left the Royal College at eighteen, after only two years of studies with Eric
Harrison. What did you do afterwards?*

At that time, military service was compulsory, and I had to spend two
years – at the typewriter! My superiors thought that this was a kind way
to treat a musician. But, of course, I went on playing, and all my free
time was spent making music. When I finished with the army I went
back to College, continuing my studies with Eric Harrison for another
two years. I started to play in public, and as I was a very good sight-
reader, I was in great demand to play for my colleagues, and with other
musicians. I was twenty-two, and I wanted to get on in the profession. But these were not easy times, and I had quite a struggle to build
my career. I also think that I was a slow developer, although I was a
very quick learner. My teacher and my friends gave me great support,
and encouraged me to give my first Wigmore Hall Recital. That was
in 1957, when I was twenty-four, and I had reasonable reviews but it
said: '...somewhere locked up inside him...' This made me re-think
my attitude and my whole playing to find out what was lacking in my
artistic expression and how I could then bring about an 'unlocking' of
my personality.

Eric Harrison suggested that I should study with a pianist and a very fine musician whom he greatly admired, Ferdinand Rauter, a Central European pianist who settled in England during the war. Rauter became very involved in Rudolf Steiner's philosophy, 'Antroposophy', and with a group of well-known young artists, was arranging weekly concerts at the Rudolf Steiner Hall, near Baker Street, in London. Rauter's approach to music was completely different to anything I experienced in the past, and my own playing was greatly influenced by his honesty and musical integrity.

In 1961 I was appointed professor at the Royal College of Music in London, and this was a great honour for me. I was only twenty-eight at the time, and this new responsibility made me aware of my own and my students' problems. I learnt a great deal through teaching, but I was anxious to continue with my career and did everything possible to develop as an artist in spite of the many hours of teaching. I was planning my second Wigmore Hall recital which I gave in 1962, and this time the critics were quite enthusiastic about my performance of the *Hammerclavier* Sonata. I had spent the whole summer vacation learning the Fugue, trying to memorise it securely. I did not have too many concerts then, so I could take time over every detail. It was a hot summer, and every morning I got up early to be at the piano. After a few hours work I went for a walk, and then I spent the evenings relaxing with my electric trains and engines, a hobby which has given me great joy over the years.

Did you think that you were now ready to start working on the complete set of the Beethoven Sonatas ?

It was Ferdinand Rauter who made me do this. He simply told me that he had arranged with the Rudolf Steiner Society a series of eight recitals, every Tuesday evening, when I was to play the 'Thirty-two'. I accepted the challenge and, indeed, I was grateful for such an opportunity. I had already played or taught about half of the sonatas at different times and now, at the age of thirty, I thought that I should face the demands of such a task. Rudolf Steiner's teachings had opened new vistas for me, and I accepted the challenge with great humility, trying to serve Beethoven's music to the best of my ability. And so, from one Tuesday to another, I was preparing another group of sonatas, and, surprisingly enough, one of the sonatas which I had not performed before was the *Pathétique*.

Since then I have presented the 'Thirty-two' several times in public recitals, and over the radio for the BBC. I was indeed very thrilled when the record company Nimbus invited me to record the whole cycle. This was a different kind of challenge, as everyone knows that playing for an audience is one thing, and playing for a recording engineer in a cold studio, when every sound is listened to almost clinically, may be a stifling experience. But, I must say that Nimbus are anxious to create an optimum atmosphere in their studios, so that the performances are as satisfactory as in a concert hall in front of an audience.

I understand that these recordings have been produced without being edited, without any interference with the flow of the performance. What did you think of the end result?

Yes, it was the attitude of Nimbus to artists, and to the quality of their recordings which fascinated me. They want to capture on the disc the spontaneity of a performance, with its unique climate, and they are convinced that this can be realised only if the playing has continuity, without the interruptions of special cuts in the middle of a phrase, to replace a wrong note or two, or when a complete section has to be replayed. This search for perfection to impress the critics and the audiences can deprive a performance of its reality. I remember Schnabel's famous remark when asked to play again just one section of a concerto: 'I may play it better now but not as well as I did the first time.' I know exactly what he meant. Nimbus has another reason for not editing the records. They believe that the sound is finer because tape noise is eliminated, and the end product is more satisfying.

For me, it was quite an experience to record the sonatas in chronological order, starting with the first one and going through the entire cycle, as if I was watching Beethoven's own life and artistic development. It took about a year to complete the cycle. There was no hurry. Sometimes the playing came off from the first time, and we all felt good. At other times I might have made an unexpected mistake or a mishap would occur, and everything had to be scrapped. We had to go all over again. It was always back to the beginning. You could not do bits or sections.

Were you satisfied with the artistic result?

On the whole yes, but, of course, an artist is never fully satisfied, and he always believes that he may have done, perhaps, better in that passage, or... This first set of recordings is now virtually out of print and Nimbus has asked me to record the 'Thirty-two', this time on compact discs. This seems to be the last word in recording techniques and, indeed, when listening to one of these discs, it is as if one hears 'real' sounds for the first time. Unfortunately, compact discs can only be used with special record players, which are activated by laser beam instead of the old arm with a sapphire or diamond needle.

I have already completed almost half of the records, and am greatly looking forward to finishing the entire set.

Do you think that your conception of these master pieces has changed over the years?

I should hope that I have grown during these past seven years, and I may bring to my playing a more mature artistic experience. I must add that although Nimbus are doing everything they can to create the right climate for the artist while recording, I still prefer playing to an audience, in a concert hall. I would much rather play to people, because the reality of the performance exists between the performer and his listeners. It is not inside oneself as the player, nor is it totally inside the hearer. It is between the two – perhaps like what one might call the mystery of an interval. If I play a C and a G, the C and G are both self-contained sounds – but the reality of the music lives in the interval, in between the two sounds. We may call it 'atmosphere', 'communication', or whatever you like, but it is the mystery of the interval which excites both the performer and the listener. On the other hand, when I played all the 'Thirty-two' over the BBC radio, I found that an exhilarating experience, perhaps because I was unaware that my performances were taped, and I was trying to play to my invisible listeners. Somehow I felt their presence.

Your career had a slow start but, surely, your recognition as a great artist by critics and the public was not so slow. The glowing press notices must have influenced the impressarios, and also, having been appointed professor at the Royal College at the age of twenty-eight was a notable recognition. Were you able to combine the two activities, the teaching and the concert career ?

It was not easy, but thanks to my early training I was able to cope with the two parallel professions. I am a fast learner, I think because I do a great deal of my work in my mind. I do not start to play anything until I really know the work very well. As to my teaching, I am very thankful that I did it for so many years. I think that I have developed in many directions because of my students' needs – which were a great lesson for me, as I had to find helpful solutions. When I was younger, I tried immediately to show them 'how I play a certain passage', but with the years I realised that my attitude had to change. If a student comes to you and needs your guidance, you should approach the problem with a certain innocence, and allow him to speak to you through his playing, and then you will understand. It is the same with a great work: you must listen to that work to see what it has to say to you before trying to interfere, imposing your own, probably inadequate, ideas and personality. In the end, these get in the way. I believe that if you want to be a true interpreter you must allow the work to speak through you, while you, the performer, become almost transparent. Not that you are inactive – on the contrary, your whole being is involved. This means that you must listen with increasing perception and depth of feeling and response. It is the same with the student.

Try to listen with the same perception to understand what he is attempting to express. Your duty is to help him co-ordinate his responses to the music he is playing, and you will find that the music will shine through him.

Your own teachers believed that if you want to be a pianist you must first have a secure and brilliant technique. Did you try to pass on the tradition of the grand school of piano playing to your own students? After all, you belong to the Busoni tradition, almost in direct line, through your own teachers.

Yes, I was always greatly concerned with this aspect of teaching, and I was working with my students towards an integration of their musicianship and physical aspect, as I believe that everything comes from a central concept. If the approach to keyboard playing is correct, and the body is in the right state of balance, with the right relaxation, and, at the same time, the right alertness, somehow the playing gains in dimensions.

In my teaching I use simple diagrams to make everything as clear as possible before we start to play. First of all, there must be a secure framework: the body in a balanced posture, with an erect back, which I call the 'pin-man', is represented by a vertical line. He relates to the earth through his legs and the stool, the pianist sitting on the edge, to allow flexibility of movement, while his head is directed upwards, lightly, as if the whole body is up to the neck in water. There should be no tension in any part of the body. I may spend several lessons with a student until this balanced posture is experienced physically and becomes part of his piano playing. Then I draw a horizontal line, representing the arms, with the upper arms slightly raised along the body, awake and alert, allowing the forearms to hang loosely and heavily. If the body posture is correct, everything else falls in place. The student then must develop an awareness of the sensation of buoyancy in the upper arms, peaceful forearms, the weight of the hands hanging from the wrists, with relaxed fingers, naturally shaped, as if ready to touch the keys.

Once the student has acquired this balanced posture and understands how to use his arms, hands and fingers, he learns to become active within this framework without upsetting it. We work towards experiencing a new alertness: be becomes awake, alive, freely upright, and he begins to listen in his mind to the piece he wishes to play. The question I ask him is: 'can you conceive the piece, can you hear it, does the piece live in your mind while keeping your arms still?' Your aural experience is expressed in the alert and awake posture. But, until you learn to hear the whole piece in your mind there is no point in starting to play even a single note.

Not only should one listen to the inner sounds, but also to the outer sounds, coming from all directions, from space. The student gradually realises that when he hears clearly the music in his imagination, a whole sphere of physical gestures is born within the head, gestures that will form an integral part of the musical expression. Then, the energy of what he hears in his mind comes down, through the stretched arms, through the wrists, hands and fingers, through the keys, and beyond. There is complete and total connection and, if the posture is right, without any strain in any part of the body, it will allow these processes to happen.

The fingers have to be active and, of course, a basic 'finger culture' has to be developed. I belong to the school of playing from the key surface, just as one walks, not stamping the ground, and I have always worked with the students trying to develop their independence of fingers and a highly sensitive control of the keys.

You have been able to combine your teaching with your performing commitments for over twenty years. What made you decide to give up your appointment at the Royal College?

I was approaching fifty, and I had to take a decision about my life as a concert artist. I want to give everything I have and I can to my playing. My teaching became more and more demanding and, at the same time, my career was making increasing demands on my time and on my energy, and after many weeks of thinking I have taken this decision. For the same reason I left the *Parikian, Fleming and Roberts Trio* after seven years of intense and joyful collaboration. I feel that I must devote the rest of my life to my solo and concerto performances, and I need my whole concentration for this. I must add that these have not been easy decisions. I am giving all my time to the work I have chosen, and this can be very lonely, and I may find myself very isolated. Yet, I think that it is worth having the courage to hang on to what I believe in with all my heart and my conviction.

Piano Journal VOL 6 NO 17 1985

Tamas Vasary

You are now established in London, and have made a name as a pianist and conductor, often appearing in both capacities. You were known as a child prodigy in your native country, Hungary, and in your teens you won the coveted prize in the Liszt Piano Competition. When did you decide to become a conductor — as a student, or only when you came to the West, after 1956, when many Hungarians left the country?

As a child, in Budapest, I played the piano, and I found everything easy and exciting. I must have had a natural keyboard facility, and I could cope with quite difficult works at an early age. I was nine when I gave my first concert, playing pieces by Scarlatti, Schumann, Chopin, and Liszt. I even dared play Chopin's Sonata in B Minor and several études when I was only eleven, and at fourteen I won the Liszt Piano competition prize, playing, among other works, the Ballade in D Flat. Then I entered the Liszt Music Academy, in Louis Hernady's Class. He was an outstanding teacher and had trained a number of fine artists, among them Peter Frankl. But I was not happy. These were very difficult years for my musical development. As a child I had great facility and I just played without thinking too much about how I played. I loved music, I was eager to learn more about the piano repertoire. Once I became a student in the Academy I started to be very rational and conscious of how I should play, how I should interpret the great works we studied, how I should develop a truly virtuoso technique, and so on. I wanted to control every gesture, every note, rationally, and what I had achieved until then intuitively seemed to have disappeared. I lost all spontaneity in my performance; I even lost the joy of being with the instrument. Instead, I developed a rough, almost brute technique, and my playing reflected my state of mind. My teacher was very concerned. He insisted that the years as a child prodigy were over, and that it was time to become a serious musician. He gave me many technical exercises and studies, and insisted that I should broaden my repertoire. The result was that I became entirely dominated by his strong personality; I was trying with all my heart to play as he would have wanted, and I could only think with his head. In my desire to satisfy him I completely lost my own personality. I realise now that he had the best intentions, and he was anxious to help me get through this difficult time. He forbade any public appearances for the next four years, even in the Academy students concerts. The effect was exactly the opposite, and at one moment I thought of giving up playing the piano altogether. I then leaned more towards conducting, and hardly touched the piano. Physically, I also encountered serious difficulties with my hands and wrists, probably through many years of overuse, or perhaps incorrect use, also being born with very long arms, and a body which is not too robust. I had pains in the wrists and in the hands and I realised that I was maltreating my own body. You see, if you have a very fine blade you can't cut wood with it unless you use a special technique, and then, it cuts even better than a hatchet. The piano, and a career as a pianist, were out of my mind at that time.

However, in life, very often what appears as a disaster sometimes turns to the good. In the early Fifties, I went through a traumatic experience. I was shattered, when both my parents were taken to a special prison for political detainees. My father played an important role in the Nagy government, but when the Russians took over there were many sad changes, as his activities were not to their liking. I found myself having to earn my living, and the only thing I could do was to play the piano. In my distress over my parents' situation I could not think about my own physical and psychological complexes and, there I was, giving concerts both as a soloist and accompanist. There were many opportunities for young artists to appear in the 'Russian style' of concerts, with half serious, half light music or jazz, with various types of musicians: singers, violinists, wind players, pianists. Thanks to these concerts, I had my first appearance in Moscow where, to my surprise, I had great success, and I was invited to play on the radio. Afterwards, my status changed in Budapest, and I appeared as a 'serious' artist. My whole attitude towards myself, towards my own playing, had also changed, I was growing up. It was rather unfortunate that because of my parents' and my own misfortune I had become less introspective and found my equilibrium.

Many Hungarians were leaving the country at that time, around 1956, and I was one of them. I went to Belgium to take part in the famous 'Queen Elisabeth Competition', in Brussels, and I won a prize. When the Queen was told about my plight and about my parents' arrest, she used her influence with the Russians and obtained the release of my parents, who joined me soon afterwards.

It was not easy for them, nor for myself, to adapt to the new life, and I had several difficult years, full of disappointments, in spite of having won such an important prize. On the other hand, those years helped me to think more deeply about my role as a musician, about the spiritual aspect of life which is so important for me, about many things. I tried to understand why certain events touched me more deeply than others, or how is it that sometimes, a chance meeting may have lasting effect. Indeed, it was such an unimportant event that completely changed my whole life and career. One evening, I played in a salon in Brussels, and a very kind man, a businessman, heard me and wrote immediately to the Deutsche Gramophon company, recommending me to make some recordings. To my amazement, I was invited to play some works by Liszt. Georgy Tzifra, the Hungarian pianist, had recently arrived in the West, and he literally conquered the musical scene. Deutsche Gramophon was looking for another Hungarian pianist to stand up to the rival company, and this was my luck. One single recording, and I was launched! From then on my career took a vital turn, and I never looked back. To be successful, it is not always the talent or the serious work which are needed. It is a particular happening, a chance, which comes at a precise moment. Of course, the work which an artist has done along the years 'gives more chance to the chance'.

In the same way, the evenings when I heard Clara Haskil, that unique pianist, playing all Beethoven's sonatas with the violinist Arthur Grumiaux, in Paris, were a determining factor in my artistic development. I went to the three recitals, and from then on I had only one desire – to be able to study with Clara. I went to the artists' room at the end of the concert and I left her a note with my name, address, and the newly launched recording, asking her if I could come to Switzerland to play to her. I was very apprehensive about whether she would ever get in touch with me, and during the next five weeks I could think of nothing else. I even dreamt that she wrote to me inviting me to Vevey to play to her. Indeed, the morning after my dream, a letter from Clara arrived. This I have treasured ever since, not only because she actually accepted to see me and listen to my playing, but because she wrote the most comprehensive piece of criticism I have ever read about my playing. She was very humble, both as a person and as a musician. She wrote that she could not teach; she would not know how to explain anything about technique or piano playing, but that she would be happy if we could play to one another and talk about music.

This I did. Occasionally, though very seldom, she would make a remark about a phrase, or about pedalling, but she would just say: 'You play your way, I play mine'. These were unforgettable moments, perhaps the most extraordinary hours I have ever lived. It was her spirituality, her simplicity, if one can say, the purity of soul, which came through in her music. Clara had most beautiful hands, which moved with supreme elegance and control over the keyboard, and every single note was exquisite. At the same time, there was an amazing rhythmic vitality in her playing. Her influence over my development was what I needed at the time, and I was grateful that I could stay in Vevey (I remained there for twelve years!) and be with her.

I always had what is called a virtuoso technique, but came to realise that this is not what is needed, nor what I really wanted. Technique for me is nothing else but the means to express the music. In fact, a pianist needs supreme technique and control to play a cantilena in slow movement, to bring out the poetry, the profound expression and spirituality. The two pianists I admire most and who fulfil this ideal are both women: one is Clara Haskil, the other Annie Fischer. When I go to a concert I am not interested in watching an exhibition of virtuosity; I want to receive what is being communicated, I want to be moved. For many people, though, the word 'technique' is synonymous with speed, bravura, accuracy, and although these qualities are important, and the public loves to watch real keyboard wizardry, they are not really necessary. Great music does not demand such prouesse, neither am I really interested in it.

When did you start conducting and playing at the same time? It must be very rewarding to be able to integrate these two aspects of music making into one experience.

I was always interested in conducting and, as I mentioned earlier, I studied it during my student years in Budapest. The piano repertoire is vast, but I was fascinated by the possibilities of an orchestra, and studying symphonic works was very rewarding. About fifteen years ago, I had my first opportunity to appear both as pianist and conductor, at the Montreux Festival, in Switzerland, when I was engaged to conduct the Hungarian Chamber Orchestra. I realised then that I was much happier playing and conducting at the same time than as a soloist under another conductor. Strangely enough, I don't feel nervous when I have the whole responsibility, that of my own playing and of the orchestra.

This I also consider the highest form of music-making; I feel a part of a whole ensemble. When I play a concerto with my orchestra, I do not think of myself as a solo performer, and I try to get from the other players the collaboration I need for my interpretation of the work as a whole. I do not believe in an orchestra 'accompanying' the concerto, and that is why I feel rather inhibited when there is another conductor between me and the orchestra. This makes me rather nervous, and I don't think I am at my best.

Besides, although my physique is not very robust, I do not find conducting while playing – and sometimes I can perform two concertos in one evening – unduly tiring physically. Mentally, yes, but it is a most satisfying artistic experience. One is absolutely inside the music. I am responsible for presenting some of the greatest works. Recently I gave a whole Beethoven programme in the Barbican, with the London Symphony Orchestra, which included the C Minor Piano Concerto, Egmont Overture and the Seventh Symphony. And next November, in Brighton, the programme will consist of the Emperor Concerto, Schubert's 'Unfinished' Symphony, and Kodaly's *Variations on a Hungarian Theme*.

You have now been living in England for nearly fifteen years, and you have made your headquarters over here, but your concertos take you all over Europe and even further. There is continuous stress caused by your travels and your performances, having the responsibility of a whole orchestra, as well as that of your own well-being. You must be ready for the platform without sometimes having time to get to know the instrument. Earlier in the interview you mentioned that, even as a young pianist, you encountered both physical and psychological problems. Have they been solved, or are you still suffering from these old ailments?

Although I enjoyed my public appearances as a child, I sometimes experienced real fear, which would turn into illness, getting high fever, and the concerts had to be cancelled. I was too young to understand that it might have been a psychosomatic reaction. Later on, when I had to accompany a violinist in a broadcast, I got another attack of fever, and I thought that I would have to cancel this concert also. To my surprise, there was an announcement on the radio that the concert of the two young artists cannot take place because of the violinist's indisposition. As soon as I heard this, my fever dropped to normal and I was quite well again. I realised then that I had been the victim of my own fears, but I did not know what to do about it. To make things worse, I developed inflammation of the tendons while over-practising for the various competitions, and the doctors recommended a period of rest for my hands. This was a great shock for me. After the period of rest I started to play again, but my confidence had also suffered, and every time I was facing an audience I was consumed with fear, wondering if I could rely on my hands. At times the pains were unbearable, and I decided to consult a specialist, an orthopaedic surgeon in Lausanne, Switzerland. He examined my hands thoroughly and asked what my profession was. When I told him that I was a pianist he answered: 'A great pity! But you will still be able to play for another three or four years'. What a verdict! To say that I was desperate it is not enough. I saw all types of doctors and therapists, each one recommending another useless treatment: waxing, ultra-sonic waves, oral medication, some insisting that gymnastics of the hands will help, while others that the hands should rest – even a sling was ordered. Nothing helped. I went on playing, in spite of my ordeal, hoping that one day everything will be all right.

Once again an unfortunate situation proved to be beneficial. I was invited to make a recording of the Rachmaninov concertos just when I was suffering from an acute food poisoning. I could not eat anything for three or four days, and I could hardly sit at the piano. When I tried to play, although so weak, my hands felt light, very flexible, and to my amazement, the pain had disappeared. I could hardly believe it. I had suffered agonies with my hands since the age of sixteen and suddenly, after twenty years, a miracle has happened. I was not quite sure whether there was a connection between the diet and the condition of the muscles. When the doctors insisted that I should eat plenty of meat, especially steaks to regain my strength to be able to make the recording, my hands deteriorated again. There was no doubt that the diet had something to do with the ease of my pains in the hands and arms and from then onward, I made a thorough study of various diets, and now I am a strong believer in the value of correct nutrition. I have reduced my meat consumption in general, and while preparing for concerts I abstain from meat and alcohol, but I take plenty of Vitamin C, in very big doses, particularly before a concert. I do not know how it works, but in my case, it certainly helps my muscles to remain elastic.

I have always tried to control rationally every gesture, and my physical movements in piano playing. I began to study them carefully to find out what I was doing which could cause or aggravate the pain in my hands and wrists. I have very strong views about ideal physical movements which are the expression of musical intentions. These movements should, at the same time, be instinctive, natural, just as the movements of animals. I then studied the animals in movement, and I am still amazed at their superb muscular co-ordination. I also watched athletes, who are much more concerned with their body movements than we pianists.

Only thirdly I studied pianists while playing, and I mean the pianists whose technique I admired. Watching a cat ready to jump upon a mouse is the greatest lesson. There is tension, but not stiffness, a sort of 'loose' tension, just the right balance between tension and relaxation. In the same way, a pianist must have the right tension when pressing the key down. Of course, every hand is different, but there must be a right relationship between the pianist's body, his hand, and the instrument. When you hear a sound in your imagination, there is an impulse from the brain and there is a will to transform that impulse into a movement, that is, to press the key and produce the tone. Yet, there are a million ways to produce that tone from the instrument, and I am convinced that the body will find the right way. We must learn from the body, and not vice versa, because the body is older than our rational thinking. This is not easy, though, because we are rational thinkers, and this interferes with our instinctive movements.

In recent years I have also become very interested in young players, and I want to help them in their work. I do not enjoy teaching on an individual basis, I prefer to work in a masterclass situation. This is also good for the young pianists who have to play to a critical audience – their colleagues as well as the teacher – and hopefully they may learn to cope with their nervousness. Above all, I do want to make them realise how important it is to be able to express themselves with joy and love in what they are doing. We live in an era when there is tremendous competition in our education. Children are told at home, and in schools that they must do well, that they must do better than the others if they are to succeed. Later on, the young pianists forget to play for themselves, for their own happiness. They study in order to get good marks or win prizes in competitions. It is rather unfortunate that these competitions are here to stay. I, personally, consider them harmful for the soul. It is true that quite a few pianists thrive under such conditions. But there are many who get bitterly hurt and cannot stand up to the strain, and these I try to help. My aim is to make them feel good whether they succeed or not and, perhaps, help them to learn something from my own experiences and my struggles.

In my work with young pianists, I do not impose any teaching of technique as such, I am more interested in making music, and I do not think that technique should be taught separately from music. But I think that it is of great value for them to realise what is right and natural in piano playing, and what is fundamentally wrong. To illustrate this, I drop a pencil on the piano strings and ask the student to pick it up without touching the string. This exercise requires a most complex movement, and great precision. If the fingers hold the pencil too tight, he cannot move it, if too loose, the pencil will drop on the strings. This is a great lesson in 'tension-relaxation'. When coming to the instrument, the student realises that to press the key the muscles must be neither too tense nor too relaxed. I give them another simple exercise, to press the index finger against the thumb with some firmness, yet retaining flexibility in the hand, wrist and arm. There is gentle firmness and freedom to move hands and arms. He must experience the same sensation when holding the key down. There is no need to 'push' it, nor hold it down tightly. Once the student had learnt this elementary lesson, he will begin to use his body in a natural way. The greatest difficulty for me when giving a masterclass is to help an advanced pianist to change unnatural movements in his playing – movements which have been firmly established during many years of wrong use of his body – into correct, natural ones. To eradicate a wrong technique is difficult and it takes time. But it is up to the young pianist to become more aware of what he is doing, just as I have done. He may listen to my advice but, ultimately, he will have to learn through his own experiences. After all, we learn through our own learning.

Piano Journal VOL 6 NO 18 1985

John Lill

You were one of the first British pianists to have won the formidable Moscow
Competition, when barely twenty years old. A great musical event, considering that
England was often criticised for its failure to train young performers to match the
Russian and American instrumentalists. What is your view on this sore problem,
which has been aired in many music journals in the past few years?

I cannot give you a straight answer. In my case I believe it was my ob-
session with the piano since I was very young. I come from a humble
home. My parents were working very hard to pay for my piano lessons.
I remember my mother taking on two extra jobs in a factory just to
help me with my passion for music.

Fortunately, when I was nine, I won a scholarship at the Royal College
of Music, in the Junior department, and from then onwards, things
were a little easier. But my parents still had to help me, as the scholarship only paid for my tuition.

It was so good that they realised how dedicated I was to my studies, as
they were not musical themselves, but sensed that I needed their support and their approval. I feel deeply grateful for their understanding.

Another happy encounter was when I was invited to the house of the
Lloyd-Webbers. Julian, now a well-known cellist, was eight or nine
years old, also in the Junior department. He needed help with some
music for percussion, and he asked me if I could show him how to do
it. I was already fifteen at the time and he invited me to his home. This
was a great moment in my life. I then met his father who was Principal
of the London College of Music, his mother, a sensitive pianist and
teacher, and, of course, Andrew. The whole family became my great
supporters and I think I really grew up as a musician in their house.
There was a great deal of music, a great deal of talk about music, and
every time I played their constructive criticism helped to think more
and more about what music is.

My teacher at the time was a patient and helpful young man, Harry Platts, who also encouraged me and I greatly enjoyed my lessons. I think that he also thought I was a very good student. I was spending all my free time at the piano, playing everything I could get hold of, then I would bring most pieces memorised, trying to give as good a performance as I could. It is true that I had a great facility and I considered the keyboard as a friend. I learnt even 'big works' with tremendous ease, and this was simply because when you love what you are doing you do not think of difficulties. You just try your best and get on with the work.

Yet I was not satisfied. I knew that I could do more and better. I watched the great artists at their recitals, hoping that I might learn some of their secrets, how they were doing certain passages, how was it that they produced those beautiful and exciting sounds and to what miraculous work did they owe such extraordinary technical wizardry? I then went home and tried to imitate my idols or, perhaps, I should say my ideal pianist, Claudio Arrau. For me, he represented an ideal on which I could, one day, model my own playing. I was searching continuously. I then started to read all the books on piano technique and books about great artists. It was a slow process, but a very rewarding one. I believe I have succeeded in developing my piano playing as far as I could at this stage.

I was not satisfied as I wanted to learn about many other subjects, as I was interested in other arts, I read a great deal of poetry and novels and I was fascinated with the study of Physics, Chemistry, and other sciences and how close these are to music. I became involved in Metaphysics and philosophical studies, still looking for some answers to my quests as to what is talent.

What else is needed in order to achieve one's aims as a musician? What is a performance, and how can one communicate ideas or how can one project a musical interpretation to an audience sitting in silence, listening intently and longing to 'receive' a spiritual message? I believe that the audience is a friend, I feel good vibrations coming towards me when I play, and I try to give the best of me, always. I also believe in the spirituality and the universality of music. I, as interpreter, am only a small vehicle. I feel as if I have been chosen and then I strive towards arriving at this, and I am grateful. I am not sure whether what I have been saying gives an idea of what young artists should aim at once they have been endowed with a great natural talent.

As to your other question about the controversial problem regarding English pianists and their performances in international competitions, I am afraid I do not agree with this on all points. There have been several important successes obtained by young British artists. On the other hand, it is true that the training of young performers is not thought of in terms of participating in different international competitions. Another reason may be the English temperament. There is a lack of feeling about being demonstrative, although there is a quantity of young talent and I must admit the artistic scene is getting more developed in this country.

You were appointed Piano Professor at the Royal College of Music when you were very young and, in the meantime, you have achieved impressive successes as a performer in many parts of the world. You have presented very ambitious programmes which included all Beethoven's sonatas, which you have also recorded, and all Beethoven's piano concertos, both in this country and in the USA. As a teacher, have you any specific views on how to train your students to be ready for a concert career?

After finishing my studies in the senior course of the Royal College, where I had the fortune to work with Angus Morrison, a highly sensitive artist and a very cultured musician, I found myself in demand for concerts. I greatly enjoyed performing and I love the atmosphere of concert halls, with their audiences, which, for me, are always a great source of inspiration. Then I was encouraged to try for some competitions, and so I entered the Moscow International Piano Competition. To my amazement, I came first. This came both as a surprise and a shock, since such a result brings with it a great number of engagements as well as great responsibility. Was I ready for it?

I was very honoured to have been invited to teach in the College, where I spent many important years of my musical development and I decided to help my students to the best of my ability. I only work with a small number of students at a time. Although I have very strong views on piano technique, I don't think I am very good at teaching in the conventional sense of the word. Such a work requires disciplined training and a great deal of patience to pursue a systematic teaching of piano technique, with 'daily doses' of exercises and studies. I don't think that I could do a satisfactory job, as I am more interested in studying the music together, helping the student to find his best way of expressing it, through his technical means. At the same time, I have come to certain conclusions on many general aspects of piano technique. I have tried to find out, for myself, and by myself, some answers to many problems I have encountered. Although general basic principles are important, pianists should be searching themselves, studying their own difficulties, analysing them to find some answers.

This year I have asked the College to allow me to take leave of absence, as I cannot give my students the time they need. I believe that it is vital for them to have the continuity of regular meetings with their teacher.

On the other hand, I believe that it is essential for established performers to help young pianists embarking on a concert career. And this I have done for a number of years. I have tried to pass on to them what I have learnt from my own experiences as performer: how to project my playing, how to bring out the voices in polyphony so that every single line is clearly heard no matter how large the hall is, how to select the balance of sounds, and so on. What you hear is one thing but what the audience hears is a completely different one and this cannot be learnt in a room or a studio. It must be listened to with the ear of an experienced performer, so that the student can learn what is needed and which aspect of his performance would need certain exaggerated representation. There is no short cut although I can only give some guidance, showing the way. After all, everyone has to find his or her own code of behaviour when facing an audience. To become a soloist means to learn from your own mistakes and it also means that you must be convinced that this is what you want to do and that this is what you want to be.

As to my own searches, I said earlier that as a youngster I had what is called a natural aptitude for piano technique and I never encountered great technical difficulties. What I found difficult, and probably my teacher would agree, was my lack of understanding of what was expected of me with regard to the details and subtleties of the music I was studying. I did not realise that one had to 'practise' slowly and with great care, I was too impatient and just enjoyed rushing through piece after piece. But this period did not last too long and I became very introspective and gradually I became engrossed in my studies. I had to find out more about my own playing, what was not satisfactory, what was good, and why. These were difficult times for me, and I realised that music is nothing but a series of challenges. I was ready to face them, and I directed my search, in an analytical way, in every possible direction.

I became fascinated with the importance of *maximum relaxation* of the body in performance. I was experimenting, trying to remember the exact sensations, the exact muscular condition of my back, arms, hands, when in a state of relaxation, and how this affected the freedom of my movements. I came to some valuable findings. When the body is in this state of relaxation, it becomes a vehicle for the projection of impulses, with arms, hands, fingers and finger-tips purely as manipulators of these impulses, and you, as performer, command a tremendous dynamic range of sonorities, which are full, warm, with character, just as you hear them in your imagination. In teaching, I try to get my students to experience this extraordinary sensation of relaxation, a feeling of freedom that cannot be equalled in any other way. At the same time, I want them to learn how important it is to use the weight of the arms and to feel that the whole body is participating. Yet, it would be wrong and even dangerous to impose rigidly my technique and my way of playing. The study of relaxation is imperative as a basis for piano playing, but there are other aspects of piano technique which have to be studied in relation to each individual. No two people are built in the same way and it is my job to observe every student's hand and body and I may then suggest certain adjustments to achieve the desired result. I think that it would be even more dangerous were I to impose certain technical aspects when working with students with small hands. In order to help them I try to identify myself with their specific problems and then I study closely the way they are trying to cope with them. I show them the importance of a relaxed body, and mainly how to use the arm weight for certain sonorities and we try certain lateral movements to reach wide spread intervals, then we work together to find the best possible fingering for their hands, or the best way of dividing the lines between the two hands. I am very much against editors who put down 'their' fingering as if these were suitable for all performers.

Do you think that it is important for students who have achieved a high standard of performance to take part in competitions, or you prefer to steer them towards a concert career without the ordeal of doing the competitions circuit?

Again, one must take into account the psychology of each young player. Some are suited for this type of contest – they thrive on it – but others, more sensitive, get easily hurt if they do not succeed. It is my responsibility to give the right advice, but only if I am asked. I believe in the right of each individual to decide for himself and I am there only to express an opinion. These competitions, with their glittering publicity, seem to be a necessary evil. Yet, many types of people want them: promoters, agents, and even performers. Some of them are eager to perform in front of a highly critical audience, hoping that some agent will take notice of them as sometimes happens, although on very rare occasions. I personally find the atmosphere of competitions charged with an excitement, not necessarily of a good kind, and that is why I avoid them. Twice I have accepted to be on the jury, but I leave this work now to my colleagues. Besides, I think that even if a young artist wins a competition he is a loser in some ways. To young musicians who are striving to achieve some success as performers, I can only tell them about my beliefs and about my thoughts, hoping that this might inspire them to search for themselves and find out what they really want to do with their life, and which directions they should take.

My constant concern remains the significance of performance and the role of the interpreter in his quest for perfection. An artist's life is a continuous process of evolution, and he may be gaining some wisdom through his experiences though he may never reach perfection. His greatest achievement is to be aware of being in harmony with the spirit of the works he wishes to communicate. I think that even the word 'inspiration' must convey the idea of being 'in-spirit', and the role of the interpreter is to get into the spirit of the music he studies, and to prepare himself for performance with all his being. The 'earth-bound' study must be done in great detail and with great care and respect for the composer's intentions. But, at the moment of performance, the interpreter must become not only the re-creator of the score, he is also the creator of his own performance, receiving the inspiration from within and from without. He is both performer and observer. At that moment, his mental awareness is on an elevated level, and he must be aware only of being in tune with the universe, allowing those outside forces to sustain his desire to serve the music, which flows through his being towards the expectant audience.

Piano Journal VOL 7 NO 19 1986

Ronald Smith

In recent years, your name has been closely associated with that of Alkan, whom many consider to be a neglected genius. Thanks to your first book, Alkan: An Enigma (Kahn & Averill), and your recently issued second book dealing with his works, you have succeeded in creating some interest among readers and performers. But it is largely through your recordings that his piano music is reaching a wider public. How did you discover Alkan?

It was Humphrey Searle, the composer, who was a BBC producer in the late Forties or early Fifties who asked me to broadcast Alkan's Concerto for Solo Piano.

He sent me a fat volume of piano music by Alkan, containing the Concerto. I opened it at random to a page which was packed with notes, masses of them, and I just wondered how on earth was I going to start working on such a piece, and how was I going to finger such music? Then I turned to the first page of the volume where it said 'Pour la main droite seule', and I went straight to the piano and started to read through some of the pieces. Needless to add, I was hooked. I became fascinated with these unusual works, some of interminable length, yet the more I played them the more impressed I was. I also tried to find as much as I could about Alkan, the man, the artist, the composer, as I realised immediately that here was a great original, not just a fringe composer. It has taken me a number of years to understand what he was really searching for in his music, and I do consider him a master of a unique calibre. It is difficult to say where he will ultimately stand, or whether his works will appear more often in recital programmes. I am afraid not many pianists include Alkan's music in their repertoire, for obvious reasons. Some are extremely demanding technically, as they are written by a virtuoso pianist for virtuoso performers, but one must not forget that young artists depend on managers and audiences, and they must present programmes acceptable to them. In America,

Joseph Bloch and Raymond Lowenthal tried to introduce his music in the Fifties and Sixties, but Alkan still remains a rarity on concert platforms. It is hoped that the Alkan Festival, which is planned by the Alkan Society during his centenary, in 1988, will create more interest among audiences and performers alike.

I have recorded many of Alkan's piano works, and I am now preparing three colossal studies, written in 1838, at the time when Liszt was revising his *Etudes Transcendentales*. It is interesting that, not only did they know each other, but Liszt considered Alkan one of the greatest pianists of the time, and admired him as a composer, although I don't think they knew about each other's work on transcendental technique.

You said that Alkan's music is extremely demanding technically, but you certainly have the right technique for these works. Most artists I interview seem to have a career which followed a similar pattern. They showed unusual ability at an early age, with the parents realising that it was their responsibility either to get a very good teacher, or for one of the parents, usually himself a fine musician, to supervise the development of the young prodigy. What about your career?

No, far from it. I come from a simple home, but my mother loved playing the piano, and she did so every evening after I had gone to bed. As a little girl she had a few lessons with a local teacher and then she taught herself to read music, mainly the popular tunes of that time, which she played with great gusto at friends' parties. She also gave a few lessons to children in the neighbourhood. I did not take much notice of the popular tunes, I did not really like them, but occasionally she would play a movement of a Beethoven sonata. Whenever I heard this music I sat up in my bed, enthralled. It reminded me of my very first years in South London, playing in our little garden on a swing which my father had built for me. I must have been two-and-a-half or three years old, but I have vivid memories of the music which came from next door where Mrs. O'Connor gave piano lessons. I could listen for hours, while the swing would move up and down, my whole body quivering with excitement. Later on I realised that I was listening to pieces like the *Moonlight* or *Pathétique* sonatas by Beethoven or *Liebestraum* No. 3, by Liszt, and other great works. These remained in my memory throughout my life.

When I was six or seven, we moved to Sussex, in the lovely town of Lewes. There was great excitement in the house when my parents brought home a gramophone with a few records, most of them with the music *en vogue*, like 'We love the College Girls', and other hit songs.

One of my enjoyments was to pick up tunes and find some chords to harmonise them. But there was just one record which kept me riveted by the gramophone. This was the Liszt *Hungarian Rhapsody No. 2*, played by the celebrated pianist Mark Hambourg. I knew every note of it, and I had only one wish – to be able to play it myself. I asked my mother to teach me, but when she heard that I wanted to learn the Rhapsody, she just laughed and said: 'But, my dear boy, this is the most difficult piece ever written for the piano!' I was seven years old, and she decided that she should start giving me lessons, systematically, or as systematically as she could, doing finger exercises and teaching me pieces from a Tutor. I learned everything very fast, and I was soon able to read music, as I was an eager pupil and wanted to know more and more, but I also played a great deal by ear. I was still hoping to be able to play my beloved Liszt Rhapsody. My mother had a copy of the music, and I saw a mass of notes and some words in a strange language. I remember asking her what *Stringendo* means, and she said: 'I think it means "plucking the strings..."'

One morning at school, the teacher, a German lady who could play the piano a bit, was struggling to play the national anthem. It was so appalling that I jumped to my feet and asked if she would let me do it. She was so impressed with my ability that she told my mother to enter me for the Brighton Music Festival. My mother had no idea what a music festival was, or what was required, but she soon found out what I had to play for my age group. That was a piece by Alec Rowley and, to our great surprise, I came second, with the comment: 'It is amazing that this boy can play at all with his cramped style...' This did not put me off, and the following year, when I was eight, I was entered for the 'Memory Class' competition, playing the Paradies *Toccata*. This was an 'Open Class' for pupils of any age, some were eighteen years old or over. I did not get a first prize, but a third was good enough for me, and for my mother's teaching. It was again my school teacher who convinced my parents to send me to a good teacher, and advised them to let me try for a scholarship at the Brighton School of Music, which was run by a Miss Maud Homsby, who had a good reputation. Her pupils performed every year in the Aeolian Hall, in London, and at the Dome, in Brighton, and she had some fine results with a number of her students. I did get the scholarship, and from then on I knew what I wanted to be. I cannot to this day remember having been taught anything specific about piano technique, but she made us sing, to hear the music and know it before attempting to play. She knew what each child or student needed, and she encouraged us, she inspired us to learn the great works of piano literature. In her school there were some talented youngsters, among them, Henry Duke, who always came first in Festivals. Matthay and his teaching were a great influence on the piano teachers and performers of that time, but I don't know whether Miss Hornsby had any lessons with him. She did not try to impose any specific method or school of technique, and she allowed me to develop in my own way. It is true that I already had some keyboard facility, I was excited with my own 'fast' playing, and she must have realised that I was anxious to learn piece after piece and I was reading everything I could find in her studio. Being so young, I was daring and I did not know what difficulties were involved. I just loved playing.

My father brought home a wireless, and the magic little box fascinated me. To turn a button and receive those extraordinary sounds, to hear many wonderful pianists and those great works, this was sheer bliss. And so I heard for the first time a piano concerto with orchestral accompaniment. It was the Liszt Concerto in A Flat played by the famous pianist Lamond, who, unfortunately, was quite old by then; these were the pre-war years. I rushed to buy the music, and then I heard it soon afterwards played by another pianist, Pouishnoff, who made quite a name in England, and Lamond gave another performance on the radio. I tried to study the concerto myself, and, to my disappointment, I realised that their playing was not very accurate; there were so many wrong notes, and the playing sounded rather strained. I shut myself in my room and just practised that extraordinary opening of the concerto, for hours at an end, trying to find a way to master it and make it sound less difficult. Surely, there had to be an easier way to execute those octaves and jumps! I was experimenting, searching, practising the octaves in all sorts of ways. I discovered that if I played blindfolded I could achieve a command of the keyboard, sensing the distances to cover with greater accuracy. I was determined to succeed. Then I studied the cadenza and the other difficult passages until I could get them to sound just as I heard them in my imagination, and afterwards I did not find them that difficult. One day I heard Dinu Lipatti's recording. Here was a pianist who played every single note just as I dreamed it, just as I wanted to hear it. This was sheer perfection, and his technique served him superbly. This is how I wanted to play, and I continued with my discoveries, reading music and learning as much as I could assimilate. But I also became very interested in composition and, while the other boys in the class were taking notes during the history lesson, I was feverishly writing my first piano concerto which, naturally, contained many 'ingredients' from

Liszt, Grieg, or Chopin. That style of music suited me.

At the time, I was working hard for my School Certificate, and I was longing to finish school so that I could concentrate only on music. Although I was not a good pupil, I was considered an asset for the school thanks to my musical abilities. I also played the violin and led the school orchestra and, of course, I played the piano for every school Fête or party. The Chemistry teacher, who was very fond of music, invited me one evening to go to a Promenade Concert in London. That was the first time I attended such a concert, and the whole evening was an extraordinary experience. The soloist was young Clifford Curzon playing the Tchaikovsky Concerto No. 1. What a revelation!

I then auditioned for the Royal Academy of Music. I was already sixteen, and great was my satisfaction when I was awarded a scholarship to study composition with Theodore Holland, a very fine musician, and President of the Royal Society of Musicians at the time. He must have liked my folio, which contained the piano concerto and a few other pieces. Holland had a fine reputation, and he has taught a number of composers who made a name in the profession. He had been a pupil of Joachim and he had just one lesson with Max Bruch, but the lessons stopped when Bruch realised that Holland never played his Concerto! When I entered the Academy I had hardly any notion of harmony or theory, and I relied on my ear for everything. I even wrote an elaborate piece using canonic devices. And it worked. But I became very anxious to learn, and I taught myself harmony, I studied many treaties thoroughly, although I was still passionately involved in my piano playing. The vast literature fascinated me, and I had great curiosity to read more and more and I certainly made good use of the Academy's library.

I must have been a satisfying student for my teacher, but I did not get the kind of teaching I felt I needed. I had a certain facility, but I did not think that this was sufficient. Perhaps it was a good thing I was not taught, as such, and I was allowed to discover, struggle, and evolve from within. On the other hand, I am sure I received a lot of invaluable background, even though this was more at a subconscious level. Besides, we were very dedicated to our work, and for us music was a matter of life or death. At the same time, we were exposed to a great deal of music every day, we heard other students either practising or performing, there were orchestral or choir practises, operatic performances, and so on. These were absorbed at many levels, and this is how a musical person gradually becomes a musician. There is a great difference between musicality and musicianship, just as there is between facility at the keyboard and technique. Facility can be acquired only in childhood, it is more a mechanical ability, and this cannot be developed in later years. That is why it is important for instrumentalists to start early. But 'technique' encompasses many aspects of piano playing: agility, the ability to produce all kinds of sounds from the instrument, and to project the musical ideas. Technique gives the artist the power to express his conception of a work freely. Paradoxically enough, technique cannot go beyond the conception, and I believe that the greater the musician, the greater his need for the right kind of technique.

My student years in London were important from many aspects. The musical life was intense and I soon realised what was expected from a young pianist eager to join the profession. Fortunately for me, the Royal Academy of Music established a new award, a Fellowship for the best students to enable them to go abroad to continue their studies. I was the first recipient of this award, and I chose to go to Paris, as I was getting very interested in French music. I was accepted to study with Marguerite Long, a pianist and pedagogue of high reputation, but, to my great disappointment, we did not get on. But, as it happens sometimes, a chance meeting may bring a great change in one's life or career. This happened to me while in Paris. I was taken to meet Monsieur Pierre Kostanov, a Russian emigrée, a pianist who studied at the Moscow Conservatoire with a pupil of the famous Siloti, himself a pupil of Liszt. He did not perform, but he was busy teaching, as many young pianists went to him on the quiet without the knowledge of their official teachers.

Indeed, meeting Kostanov was a very important event for my development. He had a profound knowledge of the physiology of piano technique, and he explained every aspect of piano playing simply and with great clarity, and he made me aware of my limitations. At last, I found what I was seeking. I worked assiduously under his guidance, and after only a few weeks I had built the technique which gave me the foundation I needed. Not that I had to spend much time on so called 'finger exercises', although he recommended the '51 Exercises' of Brahms. What he gave me was much more valuable. I learnt how to produce any tone from the instrument, I became aware of every subtle sensation of the weight of the arm or hand being transmitted to the key, of the state of relaxation needed, but, above all, I realised that a pianist must use his hands just as he uses the feet, that is, to support the weight of the body. And the secret of cantabile is what I call 'perpetual motion': there is a continuous movement of the arm in conjunction with the fingers, which are not used individually but as part of the hand, through which the tone is transmitted, while the wrist is free and flexible. I was already getting some engagements, and I also took part in an important competition in Geneva, where I received an award. On the Jury was Edwin Fischer, a pianist I greatly admired, although I only knew him from his records.

Soon afterwards, he came to London to make some recordings for HMV, at Walter Legge's invitation, and he asked that I should play the second piano in Bach's Triple Concerto with Denis Matthews on the third piano. I could hardly believe that this was happening to me, as I considered Fischer a supreme musician. Indeed, the four days of working together were a great revelation for a young, aspiring artist like me. I think I learnt in those few days more about music than I had done during all the previous years. The sheer beauty of sound he could draw from the piano and his control of every single musical phrase were a great lesson. Above all, he had a profound and comprehensive knowledge of every work he played, and all that mattered for him was to convey the absolute essence of music. This was a unique experience for me, and I felt only gratitude for having been allowed to join in that supreme music-making. Not many words were exchanged, but he sometimes mentioned that it was important to relax and particularly that 'one must never commit the sin of playing today as one played yesterday'.

And so, you had your first experience of making a record. Since then, you have made many other records and you must have witnessed great changes in recording techniques.

Yes, indeed, and I often have arguments with some of my colleagues in the profession. It is now considered essential to achieve mechanical perfection, and this is realised through what is called 'montage'. My own feeling about any gramophone recording is that it should be like a snapshot of an event that is caught and held. In this way, it has the inspiration of the performance, even though it may have a few technical inefficiencies. I strongly believe that an artist should be ready to give a good performance under any conditions, whether in a concert hall or in the studio. Of course, the audience adds excitement, as an artist needs the feedback from the hall. But most recording companies, and some of my colleagues, believe that a record should be a documentary of the work as conceived by the composer, and this should be as perfect as possible. And now, with the compact disc, you can hear much more acutely the slightest sound, even if one breathes before a phrase this is recorded on the disc, and this poses new dilemmas for the technique of montage, but this may prove more exhausting for the artist, as it means re-playing complete movements.

I have contracts with two recording companies, each one with a different philosophy. When I arrive at EMI Studios, the technician's first greeting is: 'Long takings, Mr. Smith?' – 'Yes, long takings.' I like being able to play without the interruptions inevitable when 'repair' works have to be done. But, if I am recording devilishly demanding pieces like Liszt's transcription of Beethoven's Seventh Symphony, there might be one or two missed notes. In the old system of recording, little split notes like these added to the excitement, but nowadays they simply sound like wrong notes and they appear too blatant to be allowed to remain unchecked. Well, the engineers argue that there are always the live performances for those who want them, but their responsibility is to produce recordings as near perfection as possible.

The paradox is that there is a great demand for recordings made by the great pianists of the '78' era, reissued and re-processed for the long-playing record market. The pianists who top the list are still Schnabel, Fischer, Cortot, and Hoffman, whose performances abound in wrong notes. These were usually live performances 'caught' as they were executed. Another paradox is that today's search for mechanical perfection has brought with it a high-powered competition among recording companies. And, judging by these artists' performances, it would be a miracle if any of them would pass the first round of an international piano competition. They were great musicians, great artists, but they were utterly variable in their mechanical ability to play at a moment's notice. Does this really matter?

It is known that when Schnabel had to record in a studio he felt extremely uneasy but we, pianists and particularly the students, must be thankful that these records exist. And Edwin Fischer would arrive sometimes at a rehearsal not sure of what concerto he was supposed to play. He did not practise much, but he knew every single work of the piano literature as well as all Bach's cantatas, orchestral works, and many others. No wonder that all the musicians who have been in contact with him had only reverence for the artist and the man, for he was as noble a person as a musician. I treasure the few recordings left of Hoffman's performances, for these show, in spite of their flaws, an absolute pre-eminence when comparing him with any of today's great pianists. I don't look for dazzling virtuosity; I am interested in the artist's sheer control of every single note responding to his conception of the work. Take, for instance, the slow movement of the Chopin F minor Concerto, the exquisite tones he produces with most economical means and with much less pedal than one is accustomed to hearing, bring magic to the performance. In my view, the pedal must be used sparingly, just as a fine violinist makes use of the vibrato. My teacher, Theodore Holland, often talked about Joachim's large number of different vibratos, and how he sometimes did not use vibrato at all, if the music demanded a pure sound. As I mentioned earlier, it is the artist's conception which dictates the execution.

I know that you have been interested in teaching, and you have been on the staff of King's College, Canterbury, for many years. What are the main problems facing talented pupils in such a school, where the accent is on academic excellence?

Yes, I have always been interested in music education as such, but mainly in working with young musicians, helping them find shorter ways than I did towards acquiring keyboard skill. Of course, this is not the goal, it is only the means to be able to express the great music which they are studying.

My teaching is, broadly speaking, an extension of what Kostanov taught me. Of course, I have to use my judgement about each individual as every pupil is different, physically and psychologically, not all of them are highly gifted and, especially, most of them have very little time left for their instrumental studies.

Could you elaborate on your approach to teaching and how you achieve the results you get with pupils who cannot get to the instrument as often as they wish. What is the secret of such a training?

First of all, I think that an harmonic awareness is absolutely essential for any performer, and I insist on reading a great deal of music, which they learn to analyse. Above all, I work with them very thoroughly on the 'keyboard strategy', as I believe that this is vital in acquiring the skill to go round the keyboard. I have devised a sort of game between me and my pupil who has to 'fall into' the key with tremendous speed, at my orders: 'Right hand, second finger, top E'; 'Now, C sharp', and so on. At the first mistake, it is my turn and, in fact, I have to fake sometimes that I cannot find the key to give the pupil another chance. Then, we do the same game with double notes in thirds, fourths, fifths, and eventually with four note chords. It works, and it gives them a great sense of the keyboard geography. I also have a few exercises for specific technical problems, but, in general, I get my pupils to realise how much relaxation they need, how much strength they have to acquire, and how to use their body, arms, hands, fingers, to transmit their musical ideas to the keys. I also make sure that they get frequent performance experience, learning to project their playing.

I have been on the staff of the King's College, Canterbury, for nearly thirty years, and I have watched the music of that school grow to very impressive standards, in all directions. A number of my own students are now active in the profession, and I have a few very talented young pianists; one of them (aged eight) has already appeared on the television as soloist in a Mozart concerto with the Philharmonia Orchestra. I believe it is my responsibility, and for that matter, every artist's responsibility, to care about young musicians, to give them something of our knowledge. I feel the need to do some teaching in spite of my commitments as a concert artist which leave very little time for other activities.

My great concern remains that the pressure of the academic work puts great strain on all musical pupils of the school, although music plays an important role in the curriculum: the choir is one of the most impressive in the country (as it should be, as the choristers sing in Canterbury cathedral), and the instrumental teaching is conducted by some very fine performers. Some of my pupils do find one hour every day for practising, but a few can only have three periods of twenty minutes a week at the piano.

As a teacher, I have not only the responsibility of guiding the pupils to develop their musical ability to the maximum, but I also have the responsibility of guiding them to make the right choice for their career. I have to decide sometimes if I should encourage a very talented youngster to concentrate on his music to the detriment of science or other subjects which might be more useful to him later on. There is no guarantee that such a pupil will make it in the profession, while he may well become a brilliant engineer or mathematician. What is the role of the teacher in such cases? I try to take the middle of the road and give each of my pupils a good foundation of piano technique while at the same time concentrating on his academic studies, working for the various School Certificates at O- or A-Levels. In this way, they will be well prepared for the future should they wish to embark on a musical career. There is still a big question mark, and educationalists should give great attention to it.

Now that there are a few specialised Music Schools in the country, some children have the opportunity to concentrate more on music than in other schools. But, again, is such a segregation of talented youngsters the answer?

Ultimately, it remains with each pupil to decide for himself. Those who feel as we did that 'music is a matter of life or death' will have no doubts. They will know which road to take.

Piano Journal VOL 7 NO 20 1986

Earl Wild

This has been a busy year for pianists specialising in Liszt's music, but even more so for you. The three impressive Wigmore Hall recitals on Liszt: The Poet, The Transcriber, and The Virtuoso were the highlight of the London season. I understand that you started this marathon in New York, and then presented it in other major cities. Do you often devote your programmes to one composer?

I do tend to get involved with one composer from time to time. A few years ago I was working on my own transcriptions of Rachmaninov's songs, and this took me away from almost everything else for quite a while. I spent many months trying to write those transcriptions as a true representation of the songs and Rachmaninov's accompaniments, then I recorded them, and this intense work did not allow me time to do much else. This year, which commemorates the hundredth anniversary of Liszt's death, has been a very important one for me, as I have always loved his music, and I found his transcriptions very exciting pianistically. The audience's response was immediate and, on the whole, it has been a very rewarding experience. And now, after playing many works by the same composer, no matter how satisfying they may be musically or pianistically, I shall certainly take a rest from Liszt. I need to get away from pieces which I have played too often, and come back to them later with a fresh mind when I can make new discoveries. This is what happened this time. I have played almost every piece by Liszt about ten years ago, and it was like meeting again an old and beloved friend. I think that I have also grown in those ten years.

This year, which was devoted to Liszt's music, is coming to an end. What are your future plans?

I may return to my beloved Chopin and, perhaps, include more of Beethoven's works in my future programmes. I would also love to spend some time studying the music of a rather neglected musician, Medtner, and devote a series of concerts to him. Several pianists, in the past, have played some pieces by Medtner, but I don't think they respected him enough, or loved him enough. I remember meeting Medtner's nephew years ago in New York. He could play superbly most of his uncle's works, but only when he was half drunk. We would gather at his home, and after a few glasses he would sit at the piano and play, uninterruptedly. In spite of his state, his co-ordination was amazing. But, the moment he became sober he would stop. He had no more interest in that music.

Among twentieth-century composers you seem to like the two Russians Rachmaninov and Medtner. What about contemporary composers?

On the whole I don't much like contemporary or avant garde music. Sometimes I hear piano pieces which I like, and I think they are good, like Roger Sessions's or Vincent Persichetti's, but I find myself drawn again and again to the great Romantics.

What about your own studies? Did your parents realise that you had special gifts, and did they give you the help and encouragement you needed?

I was only three and a half when I started to play the piano which we had in the house. I loved playing, and I could spend a long time at the piano, and my parents thought that I might as well have proper lessons. I cannot remember much about the teaching, but I do know that I was playing many tunes by ear, and I could improvise with ease. But I don't think I was what one calls a prodigy, although by the time I was eight years old I already had very agile fingers and I played quite well. From the age of six, I had lessons at the Pittsburg Institute from a very nice teacher, Miss Alice Walker. I liked her, and I think she was very pleased with me and with my rapid progress. I was so interested in discovering the music of the great composers and I even taught myself how to orchestrate some piano pieces. Surprisingly enough, the first money I ever made from music was for doing some orchestral arrangements. I was thirteen by then, and I first started arranging for string quartets. Then I dared go on to orchestral arrangements, and my good ear and improvisation skills were of great help.

It was only later that I began to read books about the piano and piano literature and then I found one on orchestration. I became so fascinated with the vast possibilities of the orchestra that from then on I thought more in terms of orchestral colour and tones when playing the piano.

To come back to my piano studies, I think I must have had about twelve teachers. Some I liked, but others I did not care for very much and all I remember is that they mostly looked for my wrong notes! I had to play many studies by Czerny, Clementi, Cramer, which I enjoyed. They are written by pianists for pianists, and they supply the entire background for the period up to late Beethoven sonatas. But when one of my teachers gave me Pischna and Hanon exercises, my hand began to hurt, and I realised that these were not only bad for the hand, but useless for my musical development. Hanon exercises are mediocre because you don't have to use your brain and I don't recommend them to my students. On the whole, I think that I developed my technique mostly through studying the great works. In the same way, I found that I had to spend a lot of time practising scales and then, when meeting scale passages in the music, the fingering had to be changed. Very annoying!

I started to play in public when I was very young and I think that my playing sounded rather 'technical' because my keyboard facility developed much faster than my emotional personality. I also made the great mistake of including works in my programmes which demanded great maturity and understanding and I was not yet ready. I even played the great *Fantasie* by Schumann, which really should not be attempted until one is at least forty. Clara is reputed to have played the last movement with tears running down her face. I think that this movement is so lyrical and beautiful, with moments of marvellous ecstasy. It is marked to be played slowly, but it must flow, each phrase leading to the next in a peaceful mood. And it must not be played with a very big sound in spite of Schumann's marking of ff. The pianist must be so careful, thinking about a full tone but not a loud one, not to disturb that stillness and intimacy. It seems rather complex, but this is what I feel about this sublime movement.

It was only later that I met the right teacher when I went to New York to study with the celebrated Egon Petri, who was in great demand both as a performer and teacher. He had been a pupil of Busoni, and for the first time in my life I was made aware of the excitement of producing a beautiful sound and a wide range of tones. From then on my piano playing took a completely different direction. Petri was, indeed, a great teacher. He spent a large part of the lesson guiding me towards a virtuoso technique, teaching me to think of every single tone when practising and made me get away from that facile way of playing on the surface of the keys which I had developed since childhood. First of all, he insisted on changing my finger technique. From the unmusical one based on high articulation, I was made aware of the great control one achieves when playing from the key surface with fingers 'connected' to the key, understanding the principle of leverage and being conscious of the weight of the arm and hand transmitted to each finger. From him I learnt not to 'poke' the key but 'squeeze' it gently, just as you pat an animal you love. In this way you can apply the most intense pressure, producing all kinds of tone.

Apart from Egon Petri, were you influenced by other musicians?

When I was still at High School I met a very interesting musician, Paul Dogereau. He had studied with Paderewski, with Schnabel, had met Ravel and played to him, and had been in contact with many other famous musicians. Studying with Dogereau was a new experience. He often interspersed the lessons with stories and anecdotes about his teachers and friends, and he introduced me to many works by rarely played composers, including Paderewski, and I think some of his compositions are really beautiful. Paderewski would often play for his pupils, and Dogereau tried to recapture these moments when talking about his playing. We must remember that the recordings we have from Paderewski were made when he was already quite old, and he was not practising any longer, and they do not give a true idea of the genius of his pianism. In a hall he was capable of creating an extraordinary atmosphere, he could electrify the audience and, indeed, his playing of certain pieces, like Chopin nocturnes, was exquisite. I have played Paderewski's Sonata and the *Variations in A Major*, which I consider good works, and I have actually recorded the Piano Concerto and *Polonaise Fantaisie*.

You have performed and recorded works of the piano repertoire which hardly anyone else plays. Did you do this in order to enhance your career?

I am afraid so. This is how I got into the recording business and it was important for an up-and-coming young artist to have his name in the catalogues. But once I started to study these works, I could not help falling in love with them.

Although I have done and I am still busy doing recordings, I believe that recording and public performances are two completely different things. Recordings are really a fake, not because the pianist is not good, but because you are dealing with a microphone, and that in itself is a mechanical instrument. Pianists play for a machine, not for an audience. If you play in a hall you have to play for the man in the last row, and try to communicate your music to him. In a studio, the tendency is to adjust constantly to play with a smaller tone so that it always sounds beautiful.

This brings me to the problems encountered by young pianists, the winners of international competitions. They usually become a product of the recording industry before they know enough about projecting their performances in a big hall. Then they appear rather pale when playing in public, and I think they should develop first as public performers before attempting to make recordings.

What are your views on the spate of international competitions which are now being held in almost every great city of the world?

There is one competition in the United States of which I greatly approve. Paul Dogereau, my former teacher, is the President of the Peabody Mason Foundation in Boston which offers the winner a grant of $20,000 a year for a period of two years, at the end of which the young artist gets two debut recitals, one in Boston and one in New York. I am very much in favour of such a competition. The others do a great disservice to young pianists by catapulting them too soon into a big career for which they are not prepared. Sometimes you hear of a pianist who had a glamorous career for about two years or so and afterwards he has had to abandon it. The strain was too great. Besides, pianists in their twenties need time to expand at a slower pace, they need to gain more experience. Of course, these international competitions provide such extraordinary advantages, they guarantee an immediate financial return and enormous publicity and most youngsters are eager to have a go. The saddest thing is to look at the lists of pianists who take part in competitions. The same names appear year after year, and these pianists get older without developing emotionally or as musicians. I strongly believe that if one wishes to enter the musical profession one should do so because of a great love of music and not because one wishes to achieve success quickly. We need to get over the idea that one has to be a success by twenty-one. Music is a life's work.

My advice to young pianists is to realise how important it is to make a living in music by teaching, by playing with other musicians while at the same time studying, learning many works of the piano repertoire, so that they grow into better musicians with a broader view of music in all its unity.

Although I always played and performed in public, it is only recently that I have received great recognition as a solo artist. For years I have worked with other artists, and my radio debut in 1934 was as Oscar Schomsky's pianist. I considered it a privilege to work with a violinist of his calibre, and I believe that, thanks to working with him and with other great artists, I grew as a musician.

You are now on the Faculty of the Juilliard School. What are your views on the artist's responsibility towards the younger generation, and how do you combine a busy concert career with giving enough of your time to the students?

This is a big question. I am a teacher, therefore I take my responsibility very seriously. After all, as teachers, we are dealing with their lives, but all we can do is guide them, not attempt to teach them. Because of my commitments as a performer, I can only accept a few student so that I can give all my attention to them. I select them from among the more mature postgraduate students because at that stage music is a serious matter. They know what they want to do and they also know that this is very important for them. I also prefer to work with students who have passed over their first emotional crises in their teens. Not that they are free of other problems, but somehow I think they are more able to cope with such situations.

I also like to see them every two or three weeks, and give them a long lesson of about three or four hours, instead of just one hour every week. I think this is more profitable for them; they come better pre-pared, and they also learn not to be dependant on the teacher. To be a musician you need to do enormous work constantly, alone, learning to face your own problems.

You accept only very advanced players who have reached a high standard of per-formance and who have a fine technique. What are the main problems you en-counter in your teaching?

Every student is an individual, and I try to have a different approach to each one. Technique encompasses everything. It is not just finger work, and everyone's hand is different. That is why I do not impose a certain hand position. I think, though, that the most beautiful position of the hand is so well illustrated in Michelangelo's *Finger of God*, with the hand stretched, yet relaxed, and fingers exquisitely shaped. I do make a point of getting to know each student's potential, so I study his hand and the mental connections between the mind and the hand as well as his emotional background, because these are all inter-related.

There are so many pianists with injuries from overuse, or perhaps from misuse, of their muscles. What advice do you give to your own students to avoid such injuries?

I have avoided hand trouble all my life because I understood very early in my training that some exercises cause pain, therefore should not be used. I think I know now how to guide my students. First of all I teach them to treat the 4th finger with great care, never lift it high nor force it when practising. There are better ways of gaining independence and control. As I mentioned earlier, by playing from the key-surface fingers get quite strong, yet maintain their elasticity. And a variety of tones is produced through the way the weight is placed on each finger, when pressing the keys. The hand should remain flexible, always, otherwise there is tension in the wrists and this must be avoided. I have a number of students from the Far East with very small hands. Surprisingly, they present fewer difficulties than expected, because their hands are very flexible and, unlike large hands which tend to 'sit on the chords', they are continuously on the move, adjusting to wide stretches. Whether they have large or small hands, I advise them not to use the 4th finger when playing octaves. In my own playing I use it only very rarely, because the strength of the hand is between the 1st and the 5th fingers, and this is a natural position of the hand. The moment you play fast octaves using the 4th finger there is a strain – the hand has to adjust to an unnatural position, and the result may be dangerous. I have noticed that pianists and teachers who have had problems with the 4th finger themselves usually pass them on to their pupils, and so on.

There are many aspects of piano playing that I would like to talk about. What is important is to know how and when to use the weight of the arms and hands, as this plays such an important role. A measure of the weight should always be in the hands, over the keys. Then there is no need to work hard to produce any tone, and especially a *pianissimo* tone. I try to get my students to become aware of their 'ears at their fingertips', imagining the sound they want to produce, so the mind gives orders to the fingers telling them what to do 'before it happens'.

Your students are fortunate to have you to guide them during their years at the Juilliard School, which is known for the tremendous competition which exists among the ambitious young musicians. How do they cope with this additional stress?

I have given a great deal of thought to the problems of tensions created by the very nature of our profession. There is nothing like being involved in one's work, and adopting a positive attitude. But there is no simple answer. I, personally, use a very simple technique: when I find myself tense emotionally and physically, I say to myself, 'turn it off' – and there is an immediate response. I experience the strange sensation of feeling the muscle tension going down the arm, to the hands and the tip of the fingers, and the tightness disappears. I do talk to my students about these sensations, and get them to be aware of their own experiences when there is release of tension. During the lessons, I find it easier to illustrate so that the young pianist can watch me and understand what I am talking about. A little demonstration is sometimes more telling than words.

I also try to impress upon them that if they think of the music and the beauty of each phrase, unnecessary tensions disappear. To play a phrase beautifully one needs an emotional frame of reference as well as an intellectual one, but the player must experience the flow of that phrase, and allow it 'to happen'. Above all, one has to understand the importance of breathing with the music. This I have learnt from working for many years with singers. They breathe at the right moment, unlike pianists or string players, and I advise the students to work with singers, and learn to use the hand as though they are breathing with the arm and the hand, and then the playing is so much easier. For the rest, it is up to them, and if they are motivated and dedicated, they will succeed.

Piano Journal VOL 7 NO 21 1986

John Ogdon

You are both a pianist and composer and, in your early twenties, you were one of the very few British composers to have won the prestigious Tchaikovsky Prize in Moscow. Surely, such an award has greatly enhanced your career, although you were already known in England through your performances both as soloist and as a partner in the Duo with your wife, Brenda Lucas. Most artists I interview express their dissatisfaction with the sad fact that, to be accepted on the lists of a good agent, a young artist must win a first prize at an important international competition.

I am afraid this is what happened in my own case. Before taking part in the Moscow competition I played very often in various parts of the country and I gave some good recitals in several big halls, but, it was only after receiving that important award that I became famous almost over night. Although the first prize was given jointly to Vladimir Ashkenazy (who was still living in Russia at the time) and myself, it did not matter. I was overwhelmed with concert dates both in the UK and abroad, at first mostly in America and the Scandinavian countries, but soon afterwards I was playing in almost every European country, as well as in the Far East. However, I was not very satisfied with this immediate success. Of course, being in great demand gave me satisfaction and more confidence, but it also made me aware of the immense responsibilities imposed by being launched so suddenly on the international platform. The stress which weighs heavily upon the shoulders of a young artist having to meet these new responsibilities is often unendurable.

In her book about your life and your career, Virtuoso (which, I understand will soon be the subject of a film), Brenda Lucas describes just how you collapsed under the tremendous strain imposed on your life by your commitments and how you have overcome this ordeal so that now you are able to carry on your career so suc-

cessfully. Was it a help or a hindrance, being married to another musician, indeed a pianist also?

Being married to a pianist has been, for me, a great incentive. I believe that it has been a great help to both of us to grow together and develop as musicians. We have learnt to listen to one another when playing together, and also to be more critical of our own playing. We still give many concerts as a Duo, and we consider ourselves privileged that some fine two piano works have been written specially for 'Brenda and John' by outstanding composers like Alan Rawsthorne, Malcolm Williamson, Alan Bush, and others, which we have performed many times and which we have also recorded.

Your training seems to have followed the usual pattern: you started to play very early, then your parents realised that you had unusual talent, and when you were still very young, you entered the Manchester Conservatoire (today's Royal Northern College of Music). Ronald Stevenson, the well-known composer and pianist, recalls a delightful story of how he met you when you were only nine years old. He was already a student in the senior course of the Conservatoire when he came across some music by Busoni. He became so intensely interested in this composer that he combed all the libraries in search of more works by Busoni, and he spent every free moment studying and playing them. One day, while he was feverishly practising, a little boy came near him and stood by the piano, enraptured, without uttering a word. Only when Ronald finished playing did he timidly ask what that music was. 'This is the music I would love to play one day', he added.

Yes, I vividly remember that day; I wanted to become a pianist and study composition so that I could fulfil my dream of being able to write music like that which I had just heard. Ronald was very kind, he lent me some piano pieces by Busoni and, in spite of their complex structure, I struggled through, page after page, in my simple and determined way. Surprisingly, I was not deterred by their enormous technical difficulties. All that mattered was my excitement, my joy of hearing myself playing pieces with extraordinary richness of sounds and textures.

As a young boy I never stopped to think about difficulties which I might encounter. Fortunately, at that age I lived so much in the present, I was so busy studying and playing the instrument I loved, that I never had any doubts. I was immersed in music, and that was an enriching experience.

The years I spent at the Manchester School of Music were very important for me. In spite of being much younger than the other students,

I was accepted by my colleagues as 'one of them'. Manchester was a very cultured town, and everyone was proud of its musical heritage, The Hallé Orchestra, with its series of concerts dominating the musical life. Some of the finest musical personalities had been invited to teach at the Manchester Conservatoire, and the standard of performance was impressive. I had the privilege to be accepted into Iso Ellinson's class, and my lessons with him were a continuous source of stimulation in many directions. He was not only an outstanding pianist, but he was something of a Renaissance man, with a great knowledge of literature and Art, and indeed interested in many other areas. Studying with him was an extraordinary adventure for a young pupil like me. He introduced me to the richness of the piano literature, making me aware of the styles of the different composers, and each lesson was a voyage of discovery and learning. I learnt a great deal just listening to his performances, which covered almost the entire history of piano music. He would give whole series of Bach's 'Forty-eight', then all Beethoven's sonatas; he introduced Scriabin's music to Manchester audiences, and so on. I wanted to study as many Beethoven sonatas with him as I could play myself. Iso Ellinson was a great friend and admirer of Tovey, and he gave me Tovey's edition (which he did in collaboration with Harold Craxton), but he also showed me other editions, like those of Dukas and Czerny. He wanted to help his students to think for themselves and find which was a good and which was not a good edition. In later years, I discovered Schnabel's edition, and I became very interested in his thorough study of each work. We all admired Schnabel's conception of Beethoven's sonatas and other works, and in his edition he gives both the autograph copy and his own suggestions as a possible interpretation of a particular passage. I know that some of my colleagues disagree with his unorthodox fingering, but I like many of his ideas. They make sense musically, even if they don't give the easiest solution for the student.

In my search for knowledge I loved reading music by a variety of composers, from early baroque to contemporary, and I was an avid concert-goer. Whenever I heard a pianist giving an original and impressive performance of certain pieces I wanted to study those works with that particular artist. Thus, I had quite a few teachers, and I don't remember a time when I studied with only one teacher.

With Denis Matthews I studied Mozart, Schubert, some Beethoven sonatas, Haydn. What a joy it was to be with Denis who, after listening to my playing, would start discussing the interpretation, and then would sit at the other piano illustrating his points by playing themes from a variety of works by the same composer – string quartets, symphonies, operas – comparing them with harmonic structures found in other composers, and... and... The lessons would go on and on, until late into the evening.

I think that I learnt how to play the piano from Egon Petri, himself a pupil of Busoni, who was anxious to pass on to his own students what he had learnt from the master. Not only that I was privileged to have studied the piano works of Busoni with Petri, but he also revealed to me new insights into the music of Bach, and we worked on some of the great Romantics, which he loved playing. I still clearly remember working with him on the Brahms' *Paganini Variations*. All the technical points were closely analysed, giving valuable suggestions concerning fingering to emphasise a certain tone colour or timbre. He would use the fifth finger as a pivot to turn the hand over to move from one chord to another. Very effective. He also advised us to use the third finger whenever possible instead of the fourth, because it is governed by a strong muscle, thus avoiding fatigue or injury.

Above all, he worked with me on technique. Every single movement of fingers, hands and arms was analysed, insisting that finger individualisation and flexibility are the foundation of a thorough piano technique. He also wanted me to play from the surface of the key, not articulating by raising the fingers before pressing the keys. He had strong views on how to use the instrument to the greatest advantage, and every single movement was done in order to draw out the greatest variety of tones and tone colours from the piano.

He, himself, was a superb pianist, with a unique, glowing tone which I still hear in my ears. We, the students, were trying to imitate his tone, but he did not want that. He wanted us to think intensely of how to produce a great variety of sounds, continuously exploring, listening, and particularly being careful never to allow a 'dry' tone to disturb the interpretation.

Another great musician with whom I studied was Gordon Green, who had also been a pupil of Petri before his appointment as professor at the Manchester Conservatoire. He went specially to Poland to work with Petri, who had a house in Zaccopani, a famous mountain resort. Gordon Green did not think that I needed to change my technique, as we both belonged to the same school of piano playing. I was interested to broaden my repertoire, and I found him most helpful with Romantic music, particularly with that of Liszt. I liked his grand, operatic gestures when playing, or when illustrating a point of interpretation, gestures quite suited to the style of the great Romantic composers. He enjoyed showing us some exaggerated movements of the arms, trying to get us young players to learn how to project the music when performing to an audience. A great musical experience for me was the discovery of Bartok's music, which needed a totally different approach. I decided that the best way to reach an understanding of this music was to go to the source, a Hungarian musician. Thus I met Ilona Kabos, a pianist who actually met Bartok, and who gave the first performance in London of Bartok's Sonata for Two Pianos and Percussion, with her former husband, Louis Kentner. To make me feel Bartok's rhythms, she would dance round the piano, saying: 'Listen, darling, it is no use trying to teach you how to play this music. You would only imitate me, and it will never sound convincing. Just listen again and again to Bartok's music until you feel the rhythms strongly within you, within your whole body. Only then should you try to play it. You will find that the music will come, without trying so hard to play it!' It was wonderful to have Ilona moving with such vitality and excitement. This was more convincing than using words.

Your repertoire is truly amazing, and you are one of those pianists who can play five or six different programmes in several concerts during one single month. You must have stored an immense repertoire in your memory. Yet, are there some composers with whom you have more affinity than with others?

I really find it difficult to answer your question. I get very involved; I am carried away by the specific qualities of the music which I play at the time. Perhaps I can say that I love best the piece I am playing at that moment. I am so interested in every piece of music I am studying, that I find beauty and moments of greatness in each one. It is true to say that each composer has something important to offer, and I find myself equally enjoying to play music by Debussy, Ravel, or by Busoni, Bartok, Szymanovsky, and, if I am in the right frame of mind, no other composer gives me a greater thrill than Mozart. But, it is so difficult to play a simple phrase by Mozart perfectly! Being a composer myself, I am particularly interested in the music of our time, that of my contemporaries. I am part of the 'Manchester Group' of composers, and I have given several concerts presenting a programme entitled 'John Ogdon and Friends', including works by Peter Maxwell-Davies, Ronald Stevenson, Buxton Orr, Alexander Goehr, Malcolm Williamson, Alan Rawsthorne, John McCabe, Harrison Birtwistle, Robert Simpson, Christopher Headington, and Alan Bush, most of these being dedicated to me.

Looking at some of your programmes, I see that you have performed many un-known or rarely played works. You are doing a great service to composers who are rather neglected by box-office conscious artists and agents.

Yes, I like to present works which are not too often heard and see the audience's response. I performed Paderewski's Piano Concerto in Poland, and everyone loved it. I think it should be included in the London concerts programmes; it is an exciting work to play. I also think that pianists should look for less popular works to introduce in their programmes, and I should like to recommend Medtner's *Sonata Tragica* and, particularly, Enescu's Third Piano Sonata, with its haunting folk tunes and rhythms. Also, I find some American composers very satisfying to play, and I am fascinated by Charles Ives 'Concord' Sonata, or Aaron Copland's 'Piano Fantasia'. Needless to add, Russian compos-ers like Rachmaninov and Prokofiev remain among my favourites.

You have many records on the market, and recently you have issued your first com-pact disc. You must be aware of the attitude of many artists to the methods used by the recording companies, anxious to produce only technically perfect performances by doctoring certain passages, or even single notes when there is a slight flaw. Yet, most of them still continue to make recordings, for obvious reasons. What is your attitude?

I quite like playing in a studio, although I love an audience. But the silence of a studio can be inspiring, and I respond to that atmosphere of stillness. The experience of producing my first compact disc (I play three Beethoven Sonatas: the *Moonlight*, *Pathétique*, and *Appassionata*) was most interesting, and I am very impressed with the quality of the sound of these discs. They certainly represent an important technical develop-ment. Listening to these records, you feel an extraordinary sensation of being immersed in the music which you receive from every corner of the room; you are completely surrounded by it. And, if the final result is so outstanding and brings to the public performances of high quality, this is what matters. We, artists, must also think of the work of immense precision of the recording engineers, and it is important that this collaboration should be a happy one. For myself, I am looking for-ward to continuing this collaboration and to producing more records, either the usual long-playing ones, or some new compact discs.

You are so versatile and perform music by a variety of composers, but you seem to neglect John Ogdon the composer. Is it time that you should devote at least part of your programmes to make your own music better known?

It is not quite so. I have played my Piano Concerto quite a few times and, in 1987, on the occasion of my fiftieth birthday, it will be included in the special 'celebration concert' in London, when I shall appear both as pianist and composer. I feel very honoured to have so many artistic events dedicated to me, and I am grateful to my colleagues who are participating in these events. The year 1987 is indeed very important for me and for my music.

Piano Journal VOL 8 NO 22 1987

Fou Ts'Ong

I believe you are the first Chinese pianist to have made an international career. You have been settled in England since 1955, and you have been playing for many years in almost every European country, in North and South America, Japan, Israel, Australia, New Zealand, and so on. In recent years you have been allowed to return to China to give concerts and to teach in conservatories. What are your views on music in today's China in general, and how do you find the piano playing and teaching, compared to what you remember from your childhood and your early youth?

I have mixed feelings. On one hand I am thrilled to be in China every time I have the opportunity to play and teach there. I still have quite a few friends with whom I grew up, although I left the country when I was about 18. On the other hand it is very depressing for me to realise the long-term damage done to my country by those terrible years of the so-called 'Cultural Revolution'. Physical damage can be cured with time, as the human body has immense resilience and resources. But the psychological trauma and the spiritual injuries of the Chinese people will take, perhaps, many years to heal.

The music in today's China appears very flourishing and alive. I say 'appears' because, while there are many young musicians who show great talent and amazing, almost uncanny, finger dexterity, this is not sufficient. To become great artists, and I mean artist with capital 'A', it will take quite a while for the younger generation of musicians to catch up with the cultural desert which was created during those years of unbelievable restrictions, even persecutions, when music, like other arts, was not allowed to exist. The creative artists or writers, contemporaries of my parents, were not allowed to pursue their profession; they were forbidden to write, play, or teach, thus were unable to pass on to the pupils the great tradition acquired during their studies with fine performers and pedagogues. Instead, they had to use their hands to work on the land, to build roads in various parts of the country, or to do other menial jobs. Of this generation only a handful of musicians remain. Others, like my own parents, have chosen suicide rather than carry on under such conditions. I was already in England, and my anguish when I received the tragic news cannot be described.

It is true that the students and the musicians I meet have tremendous love of music and, as I mentioned earlier, immense ability. They all have extraordinary keyboard skill which they cultivate with great devotion. Yet, it is rather sad to find that the younger generation lacks a cultural foundation on which to build their learning. The years when neither the old Chinese nor the European traditions were permitted brought culture virtually to a standstill. Yet, one would think that China ought to produce artists of great sensitivity and depth, just because the people have suffered so much. The longings and frustrations ought to find expression in Art. The reality is somehow different. Whenever I work with young pianists, and sometimes even with advanced students in conservatories, it saddens me to find a lack of intellectual curiosity, a desire to learn about other arts, about literature. They do not think that they should broaden their knowledge in other directions than music. Unfortunately, and this is true of other countries, whether in the East or in the West, we live in an era of supreme specialisation; our minds seem to work in well defined compartments, and some of the young musicians in China think on the same lines. To reach perfection at the instrument is their only goal, and they spend hours and hours every day practising finger exercises and studies set by their teachers. How can they avoid becoming pure technicians of the instrument?

Well, many musicians who have been to China to play or to teach, have come back full of enthusiasm and admiration for its achievements. The Piano Journal, for example, has published two very interesting articles, one by a well-known piano teacher in Los Angeles, Erika Chary, and the other by Diana Ambash, an English pianist. Diana described the interesting experiences meeting Chinese audiences, not only in big towns but also in more remote places, while Erika was thrilled to meet teachers and pupils at the Shanghai Conservatory. She could converse in German with the older teachers while with the others, as with the pupils, she managed through sign language and, ultimately, through music. These younger teachers, probably of your age, must have been brought up like you, in the same cultural tradition, and, although they were quite young when the Cultural Revolution set in, they must still remember what their teachers or their parents tried to instil in them. Surely, these teachers should be able to guide the young pupils in music schools, or in other academic institutions, in the right directions.

This is so. My own generation had strong cultural traditions, and such values do not die. What I am trying to convey is that today's commercialism is felt everywhere, in every aspect of Chinese life. And this is what saddens me most. When I hear that some of the most outstanding students who came to my classes have abandoned music for a more remunerative profession I get distressed. Yet, I do not blame them, but I am convinced that this would not have happened in previous years. A musician was too dedicated and entirely absorbed by his art, to leave it. It is true also that some teachers are very anxious to bring great artists and teachers from Europe or from America to the conservatories and to music schools, so that young pupils and students learn from these musicians. Listening again and again to fine performances is bound to develop more understanding, and help musicians to absorb some valuable ideas.

It might appear that I present a contradictory picture of Chinese musical life. But, being Chinese myself, and able to talk and communicate with my colleagues and with the pupils, I see some aspects which may elude other visitors. In conservatories one finds two distinct categories of piano teachers, or, for that matter, of instrumental teachers in general. Some of the older teachers who are allowed now to pursue their profession are doing their utmost to guide and to stimulate their students. Not only that they have studied in Europe before the war years, but they have also had the opportunity to listen to those unique performances on the 78 records, by Schnabel, Fischer, Cortot, and others. Unfortunately, these musicians are not performers, but they compensate by being so caring and dedicated. The other category of teachers are the younger ones, who are more limited themselves. They belong to the sacrificed generation of youngsters who grew up without any culture, and it is a miracle that they have developed as they did, as pianists, and now as teachers.

How do you explain that more and more youngsters coming to Europe or to America from China compare favourably with other young musicians, and in recent years have even won international competitions?

This is also true. They are catching up very fast with what goes on in other parts of the world and, with hard work and their innate talent, they are excelling in many fields, not only in music.

You have been going to China for many years now and, surely, you are able to impart to your students fresh ideas, a different attitude to learning in general, and your knowledge and artistry in particular. How do you structure your teaching?

My own experiences working with these youngsters have always been very rewarding. I do find them very anxious to develop, very keen to learn more about music. I work with pianists individually, so that I can spend more time on all aspects such as technique, points of interpretation, phrasing, showing them the difference between bad and good editions. I allow them, or to be precise, I ask them to copy the phrasing and other markings in my editions so that they can realise what each composer's style demands.

I also give courses on specific aspects of various composers' works. Recently I gave a course on all Mozart's concertos both at Shanghai and Beijing Conservatories. This was a completely new experience for the students. I stressed the historical and social implications in Mozart's music in general, as well as the stylistic aspects; then I made them hear the quality of sounds, the specific Mozartian tones. Above all, I revealed to my listeners the operatic character of the concertos, and the profoundly human emotions expressed in that music. But, in order to understand Mozart concertos one would have to know first his operas. Each concerto is an opera in itself, it has its own character, its psyche, that is, its psychological content, and each concerto has to be presented in such a way as to make a unique impact. The artist must at all costs avoid treating all concertos in the same way, with the same feeling. On a superficial level, the concertos in the same key (B flat – K450, K456, K595) may appear similar in character; even some of the passagework is similar. Yet, other than that, each one represents a totally different world. For my Chinese students this is not easy to grasp. Even if the natural instinct is there, the musical expression is right – and it is known that Chinese people have a great feeling for drama – in order to interpret these works in all their depth one must have a truly profound grasp of European culture. I must add that I had an extraordinary response from the pupils, whether they were six years old or eighteen and over! It only proves how great the need for such an approach is. I had brought with me my own scores and, knowing the great difficulties they encounter in getting good editions, I offered the Conservatory all the music I had with me, with all my notes. People over here cannot realise under what difficulties most students manage to study in this respect. They still have to rely on those over-edited nineteenth-century albums of classical and romantic music. In many cases, the style of performance and the phrasing would not be acceptable over here.

How do you find the audiences in China, especially now when they have many opportunities to hear foreign artists as well as some of their own rising performers?

There is nothing I love more than playing in China. I have a special rapport with the audience; I am so happy to see that my career has been followed with tremendous interest 'back home' ever since I left the country as a very young student. Many people in the audience have known me as a child, they were friends of my parents and, surprisingly, they seem to know all about my competitions, about my successes in other countries, and they come to hear me whenever I play. They even travel from other towns, and it is good to see that my records are in great demand. It is wonderful for me to play there. I feel that the public receives my special message which I try to communicate to them. I speak to them through my music, perhaps, in a very subtle way, bringing to them my deep feelings about the old China and about the new revival of the arts. Whether my message is good, I cannot tell. All I know is that it comes from the depth of my whole being, and at the moment I sense that the audience and I are one. A truly magical moment.

This unique relationship may be due also to these people's devotion to my parents. My father was a well-known and much loved writer and scholar. His books had been banned during the long years of suffering, but everyone is happy to see that they have been reprinted and are now available in bookshops and in libraries.

What about your own training as a pianist? You had the opportunity to study first in China and later on in Europe, so you had the best of both worlds. Did you find great discrepancies in the actual approaches to teaching?

It is very difficult for me to answer this question. My training as a pianist was rather odd. As a child I did not have a piano teacher as such, and I never went to a conservatory. I was an only child, and my father took complete charge of my education. He was a very cultured man, a sort of 'Renaissance' scholar with profound knowledge of Chinese traditions and, at the same time, with immense interest and love of European culture. He had travelled through many countries, had really seen the world, and had studied philosophy, languages, literature, and the arts. He also gave many lectures on Chinese culture wherever he went. Thus, I was privileged to have him as a tutor and mentor, and he found in me a very keen student, eager to absorb and learn under his guidance. He tried to instil in me the same interest and respect of spiritual values. With regard to music, he believed that this should be also included but only as part of my general education. He brought a teacher for me, a Mr. Paci, an Italian, who was not a pianist. He was the conductor of the Shanghai Municipal Orchestra. With him I had real fun; he taught me how to listen to music, how to read music; he gave me some piano lessons; he talked to me about great composers, and so on. These wonderful sessions lasted only for about one year and a half. When he died I missed him greatly, as by now I realised how much I loved music and how much I loved going to the piano or listening to records. Yet, my father did not think that it was important for me to study at the Conservatory. He still believed in the broad, 'humanist education' which he had devised for me and which, in fact, suited me. Besides, at that time there were some upheavals in the family and we had to leave Shanghai. We only returned there when I was sixteen or seventeen. I was old enough to know what I wanted to do and I decided to be a musician. I had been playing the piano all those years away from Shanghai and never gave a thought to the way I was playing. All I knew was that I loved it, and from then on I started to study music seriously. I still had no teacher, but I was working with tremendous intensity, both at the instrument and studying scores, searching, listening to the great pianists on our collection of 78's, learning and discovering the masterpieces of piano literature. Everything was so new and so thrilling. I was already playing in public, and I must have loved it. At that age I was not concerned whether I had technique or not. To me it did not matter. I was fortunate to have been chosen among the young artists to be sent to Europe in 1953, when I participated in the George Enescu Competition in Bucharest. I was just 19, and this was my first encounter with a European audience, and with musicians from other countries. I was bewildered and, to my great surprise, even amazement, I came third; the other two prizes went to the two most outstanding Rumanian pianists: Valentin Gheorghiu and Mindru Katz. The public was just wonderful, and several people came to congratulate me, comparing me with Cortot, my idol among pianists. I had been listening to his old 78's for years, and knew every single sound of his exquisite playing.

You might be pleased to hear, after so many years, what Florica Muzicescu – the great Rumanian teacher, who gave us pianists like Dinu Lipatti, Mindru Katz, Lory Wallfisch, and quite a few others – said when she came to Fontainbleau at Nadia Boulanger's invitation: 'Fou Ts'Ong was a revelation; his playing was so fresh, so unique – under his fingers the piano sounded as if it had just been created.'

Did she really say that? It does me good to hear this from such a musician. Thank you. After Bucharest, I went to Poland where, in 1955, I won the Chopin prize at the Warsaw competition. While in Poland, I played to professor Drzewiecki, who gave me some lessons for about three months before the competition. I liked working with him, and after the competition I decided to stay on in Warsaw where professor Drzewiecki took me as a student. This was a very important time for me. He was the first piano teacher I have ever had, and this was a totally new experience. All his students feared and respected him, yet they worshipped him. With me he was very different. He made it clear that he would want to hear me only once a month, as he did not want to influence 'my individual way of playing'. He advised me to carry on as I did until then, and to prepare a programme for him every month, to discuss it and, in his words, to make sure that 'I did not go out of bounds'. Those four years in Poland, guided by such a fine teacher and musician, were very valuable. Looking back, perhaps, I would have wanted to have had some 'proper lessons' on piano playing, on how to use my fingers, arms, or 'how to practise'.

I understand that you had some problems with your hands and arms. Was this because you had to develop your own way of playing? The piano is not a 'natural' instrument like the violin which gypsy or jewish fiddlers always played at weddings or other village celebrations in Eastern and Central Europe. A pianist must 'practise' many hours every day, and if he misuses his muscles a lot of damage can be done.

Yes, I have suffered from tendinitis at both wrists, but now I know how to work, although it took me a long time to find the best way to use my hands and arms. Perhaps the lack of a specific method of piano playing is at the root of my problems. It may also be because my musical understanding was always far ahead of my technical equipment. When I was very young I could achieve the results I wanted through sheer will-power and very hard work. I would just play again and again a passage until I thought it sounded right. In my case, it also happened that during the crucial years when all young pianists spend hours to develop a keyboard technique, I hardly played the piano. And this is the time when the training must be done, when the hands and fingers are very flexible. When I started to work very intensely, I did not realise that my hands were already 'set', the muscles were hardened, and at this stage it is not easy to develop a virtuoso technique. Then, when I was studying in Poland with Prof. Drzewiecki, he did not teach me anything about actual piano playing as he did with the other students. He used to say that he found everything I did so artistic that 'it did not matter how I did it'. He watched my hands and he must have realised that I did not use them like other pianists, yet he would not correct it. All he said was: 'If it sounds right it must be right'.

I have paid dearly for this lack of fundamental skill. Perhaps I also started to worry too much about it and this was not good, it added to the stress. In recent years I have found great relief using acupuncture, which has been a great help not only with my tendinitis, but also in coping with my other problems related to my work. I don't know how the other pianists manage, but I have to work extremely hard, in a very special way, making all kinds of adjustments with my hands or arms in relation to the keyboard. A very special way, indeed, and this is only fit for me.

Did you have acupuncture treatment before performances, or on a regular basis?

With my acupuncturist in China, I had treatment the day before a concert or, when this was not possible, at least eight hours before performance. But I have now met a remarkable Chinese doctor who lives in London where he runs a special 'Acu-Medical Centre'. He had the greatest influence on my behaviour, and from him I have learnt how to approach any difficulty, whether in my playing or otherwise. Instead of just trying to 'do' something, I now stop, and think clearly of the way I can do it. Instead of just playing blindly, guided only by my imagination and the desire to re-create at the piano the sounds I hear in my mind, I have learnt to sit still first, think of the best way to achieve this, plan each movement, visualise the end results. From my Chinese doctor I have learnt some ancient Chinese breathing exercises, helping to let the energy of life flow in and our of the body ('Chi'). I do these exercises every day, only for about ten minutes, slowly, using at the same time a specific movement of the chest, experiencing the flow of energy everywhere. It is so helpful, and then I feel that I can concentrate on my work, and do it with much more ease.

I have to be very careful with my hands, because I have no natural span, and I try to practice 'correctly', that is holding the hands in a special way, sometimes diagonally, not parallel with the keys, in order to prevent any damage to my fingers or wrists. The main problem is that there is hardly any music I play, with the exception of Mozart or some Debussy, which does not require stretching. The B Minor Chopin Sonata, for instance, is so demanding and, as I said, I must think of the adjustments I have to make to compensate for my lack of flexibility.

You might like to know that I have made some studies of pianists with small hands, as so many Oriental women pianists have not only very small hands, but also short arms. There should be no stretching; it is dangerous to force the span between fingers. What is needed is a rapid lateral adjustment, and it is surprising what feats these pianists can do by moving those hands quickly along the keyboard. In your case, did you find that by playing many Romantic works which are very demanding technically, your hands have been affected?

I don't think this is the reason. I do play a lot of Chopin's music, but I have always had a natural affinity with its musical language, which speaks to me, and I feel I understand it. Although some Chopin works, like the B Minor Sonata, which I just mentioned, are more demanding, when I play it I do not think of the technique, I am only concerned with music and the sounds I wish to hear from my piano. In fact I do not play many other Romantic composers, I play very little Schumann, and of Liszt I only play the Sonata. I am fortunate that I am able to choose my programmes, and I can very often play the music of Mozart and Debussy, two composers I love profoundly apart from Chopin. Although their piano works are not taxing technically, I think they are very difficult to play because of their extraordinary quality of tones and their exquisitely subtle colours. For me, these offer a continual search for sounds to express their true meaning.

You have been living in England since 1959, soon after the Warsaw competition. How did you find the English public?

Coming straight from the Chopin competition, with such a prize, I was immediately invited to play, and my career grew steadily. I feel that this is very much my home. I travel a great deal all over the world, but it is good to come back. Here I can work; I can prepare my programmes for concert tours, for recordings, broadcasts and television appearances. I do some teaching, but not on a regular basis. I love working with young musicians, although I sometimes find teaching rather frustrating when working with a pianist who does not have the right sensitivity. At such times I believe that it is no use trying to 'give to him'; he must have music 'inside him'. The teacher's role is to bring out in a student the potential which is in him, even if, perhaps he is unaware of it. I prefer to work in a masterclass situation and, surprisingly, I play best when demonstrating to students, and it is very exciting to get the right response from them. I think that it is of great value for them to listen to their colleagues; they learn so much hearing the teacher's comments on points of interpretation, and especially, hearing the sounds and the texture needed to express that particular music.

You are often invited to be on the jury at competitions. Do you find the standard of performances different now compared to the early Fifties when you yourself were a participant? And what do you look for when judging these young pianists' performances?

There are many virtuoso pianists, but I am afraid I do not hear many young artists of great individuality. Sometimes I say to myself that 'this one has been listening to a lot of Horowitz' or 'that one is trying to copy Richter'. But, the way they play the works has really very little to do with the way these great artists play. Of course, young pianists do everything they can to present interpretations which would impress the jury... I am looking for something else, though, and the qualities I expect in a young artist to succeed in this profession are rare. Alas, this was always the case. If one looks at the pianists who succeed in their career, one can see that only very few make it, in spite of the great number of winners in the many international competitions which are being held in various countries. However, competitions are important for the piano profession, with all their good and bad points. They are also part of the commercialism which has invaded the arts world.

Piano Journal VOL 8 NO 23 1987

Peter Frankl

You came to the country after you left Hungary in 1956, and after having spent some time in Paris. As a pianist, surely you are the 'product' of the Hungarian school of piano playing which developed in the true Lisztian tradition.

This is true. First and foremost I should like to talk about my earliest development in Hungary, as I entered the Budapest Music Academy when I was six and stayed until I got my diploma, at 20! Fourteen years of studies and of going through a vast repertoire under what I consider very fine teaching. At first, I was in the Preparatory Class, where students embarking on the profession were given the opportunity to train as teachers. One of these students taught me until I was 11, but, due to my rapid progress, I was soon accepted into the class of one of the professors, with whom I studied until the age of 15. From then on, my professor was Lajos Hernadi, a pupil of Dohnanyi and Bartok in Hungary and of Schnabel, at the Berlin Hochschule für Music where he went to further his studies. One must not forget that Hungary's musical life, geographically speaking, very closely linked with Germany, France and Russia, and the trends in these countries were bound to affect it. The influences from within were also very strong, and the musicians, and here we talk more about pianists, were very proud of Liszt's heritage and tradition. The greatest musical personality in Hungary at the beginning of this century was undoubtedly that of Dohnanyi who embodied all the aspects of music: a truly great pianist who, in his young days performed whole cycles of Beethoven and Schubert works, long before Schnabel; a very fine composer, and conductor. Above all, he was greatly involved and anxious to maintain and develop the Hungarian musical life as a centre of European culture.

There was another great influence which dominated Hungarian music, that of the folk music and great composers like Bartok and Kodaly played an important role in the development of Hungarian music, or for that matter of the music of the twentieth century. The richness of the folk music, its rhythms, melodies, the structure, the modes etc., was bound to inspire composers like Bartok or Kodaly, who absorbed these characteristics and used them in their own music, getting away from the diatonic system, or combining the modal and diatonic systems, with true artistry. Bartok is very important for us pianists, because he was an extraordinary pianist himself, and brought new dimensions to pianism, while trying to recreate on this instrument the character and the timbres demanded by the pieces in folk music style. Although many pianists still think that to play Bartok's music one has to use a 'percussive' touch, that is not so. In fact, pieces like *Allegro Barbaro* are very misleading as to Bartok's playing and teaching (he became a professor at the Liszt Music Academy). Unfortunately, I never heard him myself, as I was too young – actually I was not yet born when he left Hungary to settle in the West – but my teacher, Lajos Hernadi, was a pupil of his and now we are fortunate to have a number of recordings or public performances which have been issued in Hungary. These are, of course, not of a quality of reproduction to which we are accustomed, but, musically speaking, they are of real significance. Here we have Bartok, the Romantic virtuoso pianist performing music by Chopin, Brahms, Debussy, and his playing is simply staggering. Actually, he made a name at the beginning of his career by giving recitals of piano transcriptions of operas by Wagner and by a young composer of the time, Richard Strauss, playing a transcription of *Don Juan*. Not many recordings existing at that time yet operatic arias travelled fast thanks to these piano transcriptions which were very much in fashion.

I was fortunate to have grown up in musical Budapest with its great tradition. Like most middle-class Jewish families in Hungary, my parents wanted the children to play an instrument. They bought a piano and I started to have lessons with a young teacher. I was no prodigy, but I enjoyed playing and soon I entered the Liszt Academy of Music. My training there, naturally, consisted of many technical exercises, studies by Czerny, Cramer, and others, and the student-teacher was very conscientious in this respect. I am very grateful now at the way I was made to commit to memory the pieces I was studying. Phrase by phrase, each piece had to be practised slowly, memorizing each hand separately or, if I played a Bach fugue, each part had to be learnt by heart. This approach has been very helpful to me all through my studies and I greatly recommend it. One is never afraid of memory lapses when one is able to play each voice, and begin from any point in the score.

Hernadi had a determining influence on my development as a pianist. He instilled in me a great understanding of the various styles of the composers, and made me aware of the particular sounds which are characteristic to each composer. As a pianist I learned to listen and produce the right sounds to bring out the character and the personality of each work. To play a work by Beethoven, one would use a completely different approach to the keys, to produce a rich, deep tone, than, let us say, when playing an impressionist composer. But, of course, this is too simplistic an approach. There is much more to it. What is important for us pianists, is that we should know what kind of tone we want to produce. Moreover, not every sound must be beautiful! Of course, a beautiful tone is and must be part of the pianist's equipment ... but often there is a need to give a shock to the listener as the music demands it.

Hernadi was a firm believer that fingering plays and important part in piano playing and we were made to copy those marked in his scores and then practise only in that way. He was convinced that to play any piece well, you have to establish the fingering right from the start, and stick to it. No pupil would ever dare try another fingering, even though it did not suit the hand. He did not understand that fingering depends very much on the structure of the pupil's hand, and, in spite of some excellent ideas on how to finger certain passages, I sometimes encountered great difficulties only because it did not suit my hand. Yet, everything that I learnt as a child is still very securely in my memory, perhaps because a child is more perceptive, but also because I was made to study very thoroughly each work. I find myself instinctively using the fingering laid down by my old teacher, though sometimes I have the urge to change it. Strangely enough, I become rather insecure and my fingers seem to take me just as they have been used to.

You have developed as a pianist in Hungary, but your few years in Paris and the subsequent settling in London must have greatly influenced your development into a mature artist.

Strangely enough, I did not find Parisian audiences of the same calibre as London ones. For instance, I noticed with regret that few pianists played Mozart concertos and one would hear, only occasionally, K488, K466 or perhaps K491. But when I arrived in London, I found that the audiences were, right from the beginning, very receptive. Here I was not only allowed, but encouraged, to play the works that I loved most. Thus I was able to study, and perform, all Mozart's concertos, and indeed to record all the piano works by Schumann and Debussy (for Decca and Vox companies). I do play a great deal of Beethoven – in recitals, with orchestra and also with chamber music ensembles as I am privileged to work with very fine artists. Romantic composers are part of my repertoire including Chopin and Brahms, particularly the second concerto in B flat, which is so much loved by English audiences. Interestingly enough, as much as I love and respect Liszt, I have played very few of his works apart from the Sonata, which I consider one of the finest masterpieces of the nineteenth century. I used to play most of his orchestral works, but now that I am able to choose my programs, I only play the second Concerto. Besides, an artist cannot be expected to play all composers and all styles equally well and, although I consider myself rather 'many-sided' in this respect, there are composers which I choose not to include in my repertoire. There are also works of my favourite composers, like Chopin or Schumann, that I do not wish to play, at least for the time.

I have now come back to Chopin after many years of a sort of 'pause'. I think that it is only understandable that an artist grows all the time and that there are certain stages in one's development, when certain works become stagnant, perhaps from overplaying.

It is so very rewarding to come back to works which I have played when I was too young, perhaps to realise their profound meaning. I approach them with a completely fresh mind. I find, for instance, that now I have a special affinity with Schumann, although at one time, after recording the 'integrale', I had to leave him aside for a while. Perhaps I feel this about Schumann because he is not a musicologist's pianist. Although he was himself a great thinker and an original writer, musicologists seem to minimize his value as a composer. I now plan a recital, with the three Schumann sonatas in one evening, and will play them in London and New York. I have already attempted it two years ago and I believe the audience loved them. What I am trying to do is to prove that these sonatas deserve the right place among the great works of the romantic era. Musicologists insist that Schumann was no symphonist or that he had no sense of form. Yet, to play these Schumann sonatas in one recital is not unusual, although certain shortcomings with regard to their structure are apparent.

I do not do any teaching – officially, but I sometimes give master-classes and occasionally I listen to young pianists who come to me for advice before a concert or when they study new works. It is true that the standard of piano playing nowadays is higher than ever, yet there are fewer great artists and individuals. Too many pianists are forgetting that they are performing 'music'. They are playing the piano … My

144

first advice is that a pianist should not even think too much pianistically. Before playing even the simplest phrase, he should think it vocally to find where a singer would breathe. Breathing is so important in piano playing. In my own work, when I have any difficulty with phrasing I always try to sing because I feel that the most natural instrument is the voice. I encourage the young musicians to listen to singers and particularly to operas. Besides, how can one play a Mozart concerto, or even a sonata, without knowing his operas?

When a student has certain technical difficulties, I show him how to approach them musically, and invariably this works. Here is another example of a pianist's preoccupation with technique separated from music.

Above all, the pianist should be more aware of the sounds, and the quality of tone demanded by each composer – as I have said before – and by each piece. I had to work very intently to learn how to produce different kinds of tone from the instrument and, when a young pianist asks me 'how do I do it?' well, I try to explain. It is not easy without demonstrating at the keyboard. For instance, if you hit the keys you get a big tone, a loud sound, hard, harsh, and moreover, it dies away immediately. Such a touch does not carry. To produce the tone you hear in your imagination, a round, full sound, you have to bring the sonority, so to speak, out of the instrument, you have the feeling that you are playing directly on the strings and make them vibrate.

Another aspect of today's music making is that so many pianists are too faithful to the printed score, particularly to the Urtexts … and there are more and more authentic editions coming on the market. Of course, I believe in studying them and finding for oneself how certain phrases should be played, but this rigid purism leaves very little to the imagination and the playing becomes rather sterile. It is true that in the romantic period performers went to the other extreme and hardly anyone took any notice of what the composer wrote! There are two pitfalls which I advise young pianists to avoid: too much purism when reading the scores and being original for the sake of it. I like to quote Casals when he was asked if he would do an edition of the Bach Sonatas: 'I cannot do an edition because I am playing them differently each time, and if one writes down the way I am playing them today, everyone will think that this is how I think that these particular works should be played. But this is not so. I make many changes because I am always trying to improve certain aspects of my interpretation, using different bowings, different fingerings. How can one produce a "definitive" edition?'

Abbey Simon

You were very young, a prodigy, when you were accepted at the Curtis Institute during the 'golden era' of Hoffman, Saperton, and Vengerova. Looking back, do you think that the training at such a prestigious conservatoire gave you what you needed to develop as pianist and artist?

When I was accepted at Curtis I was just eleven years old. Naturally, my parents were as thrilled as I was for such an opportunity. To study with Hoffman at that time was the Mecca of piano students, and every young pianist's dream was to enter such an institution. Hoffman was a great name in the piano world, and he was very dedicated to Curtis when he became Director. It was decided that I should study with David Saperton, a renowned pianist and teacher, the son-in-law of Godowsky. All his pupils lived in awe of the great 'Pops', and at every lesson we were told what Pops said, what Pops would say about certain phrasing, about different sounds, about fingering, rhythm, etc. Mr. Saperton did take me once or twice to play to Pops when he thought that I was, so to speak, ready. Godowsky showed interest in my ability to improvise, a rare occurrence among the Curtis inmates. They were too busy practising for hours on end the études of our daily diet: Czerny, Crammer, Moskowsky, Chopin, Liszt, as well as the vast repertoire demanded for examinations or concerts. I remember playing also for Vengerova, but I don't think she was interested in other teachers' pupils. She was too much of a prima donna, and she certainly acted like one.

The emphasis in the teaching was on the beauty of sound, on learning how to produce a variety of tones – always rich, beautiful, and vibrant. All the students had one ideal, to imitate Hoffman's tone and his rubato. At the same time, the idea of a virtuoso technique was inculcated early in our mind, and we knew that unless one developed great agility, great stamina, there was no hope to succeed as a pianist.

Life at Curtis was very insular. Most of us were very young and, liv-

146

ing in a small school we spent a lot of time together, as a family. We often played to one another, and I think that we learnt a great deal in this way, perhaps more than from our own teachers. Competition was a stimulant. Of course, the teacher was a demi-god, with great authority, and no one dared question his statements.

The study of piano repertoire was oriented at that time more towards the Russian school. We did play some Bach, usually in transcriptions and hardly ever the authentic works. It was either Bach-Busoni, Bach-Liszt, or other transcriptions or arrangements. The great Romantics were prominent on our programmes, and some of the 'popular' Beethoven sonatas were also included. I believe the emphasis was on developing beauty of tone and personality. Each one of us hoped to conquer the world of piano, and we were encouraged to learn to project our playing, to think in great lines, and to communicate it to the audience. We were reminded again and again that one plays a musical instrument with the ears. 'The more you develop your ear the greater chance you have to become a fine artist!'

When Rudolf Serkin joined Curtis, in the early Twenties, the attitude towards interpreting the classics took a new turn. He brought great changes in the choice of repertoire: Beethoven and the classics were taught much more than before, and the students were introduced to the great keyboard works of Bach. Sadly for me, I had already left Curtis for New York, and missed the chance to study with Serkin. I was already eighteen, and felt that I needed a change of direction. I won the coveted Naumburg Prize, and this was a great help in launching me on a career. But I was very anxious to learn more, I was searching for some valuable experience as a musician. This opportunity came my way quite soon, when I met a very interesting musician, very cultured and with great knowledge of piano repertoire. She was Dora Zaslawsky, of Russian origin, but trained in Germany. She had studied with Backhaus, and working with her opened a whole new world for me. She introduced me to works which I did not know, and she taught me to respect the composer's score with great humility. Studying Mozart, Haydn, or Bach with her was a totally new experience. It was for the first time that I realised that Bach's ornamentation should not be played haphazardly but well thought out, well studied, according to the 'performance practices' of the time. Perhaps, I can say that Dora gave me what I did not receive from Curtis, I was by then a 'grown-up' young musician, eighteen years old, with a more mature outlook which one cannot have as an eleven year old boy, no matter how great the talent.

After your successful debut in New York, you went to Paris to try to build your career in Europe as well as in the United States. Was there a great difference between the American and the French audiences?

I don't think there was a great difference. I arrived in Paris in 1949, planning to stay some six months, giving concerts and getting to know the French musical life. My six months turned out to be thirty years! I just loved Paris and Europe. I returned many times to the United States, giving concerts, teaching, but my home was Paris for many years. Later on I moved to Geneva, and I still spend several months there every year.

My stay in Paris brought me one of my greatest musical experiences. I had the opportunity, in the early Fifties, to meet Georges Enesco, who agreed to work with me. He was already very ill and he looked old, although he was not that advanced in age. I played for him Beethoven's Sonata Op. 109. He listened intently and then sat down at the piano and played the entire sonata, from memory. He gave such a supreme performance of this late Beethoven work that I felt I was hearing it for the first time. He did not play like a pianist, although he had an extraordinary technique. He was music itself at that moment. I had a few other sessions with the great master, but, soon afterwards, Enesco died. It was a great loss for me, I felt as if I was robbed of the most valuable influence just at the time when I most needed it. Studying with Enesco, although for a short time, greatly enriched my life as a musician.

The musical life in Paris offered a great variety of trends, and it felt good to be in the midst of those exciting events. I met then Harold Bauer, who was making a good name as a pianist. He was a rather controversial personality with an original mind, and was considered by his colleagues something of a phenomenon. He had come to Paris hoping to make a career as violinist, but he found himself instead in great demand as a pianist, either as accompanist or in Chamber Music. He never trained as a pianist, yet, his playing was of a very high quality. He had some strange ideas, for instance, that one does not have to practise in order to be a good performer. All one needs is a profound knowledge of the score! It certainly worked for him! I went on to study with him, and I greatly enjoyed our sessions together. I remember bringing the Brahms *Paganini Variations* to a lesson. He offered many inventive ways of approaching this complex work and many different and imaginative possibilities, and these made me aware of the wealth there was in every single piece of music. Ultimately, he expected me to find my own solution. It remained with me to decide what I wanted to do.

While you were living in Europe you took up a teaching post in the United States. How could you combine your concert career with the demanding work with your students at Indiana University at Bloomington?

It was not easy, but I loved both my work as a performer and working with the students. As you may know, the quality of students at Bloomington is impressive. I was also rather privileged that I could choose my students and I could limit my hours of teaching. Gradually, the Music Faculty grew too large for my ideals, and I then joined the Juilliard School about ten years ago. There, again, I teach a small number of students because I want to give them my whole attention. I often think of Hoffman, who once said that 'the secret of a great teacher is to choose talented pupils!' Well, I don't think this is quite true. It is our responsibility to give to the next generation what our teachers gave us, but, also, I am able to offer them my life-long experience as a performer who never stopped learning.

When working with young pianists I emphasise how important it is to be aware of the melodic lines, and at the same time to think of the music both 'horizontally' and 'vertically'. The inner voices must be clearly heard as if using a whole orchestra, not a solo instrument. When playing chords, each voice should have its own colour, the pianist following the lines of each voice moving towards the next chord or resolution. Of course, the quality of the sound must always be the aim, and the beauty of tone should always be cultivated. I am one of those teachers who illustrates at the piano, whether this is right or not. There is no danger that the student will not learn to think for himself, because he will only imitate what I am doing. On the contrary, I think that this is a very good way of bringing to the notice of a young pianist certain points of interpretation which he will have to think about. Ultimately, each one of my students will bring his own personality into his performance.

There is a school of teaching which advocates that there should be three stages when learning a new piece:

(a) Learn the notes
(b) Study the interpretation
(c) Memorise it

To my mind this is a wrong approach. The music should be approached and studied in its totality, thoroughly, right from the start. When you have a complete musical idea of what the piece is about, when you have analysed it, have studied the phrases, every detail, the work does not present any difficulties and, especially, no memory problems. This is the only way to master the pieces. This is what Harold Bauer was trying to convey to us, and I have always done a great deal of my studies away from the instrument, getting to know the score first and foremost.

As a performer you had to learn to face an audience, and as a teacher you have to help your students who hope to join the profession. What advice do you give them before going on the platform.

I have observed my own playing on different occasions, as well as my students' behaviour when under stress. There is no substitute for thorough study, from every aspect. I came to a very simple conclusion, that the essence of a good performance is knowing when you can breathe in every phrase. You have to discover when you can exhale and then, of course, you have to inhale afterwards. This is the secret of any difficulty. If the pianist holds his breath, problems of tension will develop with, perhaps, serious consequences. I came to this simple 'philosophy' when I was learning to swim. I realised that I could do very well my first fifty yards, but, after that, I got into difficulties. I was 'out of breath' because I had not learnt how to exhale in the water. This analogy with a difficult passage made me aware of what was needed in performance.

Many young pianists listen to the established artists on records when studying new works. Do you think this is of any value?

The recordings have a great value for many performers, commercially, and for their career. I also think that if young pianists listen wisely, they can greatly benefit. There was a time, for instance, when the only recordings of the 'Thirty-two' were those of Schnabel, and how important they were for us all! Or for the students who never had the chance to hear him play. If they could hear some of the re-issues of recordings of artists of earlier generations, they would certainly have a glimpse of the true 'golden era' of piano playing. But, I am afraid, I do not think very highly of the laboratory alterations since the 'advent of the tape', with its obvious results. There does not seem to be a great difference between one recording and another, and if young pianists listen to these stereotyped interpretations, their playing becomes a perfect replica of these performances. If you go to a concert or to a competition there is too much uniformity in today's piano playing. To my mind, there is too much 'black and white' playing and not enough 'colour'.

And, as we are on the subject of competitions, I should like to state my views here and now. While competitions offer many advantages, there are also many bad points, which, I am sure, have been aired again and again. The problem is that these days there are too many competitions, and this has become an established 'system of classification'. As a rule, there is a first prize in every competition, with several other prizes, and the juries decide which pianists deserve to receive these prizes. I am strongly opposed to the idea that every competition (and there are by now over one hundred!) must award a first prize. How is it possible to launch every year over one hundred first rate artists? No, this situation cannot continue. The International Society of Piano Competitions should lay down new rules, and one of them should be concerned with the final stages of every competition. The jury should take a vote, at this stage, on the question: 'Do we award a First Prize or not?' In this way, a great deal of confusion and suffering will be avoided, and only a small number of young artists would be launched on the concert circuit. In many cases, the winner fulfils the engagements attached to that particular competition and, if he is not an artist of a certain calibre, he enters into oblivion. The winners are, in such cases, the losers!

Piano Journal VOL 9 NO 25 1988

151

Joseph Banowetz

Your career encompasses a wide range of activities. You are a well-known performer, a reputed pedagogue, an editor of collections of music from beginners to intermediate and advanced standards, and, recently, the author of one of the most valuable books about pedalling. Let us first talk about your training, and about your studies in the United States and Europe. Were you a child prodigy, like most pianists of your generation?

My development followed the usual pattern. I showed some ability at an early age and my parents arranged for me to have lessons with a local teacher. My progress must have been very impressive, as I just loved spending hours at the piano, going through piece after piece, completely oblivious of any difficulties or whether I was doing justice to those masterpieces of piano literature. At twelve I auditioned for a place at the Kansas City Conservatorium, which had a good reputation at the time. I presented a very ambitious programme, with Liszt Rhapsody No.6 and the first movement of the *Appassionata*. I was accepted in the class of the highly-thought-of teacher, Ann St. John, and this was the best thing that could have happened to me. She was shocked at the way I was playing all those great works, with great facility and temperament, but with such lack of understanding. After I entered her class the real work started.

Ann St John was a very cultured musician and an outstanding pianist. She had studied in Europe, where she spent three years working with Godowsky, who was teaching in Berlin and Vienna at the time. She also tried to learn as much as she could while in Europe, and went to Paris to study French music at the source with Cortot, who introduced her to the music of Fauré, Debussy, Ravel, as no one else could have done it. When she returned to America she continued her studies on Debussy's music with Robert Schmitz, who knew Debussy personally, and who wrote one of the best books on his piano music.

My studies with Ann St. John gave me an insight into the essence of the pieces we worked on together. First of all, she wanted me to understand what a musical phrase was, what music was all about, and, in order to achieve this, she gave me simple but great works like Bach two- and three-part inventions. I had never been exposed to such an approach, with reverence to the text and to the composer's markings, aiming at extraordinary precision, an exquisite tone, watching how the phrases merge into one another, structuring the entire piece. Listening to the different voices in polyphonic music, trying to play each one with the right dynamics, yet as part of the whole, was another exciting experience. I was at a very impressionable age and her kindness, her generosity, and, above all, her honesty and respect for music and the composer were just what I needed. She suggested that I should take part in the Summer Courses given by Carl Friedberg at the conservatorium, and I played for him in one of his Master Classes. He must have found my playing, or my potential, interesting enough to invite me to become his student.

My teacher was very happy about this, and another step in my development ensued. I worked assiduously, trying to absorb everything he said, everything he asked of me. Friedberg was one of the greatest musical minds I have ever come across. A pupil of Clara Schumann, he had had the opportunity to play to Brahms one day when he came to her house. He made his debut in Vienna, playing Cesar Franck's *Variations Symphoniques* with the Vienna Philharmonic, under Mahler himself! He did not try to teach the piano as such, although he was very demanding. He, himself, had a profound love and knowledge of European culture in general, not only of music, and he expected us, his students, to show the same intellectual curiosity. He encouraged us to read the great works of world literature, to go to museums and look at the painting of the masters, to get immersed in artistic life, the theatre and concerts which were flourishing in New York during my student days.

In his teaching he believed in an organised programme: to practise for hours on end was futile, unless the work was well-planned. Technique had to be practised regularly, with great concentration, listening to every single sound and endowing it with beauty and a vibrant sonority. Octave studies, of course, were part of the daily routine, but great attention had to paid to the wrists, which had to be flexible and relaxed. Friedberg understood the complex problems of the balance between tension and relaxation in piano technique.

When it came to interpretation, Friedberg insisted on using a good edition. He recommended the Urtext editions of *Breitkopf and Haertel* but these were not easy to get in the United States at that time, so he allowed us to make do with Peters'. Schumann's music had to be studied from Clara's editions. But only her first set, the 'Instructive Edition', could be obtained. The 'Collected Works', in which Brahms also had a hand, are quite different, and these came to the States only later. Carl Freidberg was not only a great artist but also a scholar, and we, his students, were fortunate to receive from him some of his knowledge and understanding of the great works. He also had the ability to make everything clear through his imaginative comments, and, above all, through his superb illustrations at the piano. Indeed, he loved showing what his intentions were through his playing. He made me realise the importance of a continuous long line in a phrase, of every detail, of getting to know what each note in the phrase was saying to me.

Freidberg was known for his studies into the working of the brain in relation to piano playing. He realised that if the mental work is committed to the memory in its entirety by studying the piece away from the instrument it can be learnt with much more ease. What Leimer has understood and expounded in his book, Freidberg was practising much earlier. His former students, the pianists Ruth Duncan-McDonald, Jane Carlson, and Jean Kyrstein, described how they had to learn every week one piece, in silence, without touching the piano, on their word of honour. Only when they arrived at the lesson were they allowed to play it, of course, from memory. They found this type of study of immense value, both in their work as artists and as teachers.

He never asked me to work in this way. It is quite possible that, at that time, he had not yet evolved this approach, or perhaps he considered me too young and inexperienced to attempt such a study.

It was actually at Friedberg's suggestion that I decided to go to Europe to continue my studies, and so I went to Vienna. There I entered the Vienna Music Academy (only later it became the Hochschule Für Musik) where I joined the class of Professor Joseph Dichler. To live in that magical town, full of wonderful music – with the Vienna Opera, the Philharmonic, splendid theatre – was a totally new experience. But my studies at the Academy had the main priority and I graduated with a First Prize. How I wished to stay longer in Europe! But conscription (in the Army) was still compulsory and I was given two options: either I stay in Europe for another year of study and then join the Overseas Service for two years, or return immediately to the United States, where I would be allowed to continue my studies at a university and join the army only afterwards. In fact, I had no choice but return to America, as

I could not envisage myself spending two years overseas in the army, not knowing whether I would be able to find a piano to practise on.

On my return I started to do some concerts, but I was still undecided what my next steps should be. When I attended Georgy Sandor's recitals (the Hungarian pianist who was making quite a name in America) I realised that he had something valuable to offer me. He was Artist in Residence at Dallas University, Texas, and I went there and enrolled in his class. Working with him was a real experience, as I was aware that in spite of my ability to get through pieces of great virtuosity, I lacked the intellectual command vital for an artist if he is to succeed. Sandor was both a great artist and a theoretician of pianism.

It was interesting to realise that at every stage in my development I was confronted with the right person, with the right artist. This time, Sandor – with his analytical mind and deep knowledge of the physical and psychological aspects of piano playing – clarified for me what I was doing, as well as what I needed in order to master the keyboard. And this is what I was searching for at the time.

I have read his treatise: On Piano Playing: Motion, Sound and Expression, and I would like to know more about his actual teaching. I find his description of the two basic motions – the downward and the upward movements of the wrist – of immense value for students. He argues that the wrist should be used in concordance with the musical expression demanding these two specific motions.

He was very clear about what movements are used, why, and when. These two wrist movements were at the basis of his teaching, but he also showed the various adjustments, horizontal and curvilinear, which make for ease in execution. Sandor did not advocate a fixed position of the hand because of the perpetual adjustments needed in piano playing. The hand could be in a flat position when certain sounds are required, but there should never be a tense, rigid hand. He recommended holding the hand in an arch, not with a high bridge of the knuckles, yet relaxed, without collapsing. The emphasis was on allowing the hand to change its position as and when necessary. Sandor was keen on conveying to his students the need to think in great lines, inwardly to hear great sonorities, so that we should know how to project the music to an audience, whether playing in a large or small hall. His own playing was a constant example, and my years at Dallas University were a real eye-opener. I now felt that I was ready to get on with my own playing and to start doing some teaching. At first I taught in the interesting Music Camp at Interlochen, where only outstanding young musicians are accepted. They have individual lessons on their instrument, have the opportunities to make music in ensemble playing to gain orchestral experience, and, if good enough, to perform as soloists. This was good for me also, as I learnt a great deal about teaching while working with the many youngsters in my care. I became very interested in my work as a teacher, and later on I became professor at the North Texas University at Denton, where I am in charge of the Doctoral programme.

You have travelled extensively — not only through the United States but through the Far East, having toured Japan, China, Hong Kong, Singapore, as well as Australia and New Zealand. Did you find the audiences in these countries very different?

I believe that audiences are similar everywhere. If they are interested in what you are doing and if they like you and accept you, they are simply wonderful. In Japan, the audiences are more sophisticated. They hear many of the great artists of our time, they have records, and now videos, of important performances; they are also in touch with what goes on in teaching in Europe and America. I have been on several juries at competitions in Japan, and I was always amazed at the young pianists' technical equipment and dexterity. The National Piano Teachers Association of Japan, with Yasuko Fukada as organiser, holds a competition every year for pianists of all ages, starting with children at the age of four, up to the age of twenty-four. The year I adjudicated I had to listen to several hundred selected pupils up to fifteen or sixteen, but when it came to the advanced group, not one qualified for a first prize. But I awarded the 'Joseph Banowetz' prize to the best pianist of that group. In recent years there has been a great change and more Japanese youngsters are now ready to take part in international competitions.

The situation is different in China. I believe I was the first Western artist to have been invited to perform, in China, a piano concerto by a Chinese composer. I gave the World Premiere of the concerto by Huang-an-Lun, in 1984, in Canton, with the Cantin Philharmonic Orchestra. It is not an avant-garde work; the composer is trying to create a blend of traditional Chinese music and western idioms. Like other Chinese composers, he is conscious of preserving the musical heritage, absorbing Western influences, and they seem to meet with a great degree of success. Huang-an Lun's Concerto was very well received, and I was invited to repeat the performance in Shanghai with the Central Philharmonic Orchestra. In 1986 I gave the first performance of the same concerto in Hong Kong, and then the China Records Company in Beijing invited me to record it, and I hope it will soon be released world-wide.

Joseph Banowetz

Chinese audiences are very eager to hear Western music played by European or North American artists, and I gave many recitals which included the great Romantic composer Anton Rubinstein, as well as the entire piano works by Balakirev (which I have also recorded in Hong Kong). The main conservatories of Shanghai, Beijing, and Shewang have invited me to conduct masterclasses. In addition, I had the privilege to be appointed 'Permanent Visiting Professor' at Shewang, and it is good to know that whenever I go to China there is 'my chair'.

The few young Chinese pianists who are sent to international competitions are quite extraordinary – they have phenomenal techniques – but only occasionally do we hear of one getting a first prize. Your experience teaching in the three principal Chinese conservatories must have given you an insight into why this might be. For example, how do you find the young generation of teachers in Conservatories?

I have worked with many young pianists, some truly outstanding, endowed with great talent, but these are few and far between. It is also true to say that the majority of students are very industrious. Once they have been accepted into such a musical institution, they devote all their time to their studies. Their goal is to attain a virtuoso technique. They are also very obedient and try to do what their teachers tell them, and this seems to satisfy them. Sadly, they spend too much time just playing their instruments instead of trying to learn about what goes on in the world of music. Their outlook remains rather limited, and often this is reflected in their playing.

I have met with some fine teaching, but again, not everywhere. If a student is fortunate enough to study with one of the teachers of the older generations, who managed to survive the Cultural Revolution, he receives the best tuition. For instance, Mr. Wu, the Head of Keyboard at the Shanghai Conservatory, has studied in Paris with Marguerite Long, and had the opportunity to absorb the trends of the rich musical life there. Only a few others teaching today in China had perhaps the same opportunities to travel, to mix with other artists, to attend concerts, and to experience a different culture. It is only natural that working with such a teacher is very beneficial for young students who live in a sort of ivory tower, without contact with the world outside China.

The younger generation of teachers did not have the same advantages and were not exposed to outside influences. Yet their work is very impressive, in spite of their own limitations. It is true to say that these teachers are very anxious themselves to learn more: hence their interest in bringing Western artists to conduct masterclasses, which they follow rigorously – perhaps too rigorously! Sadly, one cannot talk of a 'middle generation' of teachers. This age group has been wiped out by the tragic situation when artists were not allowed to function, but had to do menial work, and only a very few survived that ordeal.

There is another drawback. The Conservatories and the students cannot get good editions, which partly explains their stylistic limitations. And yet, with so many outstanding achievements, I am convinced that within a few more years they will catch up with what goes on in the rest of the world. On the other hand, many young Japanese artists lack the understanding of Western music, in spite of the wealth of printed music and the opportunities to study with the finest interpreters and pedagogues of our time.

You have shown interest in performing music by contemporary composers, and I understand that at your next London recital you will play a newly commissioned work by Ronald Stevenson, the Scottish composer (who, by the way, celebrated his sixtieth birthday this year).

I met Ronald Stevenson when I played for EPTA in Scotland in 1987. We spent a whole night playing to one another. Listening to his music, I was so struck by its originality that, then and there, I asked him to write a piece for me to perform in the United States and in my recitals in Europe, Australia, New Zealand, and, I hope, in China and Japan. I can hardly wait to receive the manuscript. I know it will be sensational, and it gives me great joy to be entrusted with its first performance. Stevenson is certainly a composer who deserves world-wide recognition, and what a pianist he is!

For many years you have been concerned with music education. You are not only a well known pedagogue, but you are also involved in giving lectures, demonstrations, and workshops with teachers. It is understandable that, because of your interest in this field, you have also edited a number of albums and collections of piano music for teaching at various levels.

I started to do some editing thanks to James Bastien. We were together at Dallas University, students of Georgy Sandor, and have remained good friends ever since. He has published many books and methods on piano teaching, as well as his very successful *The Business of Piano Teaching* for Neil J. Kjos, publisher. When they asked him to do some new editions of albums with piano repertoire for teaching, he suggested that I should take this on. I have been with Kjos for many years and I find this work very stimulating indeed. It keeps me in touch with piano teaching at all levels, which is so important for the growth of piano playing in the United States and in other countries. In my editions I include very informative introductions, with illustrations and facsimiles, to make them attractive to both pupils and teachers.

You might be pleased to know that your editions are very popular with EPTA members, who enjoy your selection of pieces, some of them hardly known, but real jewels. Your book On Pedalling is one of the most important studies of the twentieth century, discussing both the science and the art if pedalling. The late Sidney Harrison wrote a brilliant review for the Piano Journal, and many of us remember with pleasure the interesting demonstration you gave on the use of the sustaining pedal, with some unusual suggestions on how to use the three pedals concurrently.

I thought that it was very necessary to publish such a comprehensive study because the music of our time demands a completely different treatment with regard to the use of pedals. Whenever I tried to find a book about certain pedalling problems, I was surprised to see how little has been written about them in the 20th century. In my book I wrote most of the chapters on the action of the pedals and the types of pedalling, trying to help young musicians in their quest to interpret the great masters, and demonstrate how to create a rich palette of sounds. I decided to consult some of my colleagues who have made in-depth studies of certain composers. I invited contributions from some of the experts in this field: Dean Elder, a student of Gieseking and the finest Debussy interpreter of our time, wrote the chapter on pedalling Debussy's music; Maurice Hinson on Chopin's work; William D. Newman on the use of pedals in Beethoven's music. I have also included essays on how to pedal piano music from Bach to contemporary composers.

Ultimately the students will have to make their own choices. Knowledge is very important but it is only through intense listening that they learn, not only about pedalling, but about all aspects of music-making.

Piano Journal VOL 9 NO 26 1988

Jerome Rose

I have known about you for many years; first as performer, through your recordings of Liszt and other Romantic composers. You are also known for your research, having edited some unknown piano music, as well as music for teaching. You present this together with a cassette on which you play the pieces, so that pupils get an idea of how they should be performed. As a teacher, you have made your mark, having been a piano professor, and having conducted masterclasses for some twenty- five years. In recent years you ventured into new areas, as a promoter of music festivals, trying to fill a much-felt gap by bringing to the notice of the musical public certain works which otherwise may never be heard. In 1981, thanks to your imaginative initiative, London had one of the most exciting festivals on 'The Great Romantics'. And, in 1986, also thanks to you, the centenary of Liszt's death was duly celebrated in Washington DC, when some of the greatest Liszt interpreters and scholars participated. In the same year you performed the A Major Concerto with Georg Solti conducting the Chicago Symphony Orchestra.

It was a real pleasure to meet you, at last, on a happy occasion in New York, when you were going to rehearse with the other nineteen pianists or so, for the Carnegie Hall 'Marathon', to mark the completion of the 500,000th grand piano by Steinways. I understand that this famous piano carries the signatures of all the artists who participated in the marathon, and will be auctioned for charity.

Let us talk first about your extraordinary discovery, namely the transcription of twelve Chopin mazurkas for soprano and piano by the celebrated singer, Pauline Viardot, a contemporary and friend of both Chopin and Georges Sand.

This is, I am happy to say, one of my greatest discoveries. I found six of the transcriptions in the British Library, and the other six (which include two duos) in the Library of Congress in Washington. As a young girl, Pauline spent some time at Georges Sand's summer house at Nohant, where she must have had the opportunity to meet Chopin. She was married to the director of the Italian Opera in Paris, and soon became the darling of the Italian Opera, together with her sister, Maria

Malibran, who, sadly, died very young in a riding accident. Pauline was not only a renowned singer, she was an accomplished musician, having studied for a while with Liszt. She was also an established composer, having written over one hundred songs and four operettas on texts by Turgenev and Pushkin, writers she met during her husband's work as opera director in Russia. Chopin must have liked the songs, for in one of his letters he mentions that he was appearing in the same concert as Pauline Viardot, who was singing her own transcriptions of some of the mazurkas.

The International Music Co. has recently published my edition of the mazurkas transcribed for soprano and piano by Pauline Viardot, on poems by Louis Pomey, with a detailed introduction, giving information about the sources of this important discovery. In December 1987 I gave the first performance of the twelve songs in the New York Public Library with the soprano Catherine Sieszinka, and I hope to introduce them to London audiences in the near future. Although I have known and loved the Chopin Mazurkas since my childhood, I do find these transcriptions very beautiful, with a quality of their own. The vocal line is the same as the melodic line of the mazurkas, and Pauline Viardot has been careful to respect Chopin's harmonies and the whimsical rhythms. She must have thought that these exquisite melodies would sound just as beautiful if sung, and she also believed that the poems of Louis Pomey fitted the songs perfectly. Chopin's intense love of the opera, and particularly of Bellini's arias, may explain why he was happy with Pauline's songs. It may also be, perhaps, because Chopin always made the piano sing, and, why not have the same melodies actually transcribed for voice?

You are in the process of recording the entire piano music of Chopin on compact disc for the American company, Newport Classic. This is a gigantic undertaking, not only because of the magnitude of the programme, but also because of the strain created by modern recording techniques. Is this company one of the few who demand 'direct to disc' recordings, or are they edited?

This is a most exciting, although exhausting, venture, and gives me great satisfaction. I have already completed the four Ballades, the Fantasie, and the three Sonatas, having included the very rarely performed great C Minor one, besides the two well-known works, the B flat Minor and the B Minor. As soon as I return to the States, I shall carry on with my assignment, and hope to have all the discs issued, worldwide, in the very near future.

To answer your second question about recording techniques, the discs will be edited. I much prefer to know that if I make a mistake – after all, we are only human – that this can be corrected without having to retake the entire movement, until both the engineers and myself are satisfied. I did a 'Direct to Disc' recording not long ago, and, although I agree with most artists, that in this way the spontaneity and that extra quality of the performance is retained, I did not find the experience one which I would like to go through again. I remember vividly having given one of my best performances of the first movement of Schubert's posthumous A Major Sonata, but when playing the second movement there was a slight flaw. Everything had to be played again – as both movements were on one side of the disc, while the third and fourth movements were on the other side. My whole attitude changed, and when I played the second time I was too careful, too anxious not to have to play these two movements for a third or fourth time and, obviously, the performance was not as free and intense as I wanted. I had to have a short rest to be able to start afresh, and only then was I able to complete the recording. Of course, it depends on the temperament of the artist. For myself, as much as I love unedited performances, these may not necessarily be my best. Making records in the cold, clinical atmosphere of a studio is in itself a strenuous exercise, and I welcome any opportunity to feel less tense about my performance. Besides, I love playing to an audience, I need the excitement of a live performance. Rachmaninov was known to have avoided playing on the radio. He insisted that music was not something to listen to in the comfort of the living room, relaxing in an arm chair with the feet up. He felt that an audience should go through the ritual of dressing up, going to a concert, and listening in a hall together with many other people, all of them joined into one big mass at the moment of the musical communication. Yet, if you would ask me whether I want to give up making records, the answer is an emphatic 'no'. The recordings are a vital component of an artist's career.

You have recorded Liszt's entire piano music on the Vox label. What happened to all those valuable records?

Fortunately for me, my new company, Newport Classics, will soon reissue them on compact disc, and will distribute them together with my recordings of Chopin. We all know too well that the recording industry is continuously looking for new names, new artists, and unless one is constantly in the public eye (or ear?), many records get deleted from catalogues.

I am afraid this has been the case with one of the greatest artists of our time, Solomon. I was asked to write his obituary for one of the national newspapers, and I looked in the current catalogues to find out what recordings were still available. To my astonishment, there were only a handful, although he made over one hundred records in his lifetime. Fortunately, the BBC library possesses a large number of the tapes of his many broadcasts, and from time to time we are offered a wonderful treat. Perhaps the same can be said about Myra Hess, one of the finest pianists the world has ever known. What do you think should be done to preserve this great heritage?

This is a very sad state of affairs, and I believe that it is our responsibility to convince the recording companies to maintain such prestigious recordings on their catalogues. These should not exist only in archives of historical recordings, but kept alive, continually played on radio or through other media, so that young musicians can use them as models of supreme interpretation and pianism.

You have reached an important stage in your career, giving concerts in many parts of the world; as you yourself say, the world of music seems to get smaller and smaller, since distances are almost eliminated. Do you think that, for a young musician to succeed, his talent should be sufficient, or that a great talent will only develop in the right direction through the right teaching?

I certainly believe that good teaching is vital for the right growth of a talent. I was very fortunate in this respect. I must have played the piano from a very early age – I can hardly remember a time when I was not climbing on the piano stool and listening to my playing for what seemed to me hours on end. I was born in California, and my parents did what they thought was right, by bringing a piano teacher to the house when I was four or five. At the age of nine I played the Haydn Concerto in D, gave several recitals, and soon afterwards I entered the San Francisco Conservatory. At fifteen I made my debut with the San Francisco Orchestra. Yet, I do not consider myself as having been a prodigy. I owe a great deal to my wonderful teachers. The first great influence I experienced was when I was nine, studying under Marvin Mazel. He guided me during those informative years, looking after my technical development, but also encouraging me to listen to orchestral music, to read many scores, although I had a natural desire and curiosity to learn anyway. At San Francisco Conservatory I studied with Harold Logan at first, then with Adolf Baller, a well-known pianist who often played for Yehudi Menhuin when touring the USA. I know that I owe a great debt of gratitude to these teachers who had the right approach for me, and who were very concerned about my development as a pianist. It was Adolf Baller who advised me to study with Rudolf Serkin, after having played in one of his masterclasses, and I went to the famous Marlborough Summer School. Serkin suggested that I should have regular lessons, not just attending summer courses, and he recommended me to Leonard Shur, a pianist of the Schnabel school. Thus I went to New York, where I took a Master's Degree at the Juilliard School, specialising in chamber music. By that time I had met the Juilliard Quartet, with whom I did a lot of playing, and I realised that making music with others was a most rewarding experience. But I still wanted to pursue the career of a soloist, as this was really what I wanted to do, and I decided to go to Europe. Every young artist of my generation believed that one needed to live, to breathe, and to work in Europe in order to reach the summit! I enrolled at the Vienna Hochschule für Musk, but after two or three lessons I realised that I had outgrown the need for regular and formal lessons. What I really needed was to listen to music, to meet other musicians who played to one another and, above all, to perform. And this is what I did. I had a wonderful time, and I think I grew as an artist and performer. I had the good opportunity to play to some of the great pianists in Vienna, among them Alfred Brendel. I also realised that winning a competition was an important factor, and I decided to enter for the Busoni Competition, which I won in 1961. As was expected, this opened many doors for my career. I gave many concerts in Italy and in other European countries, I had my Wigmore Hall debut soon afterwards, and in 1963 I was appointed Artist in Residence and Professor at Bowling Green University in Ohio, where I am still teaching. London was a great attraction for me, as it was already an important centre of music. I spent several months in London before my Wigmore recital, and had the privilege to play to Myra Hess. I remember so well playing for her the Mozart C Minor Sonata, and her insight into that profound work was simply astounding. That was one of my great musical experiences. I was then invited to make some recordings, and in the first year I made no less than eighteen records which included Schubert, Schumann, Beethoven, and Liszt.

I do not wish to be labelled a 'Romantic Interpreter'. I was really brought up in the great European tradition of Bach, Beethoven, Mozart, and Haydn, through my wonderful teachers. Marvin Mazel had studied with Joseph Levine, a product of the great Russian piano school; Harold Logan was a student of Egon Petri, himself a pupil of Busoni; from Leonard Shur I learnt about Schnabel's conception of Beethoven,

Schubert, and Mozart. It was only much later, when I was asked to record Liszt's entire piano music that I was getting more and more involved in presenting the 'Great Romantics'.

In fact I love playing and teaching all styles and all periods, including some of the twentieth-century works, as long as the music is worth studying. Teaching has been an important part of my life in the past twenty-five years or so. I find it a very rewarding aspect of my music-making, whether in a masterclass situation, or when working individually with students. I feel like Schnabel, who said that he learnt more from his students than he gave them. In many ways, I feel that my students reflect many of my own ideas, having tried some of my attempts at interpreting certain works in a less conventional manner, as I am perpetually searching. What is more important for a teacher than to see his students grow and find their own inner love? Because the greatness of music is that it is a total reflection of the inner love. Basically the purpose of the teacher is to allow the student to blossom and to grow. I personally don't believe in 'rote teaching', that is, expecting the student to play exactly as I do. I tend to allow a great deal of freedom, as I believe that a teacher will be rewarded only when the student is able to integrate his knowledge into his own creative force. Such a student will not be satisfied with just getting one good performance of a work, after having studied it phrase by phrase with his teacher and then, when starting a new piece, not knowing where to begin and which direction to take. Unless your student is learning to 'teach himself' you are not fulfilling your role as you should. I know it is possible to go again and again over one single work until a pupil gives a satisfying performance. But, I am convinced that it is more important for a young musician to learn through his own struggles, and, sometimes, he should even be allowed to fail, as he will learn so much more from that experience.

I am very interested in your ideas, and I believe that they are sound. The difficulty for a teacher is to keep a balance between allowing a student enough freedom and individuality while helping him to reach an understanding of what each composer and style requires for a serious interpretation. As you yourself mentioned, there should be some knowledge about what is basically right and what is wrong in an interpretation. It is also, sometimes, dangerous to allow a student to play in public knowing that his performance is weak and that he will fail. A sensitive musician might suffer lasting consequences from such an experience. Do you think it is wise to use the same approach with every student?

I still believe that, ultimately, a student may be more damaged if the teacher is constantly reinforcing, taking over the control instead of giving the young player the possibility to steer his own performance, to think for himself. The teacher's responsibility is to allow any student to go through the process of developing and gaining his own judgement, ultimately finding out what it is that he really wishes to attain and to create. While it is true to say that some of the students are quite mature at an early age, they develop great curiosity of mind and have a well-defined goal, there are many who are rather confused, and it is the teacher's responsibility to help them in their quest for self-discovery. There is a famous remark: 'There are no great teachers, only good students', and there is some truth in that. Obviously, there are some great teachers, but the gifts and the urge to learn must be in the bones of the student.

You are married to one of your former students who is actually a fortepiano player. How do you manage to pursue your careers, each one having to go in a different direction, yet both being keyboard performers?

It is much easier than one believes. In fact, we complement one another in our music-making. Maria Rose, my wife, is a Dutch musician who was trained as a pianist, first in Holland, and later in United States, when she became my student. We got married, and since then we have managed to work each one on his and her instrument. She became totally enamoured with a fortepiano, an instrument once used by Mozart, and I owe to her my new understanding of the enormous difference between a performance of music of the period on a modern instrument, and one on an authentic instrument. Because of her involvement in the music written for the fortepiano, I also acquired a different conception of how it should sound, of the style, the texture, the design, which actually fit that music. One can really hear the early classics as they were played when they were created, and it is only after studying them in this way that one realises how strange such a performance, with its exaggerated dynamics, appears on a modern instrument.

Recently, my wife and I have actually tried to combine our careers, and we often appear together on the same platform. The public seems to like this type of concert. We shall play an unusual programme in Holland. Maria Rose will play a Mozart concerto on the fortepiano in the first part, and in the second part I shall play a Chopin concerto on a nine-foot grand. We like to think of ourselves as an interesting Piano Duo marriage. We can communicate musically without having to worry about ensemble playing!

There is one important topic which we have not yet discussed, and which is of great concern to teachers, performers, and students. You are one of the musicians who has benefited from winning a prestigious competition. Do you advise your students to participate in the contests which are growing so rapidly in number all over the world?

I am afraid that, in spite of having been the recipient of a Grand Prize which obviously helped my career, I have mixed feelings about competitions. I believe, like some of my colleagues, that young artists should be given an opportunity to be heard through an 'apprentice system', something like a proliferation of music-making across nations which would allow talented musicians to come to the top. I cannot accept that the second or third prize-winners of any competition are so far less worthy than the first prize-winner, yet very often they are dismissed, while the grand winner gets all the glory. However, many people survive through their excellence, while some of the first prizes are completely forgotten. Winning a competition is a determining factor in the launching of a professional career. Unfortunately, the publicity machine that goes with such a prize makes it impossible for other candidates to compete with it. There is another danger, namely that these international competitions may be 'killing themselves' through their growing numbers, because there cannot be fifty winners of some fifty competitions in any one year who will become famous. I also think that young musicians should adopt a healthier attitude towards these contests. I find that my own students really enjoy them. It makes them work, they broaden their repertoire, have the opportunity to play in front of fine musicians, hear other candidates, and get together with pianists from different countries.

I strongly believe that young musicians should realise from an early stage that competition is part of their life. No matter what you play or where you play, you are always in competition, if nothing else, with yourself. You are in competition with your last performance, you compete with future performances, always striving to do better. The competition never really ends with winning a grand prize, and even then one has to continue with the next stage, and so on. Young aspiring musicians should be prepared for this struggle, and only those who believe in themselves and have the stamina should be advised to go in for it. I, myself, am amazed at the great number of pianists who still choose this profession. There must be something really wonderful in doing what one wants to do with all one's heart.

Cecile Ousset

In the past ten years or so, your brilliant career has taken you from one continent to another, from one place to another. What is the secret which makes you appear so serene, rested, fresh and elegant, and playing with such zest and joy, as well as with assurance, conquering your audiences everywhere?

You gave your own answer. It is the joy, the excitement I experience every time I play and this desire to do the best I can, to give all I have as an artist and as a pianist that is at the basis of everything I attempt to do in music. I love my instrument, I love the music I perform, I love my audiences and if I can communicate this when performing this gives me the greatest satisfaction. However, like in every other skill, it is a question of inner balance, great discipline and organisation. Whether preparing for concerts or when appearing on the platform, the artist must arrive at a right balance, an equilibrium between physical well-being, mental outlook and an intense involvement in the music. This is not possible unless the artist is convinced that he has something to offer and that he has the tools and ability to achieve his potential. For myself, I need the assurance that the work I have done will help me when facing the public. Of course there is – and there must always be room for growing, for developing as a musician, for no artist can stand still. I am very fortunate that in most countries I have made some wonderful friends who are doing everything in their power to make my concert tours as comfortable as possible. I have a piano at my disposal to go through certain parts of the score whenever I need, but above all I am encouraged to relax quietly, to be alone and this is invaluable if I am to recuperate my energies between performances. To give you just one example, my current series of the U.K. with the East Berlin Symphony Orchestra under their new, outstanding young conductor, Klaus Peter Flor, takes me to seven different towns in something like ten days, playing three different concertos. This is not an easy feat.

every time there is another hall, another piano (not always highly satisfactory), another public. As I said earlier, I rely on my inner balance, and conviction that, thanks to the intense work I have put in for many years preparing for this career, I can now stand up to the strain. There is, of course, the other aspect – the immense joy of performing, of facing a friendly audience and this gives me the energy as if I am reborn every time I play.

I owe a great deal to the training I had since I was a child. We lived in Algiers where my father was an officer in the French Army and my parents bought a piano for the children to have music lessons. I remember going to the piano when I three or four years old, just playing for myself by ear, and was thinking that this was such a wonderful toy. I was the youngest of four sisters and my mother decided that we should all have piano lessons. My progress must have been so rapid that my mother took me to Paris to be heard by the celebrated teacher, Marcel Ciampi, professor at the Paris Conservatoire. I was greatly looking forward to this experience, not realizing really what it meant and my mother was very thrilled when Monsieur Ciampi told her that he would accept me as a pupil as soon as arrangements could be made for me to live in Paris. This was soon done and I arrived in Paris to start my studies with the master (he was very well known also for having taught the two Menuhin sisters, Hephzibah and Yalta) and I could hardly wait to have my first real lesson. I have prepared many pieces to play to Monsieur Ciampi and I was so looking forward to hearing comments. It is impossible to describe my disappointment when he just said that he had something rather serious to talk about with my mother and with me before starting our lessons. I felt as if everything collapsed. What he had to say was very serious indeed. He asked me to stop playing any pieces for six months, while working on my technique regularly for several hours a day. He added, though, that he did realise that I was only eight years old, and that it was only natural that I would want to play 'real' music, to enjoy my hours spent at the piano. But he also said that talent should be treated seriously and that if I wanted to become a pianist, six months is not too long a time to devote to a healthy foundation of technique. Studies and exercises can sound quite charming when played with beautiful sound and with great facility and colour. Monsieur Ciampi was famous for having worked with very young children who have made it in the profession. Hephzibah Menuhin was six when she started her lessons and Yalta just four and a half!

I accepted the challenge and actually I quite enjoyed my regular practicing. I was doing even the 'Ciampi Exercises' with interest, having learnt to listen to every tone I produced, trying to get more and more beautiful sounds when playing scales or arpeggios or other aspects of technique. He also made me realise that even my small arm had enough weight, which I learnt how to use to produce chords with great volume of sound. The emphasis was always on listening to the sound, the chords to be played with a warm rich tone, never with harshness. The six months passed much faster than I thought, perhaps because I became more and more aware of my fingers getting stronger, and at the same time flexible, with every day of practicing. I also played many studies, covering various technical problems and I realised how right my teacher was when he said that there was so much charm, elegance and even beauty when these were well played.

Monsieur Ciampi must have been satisfied with my progress- of course, my mama was always there watching over my practicing – and he kept his promise. We started to work on repertoire and only then I understood what he meant by 'the need to have a sound foundation of trechnique if one wants to be a pianist'. from then onwards he became the great master who revealed the essence of every single work which we studied together. He talked to me, he illustrated many points of interpretation and I became more and more involved in my studies. I must have had an innate feeling for music, the right intuition but I also wanted so much to please him, to hear him praise me for the way I prepared the pieces for each lesson.

After about a year of studies he accepted me as a student in his class at the Conservatoire, and I received my 'Premier Prix' (the highest examination in performance) when I was only thirteen. You see the French system allows young pupils to finish the Conservatoire when only eleven or twelve years old! Looking in retrospect I do not believe that it is good for young musicians to find themselves in a sort of limbo with no direction to go.

While in the Conservatoire, I sailed through a great deal of repertoire. like most talented pupils, I had great facility in learning and memorizing even very long works and concertos, but I had to absorb the music, to make it my own before being able to play it, to express all my feelings. Being so young, I relied totally on my teacher, he was always there to help me, to encourage me, and having to perform it was very satisfying as, in a way, the greater part of responsibility was his. As long as I did as he taught me I was convinced that everything would come off right. It is interesting for me now, many years later, to find that whenever I play in front of an audience, I rely on that same belief which my teacher instilled in me: that I can do it!

Yet, when I finished the Conservatoire I was too young and inexperienced, and I was not ready to be launched in the profession, neither was I able to do any teaching as no parent (or pupil for that matter) would consider me for such a job. Of course, I realised that I had so much more to learn, but it was not that easy. While a student in the Conservatoire, everything was fine, I did very well in the exams, I played in the student's concerts, I got my 'Premiere Prix'. But now, I had the feeling that everyone expected 'grand' things and I was not ready. Fortunately my love of music and of my piano sustained me through this uncertain period. My teacher was always kind, we prepared many works for performances and he was most encouraging. I gave occasional recitals and these were source of great satisfaction, first preparing the programmes and then finding that the public greeted me as a musician. The truth us that I was unashamedly happy when performing. After a while Monsieur Ciampi thought that I was now ready to participate in some important competitions and this again was a highly stimulating time. There were not so many competitions then, and all the young pianists of my generation were hoping to win one of the prestigious prizes. Thus, I also took part in the Geneva, Brussels and Marguerite Long competitions and in each one I came among the top candidates. Although I was not placed first, engagements began to come my way and gradually my career started to flourish, both in France and abroad.

My major breakthrough came when I arrived in London in the late seventies. I came to London to spend a few weeks to improve my English and I was invited to stay with some musician friends who arranged a number of concerts and auditions for me. In a short time I found myself in a sort of whirlwind of recitals, broadcasts, television appearances, recording sessions, and from then on, frequent European and American tours followed. I love coming to England and I am grateful for the opportunities to play over here so often. One of my greatest joys is when I can play at the Promenade Concerts, with their unique crowd of concert-goers. They give so much to an artist, they make you feel good.

My busy concert schedule, sadly, forced me to give up my teaching at the Conservatoire where I had been teaching for several years. I have learnt a great deal through my working with pupils and I believe that every pianist should spend a period of his life doing some teaching. Having found solutions to some of the technical difficulties encountered is the best learning process. I was fortunate to have gone through those six months of training as an eight year old child when every technical exercise was systematically practised, so that I was able, as an

171

adult, to explain simply and clearly what my pupils needed to develop their technique. To practice exercises in a sort of vacuum is just as useless is just as useless as not practicing them at all. It is absolutely necessary to observe that the pupils use their hands and arms correctly, that the finger movements are free of any necessary tensions, and a natural way of playing is established right from the beginning, otherwise bad habits creep in and these are much more difficult to eradicate later on. Working with young children was very rewarding for me and their joy of being able to express themselves at the keyboard was contagious. But I had to make my choice and my career had to come first.

I still do some teaching but not on a regular basis. I work with advanced pianists who come to me occasionally for consultation lessons and I am often invited to give Master Classes in music colleges. It is on such occasions that I realise how important a good beginning is. I sometimes have to work with students with real gifts, highly musical, yet unable to play as they would want to because of the wrong way using their playing apparatus. There are moments when I ask myself 'where shall I start?' I am faced with a real dilemma and I must find an immediate solution if I am to be of any use. To work on the technique in such a short time is almost an impossibility. Usually I choose to discuss the musical aspect of the work to be interpreted and, sometimes, I am quite relieved when the student finds his 'own solution', once he has heard in his inner ear what that musical phrase should sound like, or what mood or ideas it should convey. Only then can I touch upon some technical solutions, explaining how to bring a different colour here, a warmer or richer tome there, using more weight or withdrawing it, and above all on playing with freedom, without physical tensions.

Cecile Ousset and I talked about many other important aspects of the profession:

Recording — so necessary for a professional artist; having the records distributed all over the world, and the photos on the record sleeves, with biographical notes, help to maintain the name in the fore, which, in turn, keep our agents busy.

Competitons — with their good and bad features; everyone agrees that there are too many piano competitions these days, although only few have the prestige needed to further a career. The good aspect is that young pianists have to broaden their repertoire, they are exposed to playing in front of discriminating audiences, and sometimes — as in her own experience — even if one is not a first prize winner, an agent or critic may be so impressed that he would like to do something to help the artist.

Ian Hobson

Your career as a musician has developed in several directions, each one more impressive than the other. As a pianist you made a mark as a young student, having graduated from the Royal Academy of Music with the coveted Recital Diploma when only seventeen, while you were already reading music at Cambridge, having been awarded a scholarship at the age of sixteen. After completing your Masters Degree at Cambridge, you continued your graduate studies at Yale, and soon afterwards you won competition after competition.

You have been very active as a conductor since your student days at Cambridge and at Yale, and, after gaining recognition as a finalist at the 1978 Baltimore Symphony Orchestra Conducting Competition, you have appeared on the rostrum of a number of important orchestras, having also established your own ensemble: Sinfonia da Camera in 1984.

Piano pedagogy is yet another facet of your musicianship. As a Piano Professor at Illinois University at Urbana, you are greatly involved in the problems confronting today's piano students, playing a vital role at national and international conferences.

You have also made a name in the profession as a scholar of piano literature, introducing in your programmes rarely performed works. Recently you presented a series of three recitals in New York and in London devoted to 'The London Pianoforte School', working in close collaboration with Nicholas Temperley, the editor of this long awaited edition. In Harold Schönberg's words (New York Times, May 7, 1989), 'It was a retrospective of composers who were active in London from the 1760s to the 1870s. Mr Hobson plays all the music with clear textures, strong outlines and splendidly accurate fingers'. It would not be easy to talk about each facet of your activities separately since they are, in fact, closely connected. Let us talk first about your studies.

I was very keen to learn to play the piano and I started to have formal lessons when I was five. Listening to the radio, to records, was one of my joys and, as a school boy, I became very interested in other instruments, helping with the violin when necessary and playing the organ, which fascinated me with those rich sounds. Piano remained my main instrument, and I often participated in the local festivals, where I was heard one day by Sidney Harrison. I was fourteen at the time, and he told my parents that if I intended to become a pianist, I should come to study in London. He offered to take me into his class at the Royal Academy, and thus started a wonderful relationship which lasted until he died in 1986. Even after my Recital Diploma, and as an undergraduate at Cambridge, I continued my lessons with him. These lasted until I went to Yale for graduate studies.

Sidney Harrison's teaching was most unconventional. An anecdote here, listening together to some exciting recordings there, or, often, he would sit at the piano to illustrate various aspects of interpretation with his superb pianism. It was good for me that he treated me more like an adult than a young boy. His greatest quality was to develop in his students a whole aura of artistry and self-awareness. And his generosity was always present. He must have enjoyed my insatiable quest to learn new works. I remember once telling him that if only I could find the piano score of one of Godowsky's transcriptions which I heard on record, I would be thrilled. He simply said: 'Surely, you can listen to it again and again until you may be able to play it by ear'. This I did, and I brought to my next lesson the entire piece played to the best of my ability, and the score – which I wrote down for Sidney to check.

At Yale, I was interested in many different aspects of music-making, and I was not yet thinking of becoming a performing artist. Studying for my Doctoral Degree, I spent three highly productive years, conducting, actively participating in all kinds of performances. That very stimulating atmosphere contributed largely to my development as a musician. I often think how fortunate I was not to have launched on a concert career at seventeen, when I finished at the RAM and several debut recitals were offered to me. I believe that everything should be done at the right time. While at Yale, I found myself getting more and more engagements to perform, and a beginning of a career was emerging. The agents and other well-wishers thought that winning one or two prestigious competitions would boost my chances of a successful start and, thus, I was encouraged to try the Van Cliburn in Texas in 1977. I was a finalist, and this gave me courage to participate in the following year in the Leeds competition where I received a fourth prize; 1980 brought me the Silver Medal at the Rubinstein, and then in 1981 I got the first prize at Leeds as well as another Silver Medal in Vienna. With this I closed the competitions circuit. I did not enjoy being part of these gruelling experiences, yet we all know how necessary they are for one's career.

I well remember the finals at Leeds in 1981 and the audience's excitement, and particularly that of the two Harrisons when the winner was announced. I also remember the uproar which dominated the Rubinstein competition in 1980 when the critics and the audience rebelled against the jury's decision, as everyone was of the opinion that you and Christian Blackshaw, the other English pianist and your colleague at the RAM, should have been awarded a joint first prize! Indeed, we all know under what stress the competitors perform, yet we must agree that such awards establish them on the right standing as performers. After all, agents very seldom are willing to act for an artist who has by-passed these competitions, and the media is even less interested.

Yes, this is so. I had many engagements to fulfil as part of the various awards, but I also had many other concerts both as soloist and as conductor with different orchestras. With the English Chamber Orchestra I toured the Far East, and with my own ensemble, I have done many recordings of the works which I chose to perform and conduct from the keyboard. We have issued so far the Francaix Concerto and Concertino, Saint-Saëns Concerto No.2, Milhaud's *La Creation du Monde*, and more recently Saint-Saëns *Carnaval des Animaux* in its original version. Being in complete control of the whole performance, in all its aspects, is a great responsibility, but this gives me immense satisfaction.

Having become an international artist has given me the opportunity to appear as soloist with the most major orchestras in the UK (Royal Philharmonic, Philharmonia, London Philharmonic, Hallé, Royal Liverpool, Scottish National) and in the US (Philadelphia, Chicago, Houston, Pittsburgh, Baltimore, among them) as well as in other parts of the world, in Europe and in New Zealand. This also led to having been invited to record for several companies. Arabesque Records have issued my performances of all Hummel's piano sonatas and etudes by Chopin/Godowsky, while for EMI I have recorded the Twenty-four Chopin Etudes, the Rachmaninov transcriptions and, with the English Chamber Orchestra under Sir Alexander Gibson, Mozart concertos nos. 23 and 24. It also gave me the opportunity to work with a highly sensitive conductor, Norman del Mar, and record two unusual works by Richard Strauss with the Philharmonia Orchestra, *Burlesque*, and, with the *Symphonia Domestica*, *Parergon*, a most exciting piece for left hand and massive orchestra.

And now, my new recordings on CD and on cassette include most of the works from 'The London Pianoforte School' which I performed in the New York and London recitals, with some well-known composers such as Clementi, Dussek, Field, Cramer, Pinto, and Sterndale-Benett among others, and some whose names are unknown even to experts. Having to learn all these works has been a very rewarding experience, and I have made some exciting discoveries. To think that all that music (Nicholas Temperley has edited and published twenty volumes in this extraordinary collection) was heard during that period in England – a period which many consider as devoid of any music! *Das Land ohne Musik* (The country without music), as England was known in Europe even in the late Thirties, before the Second World War. I do hope that pianists and teachers will get more interested in studying and performing these gems of piano literature. Pinto's F Major Sonata is a remarkable work. He was called 'The English Mozart' in his time, and I have played many other works by Pinto, like the Sonata in C, which I included in my Purcell Room recital as early as 1977. Dussek's Sonata anticipates some of Mendelssohn's or Schumann's harmonies, while the Cramer Sonata in F clearly shows why Beethoven had such respect for this composer.

You may have found working for these programmes an interesting and rewarding experience. For us, in the audience, it was also a valuable experience. To hear these works, the great legacy of these composers, introduced to us by an artist like you, with such commitment – 'a labour of love', as Harold Schönberg wrote – gave us a new impetus to know them better and to get our students to know them. Some of these would make quite exciting teaching material. It is also necessary for English people to obtain these recordings in this country, and I hope that they are available both in the USA and over here.

You spend most of your time in the USA, but you also come regularly over here for your concert engagements spending several months in Europe. How do you cope with this ambivalent existence?

It is true that I find myself in a rather unusual situation. In America, were I have settled since I took up a teaching position at Illinois University at Urbana, I am viewed as an English artist, while in this country, although born and brought up here, I am thought of as a musician with 'American connections'. This had a strange effect on my life and on my career. Yet, it has also had a good effect. It has given me possibilities to expand in many directions.

Working with budding musicians in the university, guiding them through their studies, also having the opportunity to perform and conduct works which otherwise I might not have contemplated including in my repertoire, have broadened my own knowledge and interests. At the same time, being able to return to England to fulfil engagements, or just to come where my roots are, is also very necessary, and I value this. My position in the university has always been very flexible and rather enviable, as the more known I became internationally, the more freedom I have to travel and perform. After all, my successes bring prestige also to the university.

I must add, though, that teaching has been a tremendous eye-opener for me. When I first started, my students were not of high calibre; very often I had to teach minor piano students. I learnt a great deal through getting to understand their difficulties, their problems. And this has helped me in my own work. Trying to apply my approach to my students problems in my own playing made me play better and better, which sounds rather paradoxical. The truth is that we learn from everyone and everything. I also had to have an open mind when working with these students, knowing that they did not aim at becoming performers. They only want to be able to play as well as possible to get to know what is out there in the world of music. This I had to give them. On the pianistic side, I looked to see what each individual needed, thus I planned a structured work to develop first their technique, the tools to express their musical ideas. I prefer to isolate the difficult passages in the works they are studying and help them to get the utmost results out of these, both technically and musically, instead of giving them endless exercises. But I also use Dohnanyi exercises for some students, for more control and finger individuality, as long as these are practised correctly, without undue stretching or strain of the muscles. I consider it of great importance for them to become aware of the state of the body in performance, and I encourage them to learn how to relax so that a balance between tension and relaxation is maintained when playing. Above all, I help them to develop mental control over their fingers, as I believe that they should become musicians first and pianists afterwards. For this they must learn to listen: to listen to other instrumentalists and singers, to orchestral performances, and mainly to their own playing. If they do not learn to listen they will never hear what the music is trying to say to them.

I often am asked by a student to assign special works to study, but, I prefer that they should decide themselves and present me with their choices. Some students are more interested in the twentieth-century works rather than in early keyboard music, and, if they so wish, why not play what they really want? They can learn so much by studying works by Messiaen, Tippett, George Crumb, or Copland and Barber. I believe, though, that they would benefit more by studying a 'balanced' repertoire, to include pieces from various periods. I cannot be rigid in this respect, because they have to learn about these different periods in their history and analysis classes, and, in fact, what really matters is that these students should enjoy what they are studying.

I have given a great deal of thought to the needs of music students, particularly of piano students, and I have contributed a chapter to the book 'Creative Piano Teaching' by James Lyke and Yvonne Enoch, dwelling on 'what I would expect, under the very best circumstances, of a student coming to me at the age of eighteen'. I tried to put down what these ideal circumstances are, and present a concentrated overview of the various aspects of piano playing. I plan to write in more depth about these problems as I get more and more involved in what we, those responsible for the training of future pianists and piano teachers, should offer these youngsters on the verge of entering this profession.

You are still a young musician, active in so many different areas of music-making. The question I would like to ask is: 'Where do you intend to go from here?'

Well, it is not difficult to answer, as all my activities are part of my career, and I love each aspect of it. You said it yourself that they are closely connected. I love performing, I love conducting, and I believe it is the duty of everyone involved in piano playing at a high level to work with young aspiring pianists. Training performers these days is a highly demanding and skilled art, and this should be done by artists who understand what projecting a performance means. Moreover, young students and performers should realise how to use their bodies and playing apparatus to prevent the spate of physical injuries in future. With regard to my research into rarely performed piano literature, again, I consider this not only my responsibility, but that of other artists of our time, who ought to bring to the notice of the public works which have been rightly, or wrongly, neglected.

Piano Journal VOL 10 NO 29 1989

Aldo Ciccolini

I have known you since the years, soon after the Second World War, when you played in London, and your appearances were greeted with great enthusiasm by both the critics and the public. With your stunning mastery of the keyboard you were immediately hailed as an ambassador of French music and also as an exponent of post-war composers. Prokofiev found in you an eloquent interpreter, and your performances and recordings inspired younger pianists to be more adventurous in their choice of repertoire. It was thanks to you that Rossini's piano music became better known, and you might like to know that the BBC recently introduced several of your Rossini recordings in their programmes. We have not had many opportunities to hear you in England in recent years, but your recordings of French music, especially of the Saint-Saëns five piano concertos, remain a model of limpidity and refinement of nuances and style.

Meeting you again, after many years, and hearing your magical recital at the Concertgebuow in Amsterdam, we were confronted by a somewhat older Ciccolini who gave us a new vision of what piano playing is, or at least what piano playing should 'sound like'. Well-known works, like Ravel's Valses Nobles et Sentimentales or Miroirs or Debussy's Preludes, acquired new dimensions as if hearing them for the first time. You created a harmonious world of tones, of interweaving voices, each one with its own timbre and colour, and this added to the clarity and fluidity of the performance. Perhaps I should let Albert Brussée tell what we all experienced that evening: 'The range of vivid colours that he coaxed from the piano [...] could only have come from Ciccolini: only someone born in Naples and ripened in Paris could produce a wealth of dazzling Mediterranean tints [...] I'll never forget the way he played his encore, Claire de Lune, so fairy-like and streaked with moonlight, with a control of touch and artistry one can only find in an older soloist, and even then only rarely.' (Piano Bulletin: 1989; 3).

Did you spend many years of searching to have reached such a control of your rich palette of sounds?

I have grown to approach the works I perform in a different way than in my youth. Yet, from my earliest dialogue with the instrument, I was fascinated by the great variety of sounds which the piano can create, but it took me many years of trials and errors until I found my own answers. Sound comes first and foremost in my approach, and I hear in my imagination all the tones I wish to bring in my interpretation of a particular work, I live with them for weeks on end until I know exactly which will be the ones to express each particular motif, each note, the entire phrase. Just as a painter selects his colours, a pianist should plan his canvas in its minutest detail.

This range of tones and shades is, of course, only one aspect of performances. The longer I have been in contact with music, the more I tried to find its human meaning which goes beyond the structure of the score, beyond the performer himself. The piano literature is immense – no other instrument equals such richness – and I have lived with these masterpieces for as long as I have been playing the piano. As a musician, one has to reach a synthesis between the music, the instrument, and himself. The instrument, as I mentioned earlier, has always been a source of inspiration and search. I could spend hours experimenting with different ways of producing so many degrees of shades and I tried to remember the actual physical sensations, how I used my fingers, my hands, arms, and what I did to the keys, what touches were creating what tones. It is a complex search, but also very rewarding – and I believe this is the only way to learn. No teacher can give you this.

I have thought a great deal about the many processes, physical and psychological, in piano playing and how we learn, how we train each part of the 'system', the fingers, hands, arms, how the whole body is involved, and how the mind controls and directs everything. For instance, it is very important to acquire a virtuoso finger technique, but, actually, fingers are only a small part of the entire mechanism. What matters is the flow of energy, its source and direction. Without this inner energy we could not perform.

Most pianists I interview seem to have had similar experiences: showing great ability from an early age, appearing in public as prodigy, and so on.

Well, yes, I did play the piano as a child, I did appear in public in my native town, Naples, when very young, and then I was accepted by the great teacher at the Naples Conservatoire, Paolo Denze, himself an outstanding pianist, a pupil of Feruccio Busoni. I learnt everything about piano playing from him. He took great care of my technique, and made sure that I was practising the 'Busoni exercises' as well as many other studies. It was not the quantity of studies and exercises one had to go through, but the quality of tone, the ease, the control that mattered. The studies became fine pieces of music. From my teacher I learnt how to listen to my own playing and become aware of the many sounds which the piano can produce, not just what the tone of the piano is, but what you can coax out of it, through your touches, through the way you press the keys. He also made us realise that unique timbre of the instrument, when pressing the key down to imagine the strings vibrate and listen to the tone dying away slowly, while allowing the key to come up gradually. Busoni understood this more than any other pianist of his time, and he taught all his students how to make use of this specific quality to enhance the performance. This is, in fact, the essence of being a musician, learning to listen to oneself before, during, and after the tone.

You were still very young when you finished your studies in Naples. What did you do then?

I went to Paris to study with Cortot, the most sought after teacher of the time. Cortot was one of the great poets and painters of the piano. The tone and texture of his pianism had a magical quality which one could recognise out of a hundred other pianists.

This was, indeed, a very important period of my life. I was in that great city, the Mecca of all young artists who hoped to find a niche in the world of music. Paris was then a great cultural centre, and there were more opportunities for young artists who had something to offer as performers. The 'salons' were still part of the artistic Parisian life, and if one of us had the fortune to be invited to play at such a *soirée*, the concert was heard by the right people who could then influence perhaps an impressario, or even a critic would have a word or two whispered in his ear. Thus I managed to give a number of concerts here and there while still studying with Cortot. Later on I was launched in a really big way. Recitals, braodcasts, orchestral engagements, concert tours abroad and recordings followed. And this I have been doing ever since.

You have been teaching at the Paris Conservatoire for many years. What qualities were you looking for when accepting a student in your class?

To be accepted at the Paris Conservatoire, candidates have to pass a very stiff entrance examination, which is really like a concert appearance, and only those who show special stage presence, as well as great technical proficiency and great musicality are encouraged to take up their studies in our institution. The French system is different from the American or the English systems of selection, as there are only a few Conservatories in the whole country, and naturally every aspiring young artist wants to get a Premier Prix from Paris. In every single year there must be several hundred candidates for the four or five places and, obviously, the competition is fierce. Those who succeed in getting in are, indeed, young pianists of unusual gifts.

I was very interested to work with young musicians and, as one so well knows, the teacher learns from a student just as much as the student from the teacher. It is this continuous learning process which makes the work with young musicians such a stimulating activity. It is a time for searching in so many directions. Every student had to go through a large part of the repertoire, as I believe that a pianist should get acquainted with a wide range of styles, to master many works before embarking on a concert career. And if they choose to take part in competitions, they must be ready to be launched on the profession, if they are among the few winners.

In my class, every student was expected to bring a new work at every lesson, which was then studied and discussed. I was trying to instil in these young players an awareness as to the many possibilities offered by the instrument, to have 'at their fingertips' a great variety of touches which they could then use to paint a picture in sound. It is through developing a sensitive inner ear that one can reach great subtleties of nuances and tones. I did a lot of playing myself during the lessons, but I did not want my students to just imitate me. I showed them a variety of possibilities of interpreting a work, or a specific phrase, but I did not expect them to imitate my playing. I emphasised again and again that it depends on them and them alone to bring to life the music they were studying.

I have now retired from the Conservatoire, but I still do a lot of teaching in various countries where I am invited to give recitals and conduct masterclasses. I find it quite interesting to meet young pianists from different backgrounds and cultures. I do not often meet with the Paris Conservatoire standard, although in some music faculties and colleges I get to work with very good pianists preparing for the Masters or Doctoral degrees.

For instance, at the EPTA conference in Holland, I worked at my masterclasses with several brilliant young performers who, admittedly, came to this music festival to prepare their programmes for various competitions studying with John Parry from the USA or with Karl Heinz Kämmerling from Hanover. These pianists had ample oppor-

tunities to appear in masterclasses (with me and with the other pedagogues) as well as in the evening recitals.

*I was very interested to observe that when you were working with these young
musicians you were first of all very encouraging about their playing — this is so
important — and that you were not trying to impose an interpretation. You made
some suggestions here and there, you discussed the tempi. In Prokofiev's Sonata
No.7 you emphasised the need to maintain a certain balance between the speed
of the first theme (Allegro inquieto) not to be taken too fast so that when the
second theme (Andantino) is played there should not be too much contrast. But
when discussing Schumann Sonata in G Minor, you suggested that the Etwas
Langsammer should be played with great expression and rather slower than is
usually performed. What impressed us in the audience was how these performances
gained in dimensions within a relatively short space of time. Do you consider such
classes of value to young musicians who seem to go to different 'masters' in search
of an authoritative interpretation, or would you advise them to study for a longer
period with only one teacher?*

Both approaches are good. It depends on the pianist. Sometimes one appearance in a masterclass situation may be sufficient for a student when
certain aspects of the performance become clear to him and, as you said,
the entire performance gains in quality. At other times, an intensive
course of technique, perhaps a change of technique, could bring greater
improvement, and it is the responsibility of the teacher taking that particular class to suggest this. Of course, it is more satisfying for everyone
to work with accomplished musicians who are more sensitive and more
responsive and usually the audience responds in the same way.

*As we are on the subject of performances, the question is: what makes a perform-
ance more memorable than others, and when is it fully communicated to the audience? I have been involved in research for several years in studying these moments
when an artist reaches his own peak experience, when the music flows and
everything is amazingly easy and satisfying. Sport Psychologists have studied this
phenomenon in the past few years, but I am not sure whether musicians have been
included. You, as an experienced artist, must have known many such happenings.*

Oh yes. I have had several such experiences although not very often,
but they have remained with me for a long time afterwards. Even now
I remember everything very clearly when playing the Rachmaninov
Concerto No.2 one evening and this happened. Not only that I felt that
my playing was different from any other times, but it seemed as if the

concerto was born at that moment. It became a completely new work, and my excitement and happiness were such that for a long time afterwards I could still not come to a resting point. In the night I remember not having been able to keep my legs still. I was going in my mind over and over again through the events of the whole evening and I would have given anything to re-live those moments. All I know is that the performance was so full of inventiveness, my imagination had free rein and I altered many of my decisions regarding the interpretation. To describe my state of mind is not easy, although I experienced tremendous awareness. I felt 120 per cent awake, ready to undertake any task. Everything seemed so right, the music just flowed and my body was totally in harmony with everything else. This *body feeling* when playing gives me a familiar sensation that my piano is not only my *instrument* it is part of my whole being, and this affinity creates in me an extra sensation of being safe yet very alert.

When I reach such a state I become even more aware of the space around me and although 'my space' does not get larger, I have a sensation that it never ends... I hear the sound of the piano going around the hall, reflecting against the walls and coming back enveloping me. I almost identify myself with the audience receiving my music as if we were one single unit. I have the strange sensation that I am at the piano but I am also somewhere else in the hall, I am everywhere. It is an almost schizoid state, transcending the normal experiences. I must add that at such moments I am in a state of complete contentment, and after such a concert I am so full of energy that I could go on playing for many more hours.

I have never understood *how* this happens or *when*, I do not wish to go through such experiences every time I appear in public. I want to know that I am in full control of what I am doing, that I can take my decisions as to the different sounds I intend to choose as for instance in the Debussy Preludes.

I detach myself emotionally, and I am immersed only in an aural experience. The aural sensations are so much part of my music-making that I often find myself getting away from my 'homework'. I hear myself play f where I had always thought that pp should be. Yet, at such moments everything sounds right, and the audience receives my message. Perhaps they sense that the artist is 'creating' and 're-creating' at that very moment. And this is what being an artist is. I hope I am right when I say that this should be the point we must be aware of, because it is from this point, from such moments that we learn to be what we are.

Piano Journal VOL 11 NO 31 1990

Leslie Howard

While talking to Leslie Howard, it became evident that it is utterly fitting that he was elected the new President of the Liszt Society in Britain, succeeding Louis Kentner. He has shown much commitment to Liszt's music, and has researched not only the entire piano works, but most of his other compositions too, going to the source, in libraries and private collections. More recently, Leslie Howard has embarked on a marathon project – to record the entire piano output of Liszt on CD. It may be apt to recall here a famous story that circulated among Liszt's fans. When he was asked in 1886, the last year of his life, by one of his disciples, Stradal, 'Master, isn't it terrible that the world does not appreciate your music?' 'I can wait...' was the great sage's (less than) humble answer. Indeed, he had to wait. But no one can deny that today Liszt is one of the most studied, discussed, and researched composers of all time.

Leslie Howard, how do you plan to carry out this enormous undertaking?

I feel very humble having been asked to complete such a task – a great challenge for any artist. I have already started the work, and the first ten CDs of approximately 75 minutes each are finished, and by the end of the year I will have completed 22 discs. One of my main difficulties has been getting hold of all the music because, in spite of all this research and of the new publications of so-called 'recently discovered manuscripts', there is still a great deal of Liszt's music in various libraries, and in some attics belonging to private collectors in Eastern Europe, where one had hardly any access previously. With the amazing changes on the political scene, it will now be possible to complete many searches, and Lisztians are waiting with great expectations for some dramatic discoveries. This is one of the main reasons why a complete catalogue has not been available, since there are still quite a few errors in assessing the true source or title when yet another manuscript or fragment is unearthed. Another drawback is that Liszt did not always bother to write the title, and unless someone studied that particular work and recognised the fragment of the score for what it was, it could remain unidentified. As recently as two years ago, a manuscript was thought to be another unknown piano concerto, until the same musicologist who discovered it realised that it was in fact *De Profundis*, which one knew about. Lisztian scholars are now trying to put together the *Grand Solo de Concert* in its original version for piano and orchestra, which so far has never been performed. Humphrey Searle did a version of this work without actually getting to the original piano part, which is in Weimar. He used a score – from Lord Londonderry archives – which has only the orchestral parts. One had then to rely on the few notes and sentences put in by Liszt himself, like: 'instead of what is in the piano version, play this in both hands', and other similar small remarks. The actual version was published much later, and considerably altered and added to, which means that you just cannot use such a version but have to go back to Weimar, find the original sketches for the piano part, and only then put the whole piece together. This is actually being done now, but it takes a long time to complete it.

If you are determined to record everything that has been discovered, your 'Lisztiana' of piano works may also serve as a more up-to-date catalogue. It is understandable that you may include in a catalogue the different versions of the same piece. But, how will you decide which piano version you will record?

I am not absolutely certain how I am going to record every version of everything. Sometimes it is obvious that he produced a simplified version, and in such a case there is no dilemma. But, at other times he adds an *ossia* passage in the score, in some cases three pages long. In the *Don Giovanni* transcription, there is a whole extra section in the middle. Perhaps he thought that many pianists might get tired performing it, so he devised a shorter passage. I do know which version I shall choose in this case, as I do not worry about my ability to 'keep going' once I start. I wouldn't be doing what I have embarked upon if I did not know that I have the stamina and that I know how to cope with the pianistic as well as the with the musical problems involved. The secret is actually not to get tense before you start, and try to maintain that state while playing. Perhaps this is easier said than done, but to perform such demanding works one has to know the 'how to'. The amazing thing about Liszt is that all his music is so well written for the instrument that – although it is difficult music (of course it is difficult from every aspect!) – once you start to study it, most problems seem to resolve themselves and you actually are able to see immediately how 'He' did it – how he moved his arms and fingers. The very rapid leaps still remain the hurdle of any pianist but, then again, if you realise what the musical content is, they are more easily conquered. If you want to play such a passage well, or a passage in octaves which lasts four pages, then you find a way of coping, which first and foremost demands that your neck, shoulders, and arms are supple and free. I have always admired Horowitz, who had such a superb technique that when he played such passages you could actually tell that he was not expending any energy to throw off those octaves. He also knew how to economise when doing a crescendo. For instance *Funerailles* is a supreme lesson on what a range of sound he had from the moment he started with a most mysterious *pianissimo* and reached that grand climax. In the same way, although Liszt carefully marked the increments of tempo and dynamics, the secret is not to deliver too much too soon. So many students and even professional pianists cannot cope with *Funerailles*, as by the time they reach the 'Allegro Energetico' they have already got all the allegro they can muster, and they get much too tense.

It is so interesting to realise what understanding Liszt had of how the pianist should feel at the instrument. Czerny must have had this insight and knowledge, and it is so touching to see again and again Liszt's admiration and gratitude for his master, although he studied with Czerny as a very young boy for only about 18 months. The dedication on the *Grandes Etudes* in 1838 reads, '*A mon Maitre, Carl Czerny*', and later on the same dedication appears on the *Transcendental Studies*. Of Course, Czerny gave him the foundation, but he had other teachers later on, and he ultimately evolved his own unique way of playing. The teachers he worked with were really composers and theoreticians with whom he had endless discussions. One of the two musicians he most valued was Fernand de Paer, a composer who wrote an opera based on the same story as Fidelio and which was even more popular than Beethoven's at the time. The other was Antonin Reicher, one of the foremost musicians of the nineteenth century – the greatest theoretician with regard to fugue writing. He actually wrote a great number of fugues, and Liszt spent many hours with these two friends, debating the many aspects of composition, often over a game of chess. He loved figures.

To play the entire piano literature is one thing, but to understand Liszt's compositional technique demands a wider and more profound approach, not only to the piano works, but also to his symphonic and choral music, and of the lovely songs he left. Although he has his roots in the past, Liszt was a great innovator, concerned with tonal colour, with new harmonies that he deliberately exploited, especially in his later years. He was not really experimenting, he knew exactly what he was trying to convey, and how to do it. Thus, he understood what a composer can obtain by dividing the octave in equal parts by two, by three, by four, or even by six, and one can find so many new approaches in the way he used the tritone or augmented triads: he had real mastery in shifting from any tonality to all other possible tonalities (he must have learnt this from Bach) by using the diminished seventh, which he also exploited in order to suspend one's belief in tonality. He knew that if the octave is divided by six, the result is the whole tone scale, which is to be found in many of his compositions, (7th Rhapsody, etc) at a time when Debussy was not yet born. Furthermore, one can find a taste of the twelve tone row, by a clever use of four augmented triads in descending procession – and this some twenty-five years before Schoenberg. I find studying Liszt's works extremely fascinating, and the more I discover, the more interested I get.

When it comes to performing, the problem is not how to get through the great works – these are so majestic and so well-written for the instrument – but how to make the less exciting pieces sound interesting. I often think of Alfred Brendel's unkind statement: 'If you play Beethoven badly, one blames the awful pianist, but if you play Liszt badly, everyone says that Liszt was an awful composer.' This is not true. Of course, I try to get all the passages of *bravura* to sound like music and not like technical exercises – there would be no point in my recording these works if this is what I do. I am also immersed in creating a wide range of tones which Liszt's music inspires one to do in the most natural and simple way. To do justice to this sonorous universe you actually need to hear in your mind the 'effect' you intend to produce, to find the diversity of tones which would be right for each particular work or study.

You talked earlier about the technical difficulties which most pianists meet, and particularly how you practice the long passages of octaves. Are there any other aspects of performance that may give us some ideas on how you actually prepare yourself for the recording sessions?

I am not working in a different way for a concert than for a recording. I do have a definite and organised way of studying. First of all, as I said earlier, I am very aware of the state of my body, that there should be no tension in the shoulders, the back, in my arms and wrists. Of course, like most pianists, I do have on my piano several studies which I always play as a warming up exercise. I do think of every detail of each piece before starting to play. I work first on fingering, trying several possibilities until I decide which feels best, and I use only that one. I think it is unwise to substitute new fingering when one plays at speed. Then I try to imagine the sounds which I want to produce ultimately. I believe in practising at a slower tempo, listening, and making sure that I achieve absolutely everything that I intend musically, and only afterwards I play the piece in the tempo I decide for that particular piece. If I get into difficulties, or if one of my students encounters some, I try to find some helpful devices. I am not an advocate of using various rhythms to develop agility, as I think every performer should have his own 'clock' inside him, but I do recommend when one has to play a long, fast passage of double thirds or two voices with one hand like in *Feux Follets* to practise first the top line legato and the bottom one staccato, and vice versa. This seems to give the player more assurance against some mishap in performance. At this stage one just cannot allow any mishaps, there is no room for them. It is true that we artists must be daring, and most of us enjoy the exhilaration of a challenging performance.

You came to England from Australia, where you spent your childhood and university years. Were you always encouraged to study music and to become a pianist?

I started to play by ear when I was about two years old, but my parents did not really try to make a prodigy out of me. My first teacher was June Maclane, a very good pianist, who had studied in Paris with Alfred Cortot. First of all, she had quite a time – and so had I – to teach me to read music after having played only by ear for several years. But, once I got to learn the notes I began to really enjoy my studying with this remarkable teacher (she is now in the USA, teaching at the University of Arizona at Tucson), who gave me a good foundation of technique and made me listen to what I was doing. We went through many works together, and I must have also had a natural facility which made my studies a joyful experience. I then went to high school where I had a different kind of teacher. Mr Britten was a musician through and through, and when I arrived at my first lesson, a cocky young boy anxious to impress him with my rattling off a few virtuoso pieces, he simply placed the score of a string quartet on the piano expecting me to read it. I got the message, and all I know is that I was thoroughly ashamed of my lack of real foundation. I could play by ear, and I thought I had learnt quite a few piano pieces, but I had no idea of

189

what was beyond the piano repertoire. Thanks to Mr Britten, I began to study very seriously all the scores in our school library, and listened to the many recordings which I could get hold of. I do remember coming to one of my early lessons when he produced an orchestral score by Vaughan Williams which, although quite difficult, I managed to play somehow. 'Very good!' was his comment, which brought a grin to my face, 'Now, transpose it a tone lower.' Well, I did try, partly relying on my good ear. Plodding through, slowly, I did hate him for this, but I also respected him, as I knew he was right. He was trying to help me become a better musician. His motto was: 'The important thing to study is musicianship. The actual technique of your instrument – whatever it is – is not worth tuppence if your general skills are not thoroughly developed.' He also encouraged me to become interested in other arts and in literature, and when I finished school I decided to go to university, as I was not yet sure whether I wanted to be a professional pianist. I studied English at Melbourne University, and I never regretted the years spent studying the great works of literature. When I finished my studies I was very anxious to leave for Europe and devote my life to music. I heard a great deal of Guido Agosti, the great Italian pianist and pedagogue, and so I arrived in Rome to study with him. This was the right decision for me, and working with Agosti opened new vistas in every way. He was not only a great teacher but also a most cultured and stimulating man. Agosti's style of teaching was very precise about what he wanted in terms of tempo relationships, but, if he thought that you were capable of using your own brain to search for a better understanding of the music, he left you to get on with your work. But, on the other hand, if one of his students did not show any individuality, he could be quite rude and difficult, and he would then insist that the student should play only as he, the master, has asked him to and no questions were allowed.

I have met in London a remarkable musician, Noretta Conchi, a student of Michelangeli, with whom I love having many discussions on the interpretation of piano music. I like to play for her occasionally. Her capacity to hear certain details or points in one's playing is almost uncanny, and she has an instinctive way of bringing to your own notice what is missing in the way you are performing, or where you fail to communicate. She is also good at finding an easier way to play a particular passage or motif which brings out just that – the communication of the musical message.

You are doing some teaching yourself. Do you find working with young musicians

190

a rewarding experience, or would you prefer to spend the time preparing for your own concerts and recordings?

I like to be known as a musician involved in all sorts of activities that actually complement each other. I love to conduct, I play the organ, and I am, indeed, very interested to work with young pianists who think seriously about their own work. I am on the staff of the Guildhall School of Music and Drama on the Advanced Solo Performer Course, but I have only one student there. I have others who come to me privately to be guided to join the profession. One of them, Robin Zebaida, a graduate from Oxford, appeared on the television, and on the radio. Recently, he had a nasty accident – he fell off his bicycle and injured his right hand just when he was preparing an important recital for one of the London venues. He came to see me, very despondent. 'All right,' I said, 'here is an interesting programme for left hand only, you will work on it, and in the meantime your right hand will get well.' Instead of moaning about his misfortune, he took the challenge, and within six weeks he had completed a most unusual programme – with Hoffman's *Etude*, a sonata by Reinecke, Brahms' transcription of Bach's Chaconne (which he wrote for Clara Schumann when her right hand was crippled by arthritis), Six Etudes by Saint-Saëns, Scriabin's 'Nocturne and Prelude', and he finished the recital with a very exciting, virtuoso transcription by Leschetitsky of a Donizetti aria from *Lucia di Lammermoor*. It was most interesting to watch Robin working for this recital which, in fact, made him produce a wider range of sounds, and a more beautiful tone then when he played with both hands. Having to create and coax from the instrument a more exciting diversity of tones, he was listening with much more care, and I think that through this enforced study he developed even more as a pianist and as a musician.

Do you encourage your students to take part in international competitions?

I do not make decisions for my students. It is up to them. But, on the whole, these competitions can do some harm to these young players, not because of the stress or the fear of not succeeding, but mainly because of the uniformity of repertoire. Although there are adequate lists requesting certain works, I find that most competitors choose the same over-performed works, either Chopin's Four Ballades which one has to hear again and again, or the late Beethoven sonatas, which seem to be a must among young artists! I would like to see competitions demanding a recital of the candidate's choice, with no restrictions imposed. But, who knows? Those Ballades and the last Beethoven sonatas may appear once again on these programmes.

What about your own plans, once the recordings are finished?

There is so much music that I have looked at but never performed in public that I would like to, and which I am leaving for much later when I think I shall have reached more understanding. For instance, I have not yet played the late Beethoven sonatas, nor Brahms' D Minor Concerto, and these events I shall look forward to. The *Hammerklavier* Sonata I have played many times, and every time I perform it I find it a very great experience. Yet I am looking forward to playing it when I am older (I am now forty-three) – perhaps I shall play the Adagio with more beauty and depth, but not so well the Fugue?

Piano Journal VOL 11 NO 32 1990

John Parry

You have achieved an extraordinary reputation as a performer, a teacher and a trainer of first prize winners at international competitions. Even here, in Alkmaar, Holland, where we are having this conversation, you have been busy for the past two weeks working every day with a group of young pianists who come year after year to the 'Holland Music Sessions' (founded by Franz Wolflkampf, Director of the Alkmaar Conservatorium). You must have an uncanny understanding of the needs of each student to give them this unusual sense of performance. So many pianists appear at international competitions, but those who possess a 'magic' quality are indeed very rare. What is your understanding of this phenomenon of peak performance, which you are able to realise so fully in your playing and transmit to your students?

This is a subject which has fascinated me for many years, and I have been asking myself many questions. I think that I have got some answers but I am still searching. When I perform I am trying to create within myself a total freedom in my spirit, in my mind, and my feelings take possession of my person so that I am able to communicate to and with the audience. At such moments we become *one* integrated unit, and I experience a two-way communication: the giving and the receiving, a very satisfying experience. To bring such a freedom in performance one has to work very hard; it does not happen without incredible concentration and discipline in the process of preparing for performance throughout the years of studies. This is probably the most difficult thing to get across to students before they are mature enough to realise that true freedom can only happen out of a foundation of disciplined and organised studies and continuous attention to every aspect of the technique and of the interpretation of the pieces one is trying to learn. So often I am confronted by students who want to impress me with their ability to perform a number of works, fluently, which they have not yet assimilated. The difficulty is to make them realise that they

193

need a change of attitude towards their approach to their own studies. Every single detail must be attended to, and for this, acute concentration and discipline are required. Until this is realised there cannot be the freedom of spirit which brings that extra dimension to a performance.

I must admit that I cannot teach this to everyone who comes to study with me. One does not really teach anything, one can only hope to develop the personality of a young musician by planting the right seed. You then can tend the plant, observe its development, observe how the personality of the performer and the musical personality become gradually more and more integrated. As a teacher, one has the duty to sense what the musical personality of each student is about. I believe that this is one of the reasons that so many teachers are not as successful as they might be. They are a total product of their own training and of their own personality which they try to impose on the students, to mould them according to their convictions. A great teacher must consider what the young musician gives him rather than what he intends to give. He must attempt to get inside the student and help him to do what he can do best, rather than try to part him with his nature. In this way the teacher directs the student into successful creativity.

The danger is the mass production of stereotyped pianists, reared on recordings of the piano literature which they are anxious to imitate. The late Arthur Rubinstein made a devastating statement summing up this situation: 'Most pianists do nothing but practise every day, from Monday to Friday, may take a rest on Friday, go on the stage on Saturday, and the next day they start all over again.'

When my students work on new pieces I insist that they do not listen to recordings until they have learnt them and have decided on an interpretation of their own. Afterwards it is quite stimulating to hear other interpretations, but it is interesting to note how often they seem to be more convinced that their ideas and decisions are the right ones. Perhaps, later on, they may make some new discoveries, as it happens to all of us when returning to old repertoire. This is the greatness of music: there are endless possibilities.

On the other hand, most students who come are already experienced performers. They have a pretty good 'working' technique, but they expect something else – and my duty is to give them that 'something else'.

There is no doubt that you cannot divorce the mechanics of how to play the piano from the creative aspect. There are so many different aspects of technical proficiency, but most students have to deal with teachers who have definite ideas, who believe with great conviction that there is only one right way to place the hands on the keys. Anything that is dogmatic becomes by nature self-limiting. 'I have learnt like that from my teacher and this has served me and this would have to serve you also; and if it doesn't it is your fault' – this attitude is still very much around in the profession. Yet, there is so much information available: there are books with so many important theories explaining various ways of 'doing things'. There are also many different 'body-types', sizes and shapes of hands, arms, and so on, that one cannot dare be over-dogmatic in one's approach.

I must admit that it comes more naturally to me to understand the problems and to help a pianist with a body similar to my own: rather short, stout, with broad, square hands. But, I often have to work with slim, slightly-built pianists with narrow hands, who, in the majority of cases, have good technique and produce a good tone from the piano. I try to understand the way they play, and then I am able to be of some help. First of all I make sure that each student understands that there are various ways of pressing the keys, and there are different touches which they must master to get the right quality, the right colour, of each musical phrase. The emphasis is, after all, on learning to listen. The more acute the inner hearing is, the finer the results – as the pianist will want to get the right tones to match those which he hears in his mind.

Teaching technique? *Everything* is technique, not only the mechanics of getting the fingers to play as fast as possible. Yet, we all know that there is no short cut and the right results will come only through regular practice of all aspects of piano technique.

I am a great believer in developing a well-controlled, sure and secure finger technique through specially devised exercises. I also recommend the use of arm weight, which teaches the player an awareness of how every area of the body feels in piano playing. It is not a question of 'doing exercises' but of how and why. As a teacher, it is my duty to train a student to acquire finger independence, to learn how to isolate the muscular aspect of the technique before going further in our studies. Yet, it is hard to believe that anything one invents as an exercise has not been invented before. Our task is to select wisely. My students learn how to use finger control at any moment, in normal hand position, in extended hand position; they do finger exercises, listening very carefully to the sound they produce, from the top of the key down to the bottom with great care, then from above and through the key, imagining that there is a weight at the end of the finger which one is trying to throw to the floor, meeting resistance, then trying to hit something in a different way, just like a golf swing. I also teach 'overlap' so that the student does not lift fingers always in the same way. It is known that speed is determined just as much by the way the key is depressed as by the way the fingers leave the key.

I try to help my students to have such technical assurance that when they are on the platform they have the confidence that they can cope, no matter how nervous they are. My greatest concern, though, is not to become stale in my teaching. It is so easy to repeat oneself, one does something which is successful and tries to do it again and again. The danger is when a teacher becomes so formalised in the way he attends to the repertoire that we hear absolutely the same interpretation at every given moment. I often recall my wonderful oboe teacher during my years at Eastman (I took oboe as a second study) who warned me: 'As teachers, we must be careful not to become caricatures of ourselves'. And this I constantly fight against. I try to be open to new ideas, always searching for new ways of accomplishing certain goals, and this is not easy.

As to my development, I played the piano by ear and could harmonise hymns when I was three years old, and what a joy it was to discover the written music.

I grew up in Minnesota, and by the age of 12 I could play fairly well, having been taught first by my aunt and having found the piano a great companion, since I can remember. I was taken on by a very good teacher, Dorothea Helennis, who decided to give me four lessons every week, lessons which covered all aspects of piano playing, musical appreciation, repertoire, etc. She was quite an accomplished pianist, having studied with a pupil of the celebrated Rudolf Ganz. From then on, I never looked back. I knew that this was what I wanted to do.

To satisfy my parents, I went first to university and spent two years in a College, but I was too unhappy not to have enough time for my music.

I then went to Eastman School of Music where I studied with Frank Mannheimer, a pupil of Egon Petri, who also went to London to study with Tobias Matthay. Thus I received several beneficial influences – a very sound foundation of keyboard approach via Rudolf Ganz, and Petri, together with the new ideas which were sweeping the piano thought at that time: the 'relaxionist' theories, through Matthay's teaching and writings. Mannheimer was a great friend of Myra Hess, and they kept in touch throughout their lives.

When I graduated from Eastman I did the usual thing; I went to Europe, where I met several interesting artists. Among them I spent some time with a Swiss pianist, Cecile Genhard, of Edwin Fischer's circle of musicians, and later on I chose to study with Carlo Zecchi, with whom I stayed several years. Zecchi himself was a pupil of Schnabel, and from him I learnt about his master's insight into the music of Schubert and Beethoven. I feel the greatest empathy with these two composers. I just think that I am able to participate in their anguish with all my being, and I also feel that the imagination in their sound comes out with so many human qualities, all very near to me. We all have a great debt of gratitude to Schnabel. It is only through his perseverence and selfless dedication that a taste for programmes devoted entirely to Schubert developed. His first Schubert recitals were a sensation in the United States, but only a handful of devotees were present. Today, *Schubertiades* are a common occurrence in almost every country.

This does not mean that I do not perform other composers – in my programme of my recital tomorrow in the Concertgebuow, I am including a very interesting and exciting work by an American composer, Paul Cooper, a major work in three movements. It is a complicated score, and one day I hope to have it memorised. Not that I have not assimilated it, but to perform it without the music I shall have to be more convinced that I can do it. I have devised a practical way to have the entire music in front of my eyes, by reducing it and pasting it on a system of cards. The whole first movement is on one card, then I have just one turn for the second movement and another for the last movement. The truth is that these cards serve only as a 'prompter', as I know exactly where I am at every step. My visual memory is very strong, and comes to my assistance at such moments.

Do you encourage your students to play the music of their time, the music of living contemporary composers?

I leave this entirely to their own decision – only when I am asked I give some advice, and then I do take into consideration the physical type of the pianist and his/her musical personality. There are not many works of this kind which I like, but there are a few composers which I love, and these I do play and try to make them known. On the other hand, I think that it is essential for young artists to be in touch with what goes on in the musical world and to perform the works of young composers. It is their duty to present this music to the public, otherwise how could these composers get to be known?

What about competitions? You are not only involved in the training of so many candidates, but you often find yourself on the juries. Would you like to bring some changes or some new ideas into these events?

Well, until somebody devises a better way of exposing young talents I am afraid there is no other choice. Yes, I would like to see a change in the requirements regarding the repertoire, as it is not possible for one pianist to feel equally at home with every type of music. In a recital programme, one chooses the works which suit the artist's temperament and personality, but, in a competition, one has to perform every style of composition. For instance, it would be so much better for the young competitors if they could present a choice of repertoire and then play one concerto. In general, I find that the most talented pianists do not do as well in competitions as they do in concerts. There is something about the highly sensitive artists who get very involved in the sharing, the giving, and the communicating when facing an audience but who become rather inhibited when they think that they are going to be judged by an austere jury.

You have won several competitions yourself, and surely you are the person to give the right advice to your students. What was your attitude when you had to play in front of judges?

This is a very subjective experience. I quite enjoyed participating in such events, and when I got a prize I was very excited. But, It was a question of how I felt; if I found the actual place good for me, the jury seemed to me encouraging, and I tried to give my very best.

So far we talked mainly about your achievements with very successful students. What about your own performances? I am particularly interested to know how you reach that 'freedom of mind/freedom of spirit' which results in those memorable performances.

It is no secret that an artist's achievements are the result of many years of intense, disciplined, and thoughtful work. And then, what happens in performance is totally different, beyond the usual experience. The artist reaches a state when there is a shift from the craft to relying on the craft, when the imagination is allowed free rein and the playing gains real magic. I am both the player and the listener, and I feel I am like a medium through whom everything just flows into the audience. Yet, my mind, although totally at rest, is very open, and I observe and feel everything very intensely. It is strange that I often go through such an experience during the last few days before an important recital. I feel it is coming, I know it is coming, and I let myself become overwhelmed by it. I do not know if during the actual performance I shall go through a similar experience. Perhaps it is a good thing that these are not daily occurrences so that they remain in the artist's mind as great, 'peak experiences'. And it is our privilege, as artists, to create such moments when we can be in touch with ourselves and with those in the audience. It is giving and receiving – a truly gratifying experience.

Piano Journal VOL 1 NO 33 1990

Fernando Laires & Nelita True

It is not often that one meets two such great artists – husband and wife – both pianists, who have made very successful careers in different directions and at the same time, maintaining a harmonious relationship. When asked what the recipe for this achievement was both of them admitted that, fundamentally, this was due to their mutual respect and admiration for each other's musicianship. It also owes a great deal to their being so different temperamentally – Fernando, with his Latin exuberance, comes from Portugal while Nelita – calm and serene, with Icelandic parentage, stems from Montana, a western state of the USA where girls, although allowed to go away for their studies, sometimes even to Europe, were expected to come back and marry the young lad next door.

Yet, both admit that it is perhaps these differences which, instead of creating conflict, brought them even closer together, complementing each other. It so happened that they met and married as mature people, well settled in their careers and this may have also been a contributing factor to their harmonious relationship. 'Had we married when we were young students it might have been, perhaps, different,' says Nelita, adding: 'We did not have to struggle like today's young pianists. There were enough interesting positions in Music Faculties and Colleges for us at the start of our careers.'

'I made my first studies in Portugal at the National Conservatoire of Lisbon,' recounts Fernando, 'with a well-known teacher, Lucio Mendez, a pupil of the famous Isidore Philipp. There were five teachers at the Lisbon Conservatoire who had studied with Philipp and I could hardly wait to finish my studies to do the same. At that time, Philipp had settled in New York where he had built a flourishing teaching practice in a hotel in central Manhattan. My teacher gave me a letter of introduction – as it was customary – so I arrived in New York, but I spent several months first at the Juilliard (my Portuguese grant stipulated this) where

I worked with Ernest Hutcheson. Afterwards I had private lessons with Isidore Philipp.

'I only studied with him for two years (in 1947 and 1948) but these two years proved of immense value for my playing and, ever since, I have thought of him as my revered Master. I came to him as a young pianist, with a certain reputation, and, as my teacher wrote in his letter, with a serious foundation of technique and musicianship. At 19, I was the youngest pianist to have performed the 32 Beethoven piano sonatas in Lisbon. My youth was the only excuse for this audacity but it must have been my teacher who encouraged me to do so.

'Until I met Philipp I had a number of teachers, and they were all very good, in their own way. But, working with Philipp was a very special experience. From the start he made me understand that he was not teaching "fundamentals" of technique, he was going with me through a process of refinement of what I already had. He believed in the usefulness of exercises and he gave me *Philipp Exercises for Independence of Fingers*, selecting several from part 1, which he thought would be what I needed for my understanding of how to produce a variety of tones. After about three months the results were simply amazing. My whole approach to keyboard playing had changed into a highly refined and controlled one. We studied some repertoire during this stage but not very much. Monsieur Philipp showed extraordinary patience by not hurrying me through this new process and not forcing anything on me. He wanted me to reach the needed changes from within my own thought processes.'

The *Philipp Exercises* have been the subject of two very important articles in the *Piano Quarterly*, co-ordinated by Dr. Frank Wilson, with Fernando Laires explaining their importance and Dorothy Taubman – the well-known teacher who had helped dozens of pianists with their hand injuries – bitterly attacking them as one of the causes of the many ailments. Laires continues:

'I intend to write a special article on 'How to Practise the Philipp Exercises', as recommended by the master himself. I remember one thing that he said, that I had to do the exercises for a while, then practise scales, so that the muscles used are rested by doing something different. We must know when to stop from an intensive activity by doing a different one, thus understanding the process of that kind of equilibrium.

'Those were also more auspicious times for us, young pianists at the start of our careers. We were not confronted by such insurmountable hurdles like our young artists today. Therefore, we were not working under the same kind of stress – a great deal of which is responsible for the many physical complaints'.

Nelita takes over: 'I had a different upbringing. Montana was not very active culturally, yet when I started to play the piano I had two very good teachers who helped me to develop a natural technique. It was only later on when I entered Michigan University that I really matured. My teacher there, Helen Titus (a pupil of Schnabel), was the opposite of Philipp. She was a very reserved, soft-spoken woman, with no sense of humour – not the sort of personality that you would think would excite a student. But, somehow, in her quiet ways, she just brought such meaning to music-making, it was so compelling, that after every lesson I couldn't wait to get to the piano. I owe it to her that I worked very hard at my technique, getting control and independence of fingers. In my teaching, this has been my credo – to guide my students to develop the tools to be able to look at a piece of music and make sense of it without being told how to play every note.

'I then went to the Juilliard and afterwards got my Doctorate at Peabody studying with Leon Fleischer, one of Schnabel's finest pupils, with whom I really did most of my training. A year in Paris with that extraordinary woman musician, Nadia Boulanger, was one of the most meaningful experiences. To be part of her circle of musicians, to hear her comments, so revealing and always so positive, taught me a great deal about myself, about what my ideals were – as a musician, as a teacher. I also had my first really bad experience in Paris that year having met the most unsympathetic piano teacher. Fortunately, Nadia Boulanger's classes made up for this.

'On my return to the States I got my first teaching post at Kansas State University at Lawrence. Later on I was fortunate to get a teaching assistantship at Juilliard where I had wonderful opportunities to perform as soloist, in chamber music and accompanying outstanding singers.

'My great chance came when I won the Concerto Competition to play with the New York Philharmonic for the opening of the Lincoln Center so I appeared at the Philharmonia Hall (now Avery Fisher Hall) and, to my great excitement, I had very good reviews.

'From then on I had a smooth path, my career just soared, I had many concerts and I was invited to present workshops – a newly established type of lecture/demonstration involving audience participation and also 'Illustrated Talks' on specific composers. Indeed, she presented an unforgettable session on Chopin's Nocturnes at an EPTA International Conference in London.'

When talking about teaching, their experiences were rather different.

'I went back to Lisbon after the two years of studies with Philipp, where a brilliant career was waiting for me – concerts throughout Portugal and I was soon invited to teach at the National Conservatoire. I spent six years, gaining great experience, working with the most talented young pianists while continuing my solo career.

'I was then sent to the United States to do a survey of the main Music Colleges and Conservatories and this allowed me to find out what was going on in the piano profession. I then decided to stay in America. Having met and collaborated with several Deans of music schools, I had their support and Texas University offered me a teaching post which also allowed me ample opportunity to play as a soloist and in Chamber Music concerts.'

While Fernando considered teaching and performing as an integral part of an artist's life – he had done this during the previous six years in Lisbon – Nelita took a long time to reach this kind of duality. 'My need to perform and my love of teaching are both very important for me but when I married Fernando I found it very difficult to cope over the years as I was torn between my career I deeply loved and my belief that once I have made a commitment to another person I wanted to give the best of me to that person. So I had to sacrifice my practising time and this had been a conflict all along. Fortunately, I always had a high energy level which has been my saving – I have learnt to cope and have actually come to terms with the demands.'

Both Fernando and Nelita have enjoyed a great reputation for their teaching at prestigious music schools, Fernando became Head of Piano at Peabody Conservatory – which gave many outstanding pianists to the profession – and Nelita was recently appointed Head of Piano at the famous Eastman School of Music in Rochester, where she had already brought some interesting and very welcome changes in the system of teaching. 'It has been very gratifying for me to have been able to influence certain decisions, thus I could bring several new members on the teaching staff who are now adding their qualities to an already strong existing faculty and this has worked extremely well in maintaining and even improving the high level of performance and teaching "in pairs". I work with one of my colleagues teaching our students together, thus they get the two approaches.

'I think that such a way of studying serves also to train young musicians for their future faculty jobs, realising how much colleagues learn from one another by working together. I must add that everyone in my department is enthusiastic about this scheme and it is also interesting to note that there had been no defections of students wanting to change professors. There is no need as they have the freedom and I do encourage them to go to other classes, to observe the teaching and also they can get the opinion of other faculty members.'

Fernando actually enjoys administrative work, in spite of his limited time for activities other than performing and teaching. He founded the 'American Liszt Society' over a quarter of a century ago, has been its president and staunch supporter all these years – with a short interruption of three years – and is now back at the helm. He realised that there was a need to stimulate research into the mass of works of Liszt, about Liszt, the enormous correspondence and, above all, to promote performances and recordings of less popular works, as well as cataloguing the vast output. Thanks to his vision, other Liszt Societies sprang up in many other countries and, today, there are 26! The *American Liszt Society Journal* and the *Newsletter* contain information about the activities of these societies, all very flourishing. They maintain international exchanges, organising 'International Liszt Festivals' in various countries, (there will be one in South America, and later on in the Soviet Union), International Piano Competitions (The Liszt International Competition in Utrecht in Holland has been gaining a fine reputation and EPTA Netherlands is one of the promoters) and, most of all, there is a continuous exchange of news and views among members everywhere.

'I also had another aim when I created the society. From my own experience, and especially today, young up-and-coming artists depend on the whim of the agents who can only think in terms of a good return for their own businesses. The Liszt Societies offer good opportunities to the young pianists to be heard by knowlegeble audiences, by critics and by agents who attend the competitions. It is important for them to be part of such prestigious festivals and some of them have been stimulated to further studies and, by now, have made a name in the profession as 'Liszt Scholars' or 'Liszt Interpreters'. It is true that Liszt Society has the support of the Music Faculties with which I had been in close contact along the years for our annual conferences and festivals.'

When Nelita was appointed Head of Eastman Piano Department, Fernando resigned from his position of many years at the Peabody Conservatory to be with her in Rochester. Being together means a great deal to them, although they often travel separately. 'For me,' adds Nelita, 'Fernando represents wisdom, he has a philosopher's outlook on life, his perceptions are so broad that even if we talk about the same things he has new insights every time. I wish I could find more time every day just to listen to him talk! More than anything else we want to have a relaxing time when we are together, almost avoiding the music and the piano during our few hours at dinners and in the evenings. We both feel that after a full day of teaching and discussions on piano music we have to find a way to resist it taking over our life totally.'

When Nelita was invited to conduct courses at Rimsky Korsakov Conservatory in Leningrad for a month in 1988, Fernando joined her as he was also invited to give concerts in the USSR. 'The standard of teaching in Leningrad Conservatory is amazingly high', says Nelita. 'and it was a very interesting time for me to understand the students' mentality, their total dedication to their work and to music, not worrying about what will happen to them when they become professional. It is true that the state looks after each musician, there are still positions in the many Music Schools throughout the Soviet Union. It was also fascinating to have many talks with the professors, most of them having a fine tradition of Russian pianism from disciples of Anton Rubinstein, Yossipova, even Rimsky Korsakov. Such exchanges should be organised from state to state, they are vital for our profession.'

Fernando travels much more now that he has left Peabody. He has a number of students at the Catholic University (Washington) and has been appointed Professor at Shenyang Conservatory in China, where he goes every year for several weeks.

'It is amazing how fast the Chinese have recovered from the Cultural Revolution which had completely arrested any progress in the Arts. The zest with which teachers and students try to absorb everything that we, guest professors, have to offer is very impressive. They are catching up and as we all know, young Chinese pianists are winning many international competitions.'

Talking of competitions, Fernando and Nelita did not have much to say that other artists and teachers had not stated before – that there are too many and that it is not possible to launch nearly one hundred young pianists in any one year as first prize winners!

Yet, the winners of prestigious competitions like Cleveland, Gina Bachauer and Maryland in USA, Leeds in the UK, Rubinstein in Israel, Queen Elizabeth in Brussels, Geneva in Switzerland and, of course, the Tchaikowsky which is not only for pianists, stand a sure chance to make a name in the profession.

Both Fernando and Nelita are often invited to be on juries and, actually enjoy it, particularly to hear young pianists and discover new talents, if not stars. They have been involved in the training of pianists for so many years that they like to witness such contests. In spite of the negative aspects, these aspiring artists being under unbearable strain, there are many exciting moments for both the jury and the competitors. Having to live and perform under tremendous pressure shows which are the ones who will be able to withstand what may come, if they succeed.

I then asked them about the fascinating phenomenon of performance, those moments which remain in one's memory for a very long time because of their uniqueness and perfection. Their experiences are very similar to those of most artists when they reach their peak. 'What it brings for me is a kind of communication which is bonding with the audience. There is such a stillness in the hall when this happens and, although I am acutely aware of everything that goes on and of everything I am doing, it seems that everything goes, somehow, through me, direct to the audience and I am performing way beyond what I think I am capable of' – this is how Nelita describes her experiences.

'I often discuss the total freedom of the body from any tension with my students, as they realise that if there is any tension, you are restricted emotionally also, not only physically. I do emphasise that, on the other hand positive tension is vital, and if you are not intensely involved, feeling that tense intensity, then you are not really playing as you should.

But she does not find it easy to convey to these young pianists what it feels like when you go through this kind of magical experience. 'They will have to find it themselves and I hope that this will happen sooner rather than later.'

Fernando talked about his great joy when performing and he has been trying to stimulate his students to adopt such an attitude. 'Unless there is excitement, and profound love of what one is doing, the performances suffer.'

I asked them if will consider playing again as an ensemble, now that they have reached such a measure of understanding in so many directions. Both felt that they should carry on with the way their careers have been shaped. They recall with pleasure the times – at the beginning of their relationship – when they played duets and on two pianos and how much they loved discovering the rich repertoire of the different periods and styles. They particularly enjoyed playing an interesting Concerto for Two Pianos written especially for them by the American composer, Leslie Bassett, winner of the coveted Pulitzer Prize. It is a modern concerto, written in a very original style, yet using the idiom of scales and chords and presenting a unique feature: each pianist is at the extreme right and the extreme left of the orchestra and the stage and this creates some eerie stereophonic effects.

In recent years, like most pianists and piano professors in the USA, Fernando and Nelita become more and more involved in the programme initiated by Dr. Richard Chronister, Executive Director of the 'National Conference on Piano Pedagogy'. He organises a large conference every two years – to prepare better-structured courses for the training of piano teachers. EPTA is also participating in this programme and it is hoped that other European and world piano teachers' associations will collaborate towards the raising of standards in piano teaching in this last decade of the Twentieth Century. The goal is to help the future teachers in their studies which should cover wide areas, not only on piano teaching and performance but also to include anatomy and physiology, and develop an understanding of the neuro-physiological processes in instrumental playing, as well as to learn how to make use of highly sophisticated equipment, which already is being introduced in many institutions.

Let us hope that there will always be room for the individual, serious and dedicated teachers who have done so much for the profession.

Moura Lympany

Moura Lympany is vivacious, elegant, and very energetic, greatly belying her impending seventy-fifth birthday. Indeed, she is able to talk about a successful career spanning more than sixty years. As soon as we met, she started to tell me about the exciting musical events that were part of her birthday celebrations in August 1991.

The BBC also invited her to play in the popular Proms Concerts at the Royal Albert Hall she chose to play the Mendelssohn G Minor Concerto, the very same work with which Moura made her debut in London at the age of twelve, exactly sixty-three years before. This year also marks the publication of her *Autobiography*, which she assures me is full of much more entertaining details than lists of concert successes.

How did you write your book? In longhand, on word processor, talking into a cassette recorder, or by some other method?

I wrote the book in collaboration with a cousin, a well-known English author, Margot Strickland (she wrote several successful books, including *Byron's Women*). Actually, I had a nasty attack of whooping cough, or something of that sort, and the doctors ordered complete rest. Not being used to doing nothing all day, I decided to put down on paper my thoughts, my ideas, but mainly I wanted to write about the lovely little village, Rasiguere, near Perpignan, in France, where I chose to live after another bout of illness. I was continually suffering from a throat infection, having developed a voice at least one octave lower, and my specialist threatened me that unless I moved to a sunny, warm and dry climate, the condition would become chronic, if not worse. So, after reading an advertisement in the *Sunday Times* about a small property in that area, I went there and it was, indeed, love at first sight. Going by car through rows and rows of vineyards an each side of the road, I arrived at the place and, without any hesitation, I just took it. I felt immediately at home, and was very attracted by the small patch of garden with a huge pear tree right in the middle of it. As soon as I moved in I set down to work at my garden, which I turned into an enchanting little place, so full of flowers that there was no room to place even a pin in the ground. It was so beautiful that I sent an article to the Royal Horticultural Society, which was actually published.

Life in the village was very peaceful, but I had to do something creative. I then saw this charming place as an ideal setting for a Festival and, after discussing this with the village mayor and his council, we set up to organise a 'Festival for Music and Wine', a week of music, good food, and wine. It has become an annual event, usually at the end of June This year it is from 22nd to 29th, and my great friend Victoria de Los Angeles will open it. I arrange the artistic events and the whole village takes part in providing midnight suppers after the concerts, cooked and served by the women in the village, the wine flowing freely, in every sense, as it is offered to the visitors by the local growers. It could really be called the 'Festival of Love' as everyone gives their services with great devotion. There is no concert-hall and we use the wine-making hall for the occasion, arranging seats – it holds three hundred and fifty – in the middle, while on all sides, the walls are covered in bottles of wine, each one in its little pigeon hole. There is no need for advertising, as the festival is well known in the region, and people flock in from the surrounding villages to savour the music, the exquisite food and wine, and the unique atmosphere. Some hundred and fifty people come regularly from Manchester with the Manchester Camerata, which gives three or four concerts in exchange for a good holiday. They hire a bus that brings them all the way to Rasiguere, and, as soon as they arrive, they all make for the river for a swim. By now about twenty Manchester families have decided to spend all their vacations in our village and they bought their own places. Of course I am expected to give some concerts, but this year I shall give only two recitals so that I can spend more time with the visitors.

I met you for the first time when we were both students of Tobias Matthay, during the war. We were travelling together from Waterloo to Haslemere, in Surrey, where a car would wait to take us to High Marlow, up on the Sussex hills, where he retired when he had to close 'The Matthay School,' in Wimpole Street in London. A group of devoted teachers, including his daughter, Denise Lasimonne, herself a very fine teacher, gathered around 'Uncle Tobbs' as everyone called him. Thus the Matthay School continued throughout the war. The students then went down to High Marley for their lessons. You had your lesson first so I had the opportunity *to hear you play and listen to the interesting comments of 'Uncle Tobbs'. You had already made a name in the profession, having won the 2nd prize in the Ysaye Piano Competition, in 1938, in Brussels, which only a year later took on the title of 'Queen Elizabeth Competition'. Emil Gilels, the Soviet artist, got the 1st prize, but, as he was not allowed to travel through Europe to fulfil his engagements, these came to you. Thus, your career took off, so to speak.*

I had, indeed, many opportunities to perform. I was in great demand both for concerts and for recordings. I gave the first performance of the Khatchaturian Piano Concerto outside USSR, which and I recorded it for Decca together with Rachmaninov's Preludes, issued in Europe for the first time.

The war was in full swing and I became known as an interpreter of Russian music, so much so, that I had to play the Khatchaturian, Tchiakovsky, and Rachmaninov Concertos again and again.

In 1956 I went to Russia with the London Philharmonic Orchestra, under Fistoulari, where I played the Khatchaturian, Tchiakovsky Concertos and Rachmaninov 'Paganini Variations', both in Moscow and in Leningrad, to capacity audiences. This was, indeed, an unforgettable experience. Another highlight of my career was performing the Khatchaturian Concerto under Khatchaturian himself. He conducted the London Philharmonic Orchestra at the Royal Albert Hall, in London, when David Oistrach played the Violin Concerto.

During the war, music played a very important role in keeping up the morale of the people. Myra Hess organised the famous National Gallery Lunch Hour Recitals, in London, which attracted large audiences even if the air raids were going on. I was privileged to play there many times and Myra and I became very great friends.

As I mentioned earlier, I was interested to see that in spite of your fame, you continued to have your lessons with Matthay.

Well, you know yourself what kind of teacher he was. He had genius and I can still say that one hour with Matthay meant more for me than all the years spent otherwise. His knowledge of the workings of the piano action, his understanding of the role of relaxation in piano playing, together with the use of arm-weight, his wisdom, all these have remained with me throughout my whole life as a pianist. What mattered to me was his approach to music. He did not teach me technique, he was interested only in music. Actually when I questioned this he simply answered: 'You have all the technique you need so let us get on with the music.' Yet, he was very concerned that I should experience fully the sensation of playing in a relaxed manner, particularly when practising. It was amusing sometimes when he would try to illustrate a point and I copied him, exactly, and he would remark, 'Why exaggerate the movements?' 'But, Uncle Tobbs, I tried to do exactly what you showed me.' 'Well, I exaggerated to make you understand better but... you don't have to be such a copy-cat, my dear!' and we both fell into a fit of laughter ... What I really learnt from him was how to produce a singing tone, the emphasis being always on beauty of tone and the importance for a performer to strive to produce sounds which are rich, warm and more and more beautiful. Talking about technique, he gave me some very important hints: to play always from the key surface, not with finger articulation, from high up, and he made me realise that the secret of secure big leaps from one end of the keyboard to the other is to be there a moment before playing.

I am very glad to hear you talk in such glowing terms about Matthay and his teaching. He seems to be rather under-rated, particularly in this country where there are still quite a few 'Matthay-ites', pupils of pupils of pupils of the great master, although in America there is even a 'Tobias Matthay Society', which holds at least one annual seminar and produce a newsletter with important information.

Yes, it is sad that his name is not what it should be. This may also be due to the fact that his books are rather difficult to read and understand. He was certainly a pioneer in his field of research and he was trying to make his theories clear to his readers but he must have been trying too hard to explain those new ideas and was worried that the people would misunderstand him. Hence, his attempt to over-explain.

It may be also the result of the generations of pupils' pupils who did not quite grasp the meaning of 'Matthay teaching of technique'. These were teachers who were satisfied to use the 'rotation' to the detriment of actual finger individuality. They did not bother to read his writings and accepted what their teachers showed them. I would like to add here that Dorothy Taubman – the well-known American teacher who has specialised in treating pianists' hands or arms injuries – bases her entire teaching on 'Matthay Rotation' for a healthy, free use of fingers, hands and arms. This seems to bring about a healing process, and pianists are able to go back to their instrument.

Who were your other teachers?

As a child I had lessons with Mathilde Verne, herself a pupil of Clara Schumann. From Mathilde Verne I learnt how to practise the Clara Schumann exercises. She believed in stretching exercises, lots and lots of scales and arpeggios, chords, octaves. When I have to play the Tchiakovsky Concerto I just play the Chopin etudes for octaves, repeating each one four times! And it does help if I play double thirds and sixths as a daily regimen. They are, indeed, very helpful for developing a sound technique and I owe to Matilde the foundation of my virtuosity. But, she also inspired me to be more aware of how to coax beautiful sounds from the piano, encouraging me to listen to every tone I produced, and she always talked about 'long lines' in phrases. Mathilde, and her sister Adele, became highly sought after piano teachers and they had several very talented children, real prodigies. One of them was Solomon who actually lived in their house and, according to him, was forced to spend the whole morning locked up in the room with the piano, practising what had been assigned to him. He never quite got over this ordeal, but he certainly 'made it', having been launched on the London scene at the age of eight.

In my case I just loved every moment of my lessons and I could spend hours and hours playing the piano. The little boy Solomon must have hated practising while I hated being away from the instrument. I did listen to my teacher who insisted that one should not practise for more than one hour, then stop, go for a walk or do something else, then play for another hour, getting four hours playing with periods of rest in between. This I have tried to do all my life and I found it very helpful. I feel that I am continually recharging my batteries.

After my London debut when I was twelve, I was accepted at the Royal Academy of Music, where I stayed until sixteen. My teacher was Ambrose Coviello, a pupil of Matthay. He actually wrote a booklet, *Explaining Matthay Principles*, but later on he turned against him.

Coviello had his own ideas on teaching relaxation in piano playing but I was perhaps too young to understand what he was aiming at. Later on I went to study with Matthay who was really the mentor I needed at the time.

When I left Uncle Tobbs — I settled in America with my husband — I went through a period of despondency. I had enough of being labelled as an 'interpreter of Russian music', a 'Romantic Virtuoso'. I wanted to be accepted as musician who plays the great works by Beethoven or Brahms and I felt I needed a great change in my attitude, in my work. Edward Steuerman came to New York and he soon made a great name both as a performer and as a teacher. I decided to study with him and this was another great experience. He had a highly intellectual approach, very Germanic in his attitude and tried to impose his musical ideas, so unlike Uncle Tobbs. I found myself at first out of my depth and felt like a fish out of water. His way of working with students was totally different from what I had been used to but then I realised that this was what I was lacking. When he played Beethoven it was so profound, so intense, and he brought great beauty and meaning to every note, every phrase, to the whole work. His lessons became very significant for me. I often remember his voice telling me to do exactly what the composer has written.

Before that, I sometimes played 'just as I felt', but with Steuerman you could not do so. If there was a crescendo mark leading to forte, it had to be done only as in the score, deciding how much volume of sound to give, how gradual the crescendo should be, then give every note its right intensity. When I expressed my doubts about whether one can play with great emotion, with all one's heart, when the mind is busy with the minutest detail he answered: 'What you have to do, Moura, is to study very intensely what is written and "put your heart" into playing it that way. This is the only way to make great, beautiful, and profound music.' He would sit in front of me while I was playing and I did play as he wanted me to. And it was very rewarding. It was interesting, though, that when he illustrated a point during the lesson his playing had greatness. But when he played in public he was under great strain, and sometimes this was noticeable, although the ideas were there, and the performances always had great intensity, and were meaningful.

When I was asked to make a recording of the Emperor Concerto for the Book of the Month Club, I spent the whole summer with Steuerman in Long Island. Unfortunately, I was given too short notice to prepare such a work. We worked just as he always insisted we should, but I gave a bad performance of it. I remembered Matthay's words then: 'You learn a work three times, and you only know it after the third time!'

My marriage did not last, so, after the divorce in 1967, I decided to come back to Europe, back to my career over here. To my great disappointment, when I went to my Italian agent, after only a few years in the States, she coldly stated, 'I am afraid you are completely forgotten. There are now a whole lot of whizzkids who are much in demand both by the public and the media.' I proudly walked out. I had to do something drastic – I am a fighter and would not accept defeat easily. I went back to my old studies, I got down to working hard at my technique, doing all the exercises just as during my student days. I realised that everything I learnt with Mathilde Verne, with Matthay, and with

Steuerman was still there, and everything came back to me magnified and enriched. Now, my whole approach was on a different plane – I had been rethinking my way of playing. If you want to grow as an artist you have to think and rethink constantly. It was really only then that everything acquired new meaning, new depths. Perhaps this was due to the shock of finding myself not wanted as an artist, or because I had to rely entirely on myself and I was playing the way I wanted, the way I thought music should be expressed, and not as I 'was told' to do. This change had a salutary effect on my playing, my performances received rave reviews everywhere, in Europe as well as in the United States, and I was once again where I wanted to be.

A few years ago I had another bad bout. I had to be operated on twice, the muscles under the left arm had to be severed and I had to do special exercises to regain mobility and to be able to stretch my arm. The surgeon assured me that within three months everything would come back to normal and I should be able to play again.

The physiotherapist worked with me patiently, every day, trying to help me move my hand with the palm on the wall, a little bit higher every time until, at last, my arm could stretch with ease. Only two months after my operation, Emmy Tillett, my agent and great friend, offered me an important engagement: 'You are strong Moura, you can do it'. I listened to her and, in my enthusiasm, I couldn't wait to start playing, practising for four hours every day – but I soon had to give up. I had no energy, no physical strength. I started to cry bitterly, and I called my doctor, telling him, 'What can I do? I think I am finished. I can't play anymore', to which he replied, 'You were told that after three months you will go back to your piano not after two months. Do not give a concert before the three months are up.' And, indeed, exactly three months to the day, I was playing Prokofiev's Concerto No. 4 for the left hand at the Royal Festival Hall. I sent tickets to my surgeon who came to hear me. 'I nearly had a heart attack when I received your invitation,' he remarked, 'to play with your left arm so soon after surgery!' And it was a triumph, both physically and artistically. It was a question of mind over matter, but it was also my determination as I had no intention of giving up, and if I was going to live I just had to get on with it and do the work I was meant to do. I have experienced a resurgence of my whole career and here I am totally reborn. And I know that my playing has reached new, different dimensions.

This is, indeed, very noticeable. When you were young your playing had all the virtuosity, the energy and youthfulness that impressed the audiences. Now there is more depth — there is a transcendental quality which is immediately communicated. How do you explain this phenomenon?

Thank you for saying this. I sometimes hear my old recordings and if I am asked whether I have changed my interpretations, my answer is 'not really'. I find these recordings very well played, my intentions are there, but, when I play the same works now, perhaps I do not play them as well as I did, 'though I am playing them more beautifully' – to paraphrase Schnabel. When he had to re-do the recording of the opening of Beethoven's Piano Concerto in G, he exclaimed, 'I may play it better, but not so well!'

I recently played the Rachmaninov Third Piano Concerto in Pasadena, California, and while playing, I experienced an extraordinary liberation. All I sensed was the flow of the music, one melodic line after another. I gave to this performance my whole being, experiencing climax after climax and it was not only a communion with the audience, but also with the whole orchestra; we became one, as if we were one soul and one body. The same great experience happened when I performed the Emperor Concerto, which I am going to play three times in Dallas, Texas, in June (also part of my birthday celebrations).

All I can say is that whenever I perform I give so much of my whole being. I feel the music so intensely that afterwards I am utterly drained, and my clothes are soaked as if I had entered a pool completely dressed. Yet, I emerge exhilarated from and by such an experience.

Future plans? As you may see, I intend go on playing and loving it.

Piano Journal VOL 12 NO 35 1991

215

Andras Schiff

Talking to Andras Schiff, one of the leading pianists of his generation, is not as straightforward as any other interview. He seems to enjoy creating an argument, and I found myself debating with him instead of thinking what my next question ought to be. He is rather boyish in appearance; small of stature, with an innocent, sometimes ironic smile on his face – especially when he makes provocative remarks, such as: 'How can one enjoy playing Bach on that un-singing instrument – the harpsichord?' At times, these asides could appear almost absurdly intolerant: 'I know many conductors without any proper background, who cannot read a score at the piano – and are even quite proud of it.'

There is no wonder that this highly-acclaimed pianist and consummate musician is so demanding of the young musicians who come to his classes. He has dedicated his whole life to all aspects of music-making – chamber music, accompanying, directing orchestras from the keyboard, devising festivals with unusual programmes devoted to one composer or to a particular period, and, in recent years, doing quite a bit of teaching in masterclasses. For his memorable Haydn Festival at Wigmore Hall, London (1988), he received the first Royal Philharmonic Society/Charles Heidsieck Award, and, in his own country, Hungary, the Bartok Prize, the highest musical distinction. Andras Schiff's achievements stretch over several continents, and his repertoire is just as vast – Bach, Schumann, Brahms, and Bartok in the twentieth century, although he tends not to go beyond Debussy. He is idiosyncratic in his tastes. He loves Debussy, but does not play Ravel. As to Liszt, not only does he not share the adulation of so many Lisztians throughout the world, nor the cult understandably developed in Hungary, but he likes to state, quite emphatically, that he has never played one piece by this composer. 'I am unsuited spiritually and physically to this type of music, and my hands are actually much too small.' For Bach or the classics, he thinks that his hands are actually an advantage, his narrow fingers getting more easily between the black keys. Yet, when asked how could he cope with majestic works like concertos by Brahms or Bartok, his smile came back with a typical remark: 'If I really love a work, I do find the way to play it. I think only of the music and what I want to convey, and my arms and hands just follow my intentions.'

You are in great demand to give masterclasses in many European cities, and you have been associated for several years with the prestigious International Musicians Seminars in Cornwall, England, where many musicians gather for the sheer love of music-making. Do you find teaching a rewarding experience?

The International Musicians' Seminars is one of the most fascinating places, and I am very happy to be associated with it. At first, these seminars were devised around the personality of Sandor Vegh, only for string players, but gradually they extended, and pianists and composers like Gyorgy Kurtag are also on the faculty. While I am convinced that artists should spend part of their life working with young musicians, to pass on to the new generations what they have learnt themselves, I have some mixed feelings about teaching and about the role of the teacher in general. The main question is: What can be taught and what cannot be taught?

I am also very concerned about the attitude of today's young people, an attitude which is reflected in every other area, not just in music. Maybe I am too conservative, but I do not approve of the antiauthority, rather rebellious behaviour of so many youngsters. In my student's days at the Budapest Music Academy, there was a 'threestep' distance between teacher and students, and we all revered our masters. These days there is too much familiarity, students even call their teachers by their first name and, so often, they lack humility which is inherent in an artist.

Furthermore, the majority of pianists who attend my classes seem to have false ambitions, they are so intent upon making a career that they lose any sense of direction, which should be guided primarily by a love of music and by the desire to become a musician. Their goal is to learn a number of piano pieces required for competitions, then try to win some prizes as a stepping stone towards making a name. At the International Musicians Seminars we have totally different ideals. We teach music as an entity and we want to be involved in music-making of the highest calibre. We do not categorise performers in pigeon-holes such as, 'this one should be a soloist, the other one would be more suited to chamber music, another one to specialise in concerto performances', and so on. A real musician is one who feels that he is fulfilled when making music with other dedicated artists. I think that there are many quite good performers amongst pianists, although there are so many different levels even among them. There are those who actually succeed in competitions, winning not only one prize but several, yet they do no quite make it in the profession. What is the reason for this? First of all, there are far too many competitions, but only very few carry the prestige of launching yet another pianist on to the already overcrowded profession. The answer is that what audiences expect from an artist is rather different from the requirements imposed by competitions. The audiences cannot be fooled by artifices. Only when a young musician has a message, has something to offer, then, and only then, the audience will accept him.

What about your own career? Did you take part in competitions yourself?

Yes, of course. This was the thing to do, and, as far as I know, young pianists were encouraged by their teachers or by their music academies to do so. An important prize would bring extra glamour to that particular institution. When I was 21 I did the Tchaikovsky, and I was placed fourth. At 19 I tried for the Leeds (1972), but I only made it to the second round. I did not mind in the least, it was an interesting experience and I thought that Murray Perahia certainly deserved the first prize. I took part once again, in 1975. I was fortunate, though, that my career took off in spite of not having won first prizes.

I was not a prodigy but I was accepted when I was a young boy at the Liszt Music Academy where I had several most wonderful teachers. Pal Kadosa, the Head of Piano, a pupil of the revered Toman, was also a composer, and I was privileged to study with him all the different styles from Monteverdi to our time, including his own music. Kadosa had several assistants, all outstanding young musicians. Among them was Gyorgy Kurtag, who fascinated me with his revolutionary music and the type of workshops he gave, encouraging young pupils to improvise, to compose, to create. I studied with him for 10 years, and a great deal of what I know and what I am as a musician, I owe to him. Whilst in the Music Academy I did some teaching, working for three years with students in the chamber music department. These three years taught me perhaps more than it taught my students. For me it was a revealing experience, and I am convinced that my love of chamber music started at that time. Working with Kurtag also made me realise what great teaching means. I make no concessions, no compromises. I have an idea and an ideal of how a piece should sound, and I expect to hear that from whoever sits down and plays it. A good teacher is one who treats each pupil individually, working with the same intensity and honesty at whatever level. It is not only that I cannot do it, but I would not know how to do it. Kurtag, on the contrary, finds teaching very much a part of his work and life: composing, conducting workshops, playing, teaching – all these are one. Yet, he does not compromise either. He can find something wonderful in the playing of an amateur, and he would not be satisfied with a very advanced pianist until the music has meaning. Kurtag's contribution to music education and to music in general is enormous, and it must be such fun for children to experience that freedom of expression through their own creation. Of course, a technical foundation is vital, but this should not be separated from music, and here lies Kurtag's strength. Mechanical exercises do not inspire a child; on the contrary, they turn him away.

I am often asked by young pianists to teach them on a regular basis. This I do not do, but I am willing to listen to them and give them advice. They also ask which teacher I would recommend. In the first case, I am trying to be as honest as possible. In most cases I say: 'Let us put this right, now....' If the pianist hopes to become professional and he has not got that great talent and the other qualities to go with it, I have to say so. But, if he wants to study music and learn to play the great works of piano literature, then, yes, I do encourage him, and I am happy to go through some works together. And if such a work could help a person find a greater satisfaction in making music, then I am also satisfied. As to recommending a teacher, I don't find this easy. The relationship between a young pianist and a teacher is a very sensitive area. I know quite a few wonderful artists, but how can I say, 'you must study with so and so?' My sincere advice is that one should learn to listen much more intently to oneself, to listen to every sound one makes. This is a way to teach oneself.

Some of them need to develop a better technique, to have the tools to interpret the masterpieces, others need to develop their understanding of these works. In each case, if one listens to the sounds both in the imagination and afterwards to hear if what the piano produces is what one intended, there is no better lesson than this. A real technique involves how you produce a tone, the sound on the piano, and what kind of sound to produce. Every individual produces his/her personal sound, like one's signature. Even if several pianists have studied with the same teacher, each one creates a different atmosphere, produces different timbres. It is a fallacy to talk about a specific 'piano school' when there is a question of the personality and the temperament of the artist. Indeed, my teachers were very demanding. If anyone in the class played a note with an unpleasant tone, or if that note was out of line in the phrase, the rest of the lesson was spent on discussing just that. Thus, I became very self-critical. You have to know what you want to do, you have to want to do it, and this means, what kind of sound, what dynamics, what colours, how many different colours you would want to bring into the motif, the phrase. And this is very much a question of imagination, of sensitivity, of fantasy.

I am afraid the subtleties of an interpretation can only be perceived fully in a live performance. The recordings, no matter how advanced the technology, do not reproduce the finest nuances; somehow the microphone catches the 'dynamic nuances' which get pressed into the disc. When one hears the old recordings of Cortot, Lipatti, or Schnabel, one cannot but marvel at their amazingly beautiful tone, and one can hear an extraordinary variety of colour, each artist with a unique timbre. I never had the privilege of hearing them myself, but those who have actually heard these great artists say the recordings cannot compare with their live performances.

Yet, you have done many recordings and continue to do so. How do you explain your ambiguous attitude?

In spite of the limitations, recordings have many positive aspects, and also present many advantages. It is not only to maintain the name of an artist in the public eye, and ears. In my own case, recording companies give me great freedom to choose what I want to record; thus, I have completed a cycle with all Mozart's piano concertos (with the Camerata Academica Salzburg), concertos by Mendelssohn, Schumann, Chopin No.1 and Brahms No.1, and other discs with singers like Robert Holl and Peter Schreier. Among solo works, I have recorded Bach's English Suites (which received the 1990 Grammy award), all Mozart's piano sonatas – and my next project is to record all Schubert's sonatas, which I am starting soon. This explains why I go on making records, as well as my loyalty to my company, Decca.

What I object to, though, is the type of editing that goes on in the studios. You may hear some very good performances on record, and you know very well that some of the pianists on the labels would never be able to play those works in the same way. The art of a musician is to play a work in its entirety, not in separate bits, doing continuously some repairs. I want a recording to represent what you are actually doing.

On the other hand, don't you think that it is of value for students and for those who cannot easily go to concerts to have some good recordings in their own homes, so that they can listen again and again to what you actually admit are 'perfect performances'?

Frankly, I would rather that they study the scores again and again, and not sit by their stereo for hours and then imitate very faithfully their models. This is not the best way to grow into a musician.

Your concert tours, recordings, and other engagements in one single year seem to exceed the number of days in that year. There are already advance notices of your projects for next season, to include performances of all Schubert sonatas in six recitals which will then be repeated in seven cities throughout the world. You will also continue with your various festivals, masterclasses, concerto appearances. What is your recipe for coping with the stress of such an existence?

I think each one of us finds special ways to deal with this type of existence which, after all, is our choice. I do try to spend some time in one place; I have several 'homes', with good pianos where I can work consistently, unless I wish to take a break. I also am able to relax in between engagements, and I am careful about what I eat. The true answer is that I must love what I am doing, otherwise I couldn't do it. I always loved playing in public, and actually I play better when I have an audience. I am inspired to give all I can to bring the essence of the works I play as a homage to the composer and, at the same time, as an offering to my listeners.

As an artist you, surely, have experienced those magical moments when the performance acquires new supreme dimensions. What do you feel about such phenomena?

I don't really know. I do not wish to appear mystical, but I believe that such moments are very mysterious, they are truly spiritual phenomena. Perhaps this is what one calls inspiration, but there is much more to it. In these times of exaggerated scientific approach to everything, one might try to study this phenomenon. But, I find these experiences so powerful, so intense, that I would even be afraid to analyse them. I can only say that at such moments, in our little way, when we perform a masterpiece, something extraordinary occurs, something which does not happen in the studio. Perhaps it is the greatness of the work, together with the inspiration one receives from the audience, which creates such a response. But, how can one know? All I can say is that these occasional experiences remain in my memory for a long time afterwards, and I wonder how they happen, yet, I think that it is a good thing that they do not occur every time one performs. No, I would not want to feel that the moment I start playing, the magical moment will be there. I like to know that, after all, I am responsible for what I intend to do, and for what I am doing. Above all, I want to be sure that I have done my 'homework' with all my power, in all honesty, and that I am ready to face my public.

Piano Journal VOL 12 NO 36 1991

Melvyn Tan

Over the past decade, you have helped to bring the fortepiano to the attention of many music-lovers throughout the world, and you are now internationally renowned, in demand for performances, masterclasses, and recordings. I heard you for the first time about ten years ago, when you gave a demonstration at the Colt Collection on the launching of a splendid book about their instruments (Stainer & Bell). You played works of different periods on the respective instruments. And what fine performances you gave! You must have started to play the piano very early, like most children in the part of the world where you came from, in Singapore.

Yes, I started to play when I was four years old because my sister, who was ten years older, was having lessons, and I got so interested in her playing that I tried to pick up by ear all her pieces. When my parents realised that I was really so keen they asked the teacher to give me lessons as well. And this is how I began my exciting years at the piano. When I was about eleven, we had a visitor to the house, and she heard me play. She was an Air Hostess, a great lover of music, and she offered to help me by taking a tape with some of my pieces to London to the recently established Yehudi Menuhin School for talented youngsters. There was great commotion in our home to get a tape recorder to record my playing in our front room. We were anxiously waiting to hear from the school and, indeed, two months later, my parents received a cable letting them know that I was offered a scholarship, and that I should arrive as soon as possible. Our good friend found a sponsor for me, as the scholarship did not pay for all my expenses while living away from home. This is how my real training started. The staff did everything to make us young people feel good, having to cope with an entirely new way of life, as well as being so homesick, since most of us were separated from out parents for the first time. But, there were many compensations. There was so much music-making, a lot of homework for various subjects, many new and very interesting, and

223

also, being with other children, all committed to their instrument. I was also very pleased that there was another pupil from Singapore with whom I have remained friends to this day. And there were the wonderful and inspiring lessons with artists like Marcel Ciampi, who came every month from Paris, and his assistant, Denise Riviere, apart from my regular lessons with a young teacher, Barbara Kerslade, who helped me through the years I stayed at the school. There was also Peter Norris, who, as Director of Music, looked after the chamber music groups, the orchestra, and, in general, arranged for visiting artists to conduct masterclasses, such as Vlado Perlemutter, who taught us the Romantics (Chopin, Schumann) and French composers (Ravel, Debussy, Fauré) or Nadia Boulanger, who insisted that we all played the 'Forty-eight'. These classes were invaluable, and I left the school when I was about 19 with a good foundation to make a career as a pianist.

I was accepted at the Royal College of Music to study with Angus Morrison, a very fine pianist and an inspiring teacher, who thought that I would make a good romantic pianist and he gave me a lot of Liszt (which I hated, but, being an obedient student did not dare say so), but also many French works, as he had made a name with his interpretations of Debussy, Ravel, and other French composers. It is customary in English music colleges for students to take a 'second study', and I was very interested in conducting. Sadly, I was not allowed to do it, as conducting could not be included as a 'second study', and I thought of taking up the harpsichord, an instrument which would use a great deal of the piano repertoire: early music, Baroque and Classical. I started absolutely from scratch, learning about the action, which is so different from that of the piano, and the technique, and playing entirely new repertoire. Strangely enough, neither at the YMS nor at the RCM was I guided towards the great classics, Haydn, Mozart, Beethoven. I did study Bach; I played some of the 'Forty-eight', but no other early composers or the classics. I should mention, in fairness, that one of the new young piano teachers, Simon Nicholls, did give to his pupils works by Mozart and Beethoven, but I was not working with him. In a way, this was a good thing, as I came to these works with a completely fresh mind, with no pre-conceived ideas, and playing them on this new instrument fascinated me. My teacher was Millicent Silver who introduced me to the French composers, Couperin and Rameau among them, and to many other Baroque works, and I became more and more interested in early music. I then went to study with Ruth Dyson, who developed my harpsichord technique even further. By that time, I was invited to give a number of concerts, both on the piano and on the harpsichord, and I started to make a name as a harpsichord player. I did a lot of practising in the two magical places, the Colt Collection and the Finchcock Museum, where I was allowed to play on any of their amazing instruments. Thus, I discovered the fortepiano, which I found more and more satisfying. And this is really how it all started. I was still a student at RCM when I decided to enter a new competition, the Overseas League Competition for musicians from the UK and the Commonwealth (Singapore was not yet independent!), and I won the First Prize for Harpsichord in 1977, and this event really decided the direction of my career. Not that this competition had, at the time, important repercussions, but it so happened that in the jury was an outstanding musician, Ellena Warren, who worked for BBC Radio 3, and who recommended me to one of her colleagues, the producer Paul Hamburger. Thanks to her, I did not even have to pass an audition, and I was engaged for my first broadcast, a Lunch Hour Recital on the harpsichord. This was such an important event for me, and I was greatly excited when another Radio 3 producer, Clive Bennett, offered me a series of broadcasts with lesser known composers: Dussek, Clementi, Haydn, and others, and he also encouraged me to play them on the fortepiano. I became greatly involved with the sound and the nature of the instrument, which I found fascinating. I still do.

How did you find building up a career as harpsichordist and then as a fortepiano player when you started in the late Seventies? There were hardly any fortepianists at that time, when audiences had not yet been exposed to the timbre of the instrument and it was, indeed, very enterprising of the BBC to present a series of broadcasts with early works on historical instruments.

I was already getting quite a few concerts, but I could not command the fees I am getting now. Neither the harpsichord nor the fortepiano were what I would call popular instruments, and it took nearly ten years to be where I am now. I had to supplement my income with teaching, which I always found stimulating. I gave harpsichord classes at the Morley College, and I also taught fortepiano at the Royal Academy of Music for two years, but there were so few students interested in this instrument, and I also had a few private students. Playing chamber music was always very rewarding for me, and I had a Baroque Group, playing the harpsichord, and later a Fortepiano Trio with John Holloway and Susan Shepherd which was very successful, and enhanced my career.

But it was only when I was offered a recording contract that my career really took off. I then had much more solo and concerto work, and

I could cut down on my less rewarding activities, although I still do some private teaching and conduct masterclasses in many countries. I still do some chamber music. For instance, tomorrow I am giving a concert with the outstanding cellist, Stephen Isserlis, when I shall play on an 1838 fortepiano. I also accompany several singers in songs by Mozart, Haydn, or exquisite Lieder by Schubert and Schumann.

Lately I took up conducting, which I always was interested in. I formed my own orchestra, together with a colleague, using young instrumentalists who are very keen to work with me. We have been playing together for over a year, and have already made our first recording, which will be issued next September, with two Mozart concertos, which I conduct from the keyboard.

I intend to record all of the Mozart concertos, but I am not hurrying. I shall do two, perhaps three, in one year – not only because I do not wish to rush through this task, but also because, beside my many other commitments, I prefer to have a period of time in between, to allow the works to mature in my own mind before recording them. I also like to perform a concerto several times, in different places, in the UK or abroad, as this helps to create the needed unity of the orchestra itself.

Conducting from the keyboard must be a new experience for you, as you have been so much a soloist all these years. How did you adapt to this situation?

Surprisingly well. I always approach the Mozart concertos as chamber music, with the soloist very much part of the texture, and this makes it easier to perform really 'without a conductor'. I place my instrument in such a way that I am facing the audience while the players are seated around me, with the wind players right behind me so that they can see my hands. This is crucial for the ensemble, as wind players are apt to enter early or late, if there is no conductor, thus there are no such problems for us. Of course, the Concert Master assists me when I have to play some of the solo sections, but, on the whole, it is a most enjoyable experience for me and, I like to think, for the other players.

What happens when you take the ensemble on tour? Do you take the full orchestra?

No, I only take up to twenty-four players – four violins, four violas, four cellos, and so on. Working together intensely during a tour – as, for instance, last year we had a long run through Hong Kong and other

226

places – we grow more and more as a unit and we develop a truly co-herent sound. All of them are such good and responsive players!

You seem to be continually searching for new grounds to expand your musical activities, and you give yourself new challenges all the time. First the series of Mozart concertos with your own orchestra and, recently, another 'marathon' – all Beethoven's sonatas! This is indeed a very daring enterprise, and it would be interesting to know how your instruments stand up to the later works, such as the Hammerklavier Sonata or Op. 111!

I would not have started the series if I were not confident that I am capable of bringing it off as I would want to.

I shall, of course, use the later instruments which were developed after 1770, from a small fortepiano to one of six and a half and seven octaves by 1845. I shall choose one which has more strength to sustain the needed sonorities, possibly one built as late as 1825, rather than one from the time when Beethoven wrote the *Hammerklavier*. What Beethoven was trying to do was to stretch the instrument to its limits, and that is why piano makers started to respond to these demands. It is only by 1825 that the fortepianos became bigger, stronger and heavier.

I have four instruments myself: one, a copy of the Nanette Streicher by Derek Adlam, an English maker; another by Johann Streicher, Nanette's son, dating from 1835, and two Broadwoods, both from about 1840; thus I have quite a good choice. But, I can always choose my instruments from the two English collections, or even from abroad when I need a special one.

On the other hand, playing the 'Thirty-two' in a series of recitals at the Wigmore Hall, is another great responsibility, and I want to do the best I can. I have already done two recitals playing the earlier ones, which, at present, suit me and my instrument. The project covers Beethoven's entire development and, to do it justice, I shall take my time, as I am doing with the Mozart concertos. This year I am doing a group of sonatas, next year I shall do another group, but I shall leave the late sonatas only until I have gained a great deal of experience in presenting only Beethoven programmes. I shall then try to play them in different places, and I will not record them as a whole until I shall feel satisfied that the sonatas have grown and matured in myself, in my mind, and that I can be ready for it. What I intend to do first is to start playing the later works sometime in November, in various recitals, and then I shall leave them and come back to them later on.

We have covered a wide range of aspects of your career. You have done many years of teaching, and you are still working with a number of students privately. Do you find that more pianists are taking up the fortepiano?

One can say that there is a sort of revival, there is greater interest in early music and in the use of authentic, historical instruments. There are also special courses in Music Colleges both at undergraduate and postgraduate levels, and consequently there is also a growing audience for this type of music. I do think that all pianists ought to try to play the classical repertoire on a fortepiano, occasionally. They would realise what sounds, what sonorities the composers heard in their mind. I myself often find that on the fortepiano I hear certain effects which seem more logical than if I would play the same work on the modern piano. I am convinced that this would open new vistas for their interpretations, as they would gain a historical conception of these works.

Now that there are more fortepianists and harpsichordists in the profession, what are their chances to participate in competitions, as we all know that winning an important prize is good for one's career. Are there any such competitions?

There are still only a few, for obvious reasons. There are not enough players to set up such events, as these are costly, and need a great deal of organising and financial support. Another reason is that the forte-pianists who are good and are already getting engagements, making a name in the profession, may not wish to take part. There is also the strain and the tension associated with such exercises. Besides, the players have to be concerned not only with their own performances, but also with their instrument and when they can stop to tune it. The most important competitions are: the *Festival-Estival*, in Paris, which includes both instruments, and the Bruges which alternates, one year for the harpsichord and the next for the fortepiano – and these give players the opportunity to be heard in the right places by the right people.

Talking of the strain of competitions, what about your jet-set life, travelling from one corner of the world to the other performing, giving masterclasses, making recordings? How do you cope with it?

This is, indeed, a most demanding life, physically, mentally, and spiritually – and one has to be really tough. I was fortunate that at Yehudi Menuhin School all of us had regular Alexander Technique lessons with an excellent teacher who was an ex-runner. Thus, he had great understanding of the needs of the body for exercise as well as relaxation. He helped us greatly to develop an awareness of the state of the body while practising and in performance, but above all to be concerned with physical and mental wellbeing, by keeping fit. This awareness has always been with me during my student years, and since having joined the profession. I am constantly concerned with my wellbeing: I swim a lot every day, and I do not allow myself to overspend my energies. It is important for an artist to be more rational and careful and know when to stop, to maintain our strength. Our career demands that we prove ourselves every time we appear in concert, even if we are tired or unhappy for whatever reasons. We have to be always on top of everything.

I try to help my students to develop this awareness of the way their muscles function, not to misuse them, particularly as most of them went through the same transition as I did, changing from the modern piano to the fortepiano. This is bound to cause some psychological conflicts as well as physical problems. But, starting from scratch, they learn everything about the new instrument gradually and there is no danger.

For me, this is the life I have chosen and I am giving all of myself to it.

Piano Journal VOL 14 NO 41 1993

Gaby Casadesus

You grew up in Paris at a time when French music was at its height. Pianists like Marguerite Long were giving first performances of Debussy and Fauré piano music; Robert Casadesus and Vlado Perlemuter were devoting entire recitals to Ravel's music; Alfred Cortot and Edouard Risler were known as great interpreters of Romantic music; and Risler had the audacity to perform all of the Beethoven sonatas — an unheard of event; Fauré was making an impact both as a composer and as a teacher, with many great artists falling under his spell such as Thibaud and Enesco — to mention only these few artists who dominated the musical scene.

This is quite true. Although I was only twelve when I entered Marguerite Long's Preparatory Class at the Conservatoire, I found myself almost immediately in the midst of all this, going to concerts and meeting some of the greatest artists who were her friends. I had my first piano lessons with my mother, herself a fine musician, who taught me until I entered the Conservatoire.

She actually took me to Cortot hoping that he would accept me in his class, but he had no vacancies at the time and suggested that I study with Marguerite Long who was at the beginning of her career. She had just started to teach, and already had a group of talented young pupils.

Her guidance was just right for us. She was very demanding, insisting on a daily preparation of technique, then we studied Bach as well as the French *clavecinistes*, wanted us to became acquainted with the composers of 'our time', especially the French musicians. She held 'Musical Afternoons' when we were all encouraged to play in front of her distinguished guests. On one of these occasions Ravel announced his visit and each one of us had to prepare a piece by him.

I played *Jeux d'Eaux* and to these days I still remember his interesting remarks which I wrote down in my score: 'Not to slow down, keep the same tempo and think of the piece as a happy, lively one'. On another afternoon she invited the celebrated professor Louis Diemer, and, after I

230

played for him, he told Marguerite Long that he would accept me as a student. Thus, I found myself, at the age of fourteen, in the so-called 'senior' Conservatoire, and at fifteen, while still a student, I obtained my *Premier Prix*, the highest examination at the Paris Conservatoire. It was very interesting for me to be in Diemer's class which until then had male students. Mixed classes were not allowed but, due to the war, there were fewer boys and more girls; thus this ridiculous rule had to be abandoned.

Many young musicians obtained their Premier Prix at very early ages — Robert at thirteen, you at fifteen, and this was not unusual for talented youngsters. What happened to these very young musicians once they finished the Conservatoire? Were they launched on a concert career immediately or were they encouraged to continue their studies with some celebrated 'masters' in France or abroad?

One must remember that Paris was a great musical centre and there were quite a few opportunities for us young players to be invited to appear in 'salons', where the elite of music lovers, connoisseurs, and even critics, came. These often led to engagements for recitals in Paris or in the provinces where music was flourishing. Even orchestral concerts were not too difficult to obtain.

Competitions were not so much a part of the usual musical activities as they are these days, but I had the luck to win one of these, the *Prix Paris Pagé* in 1924, when a very wealthy lady decided to offer a prize to a woman pianist.

Oddly enough, Robert had been the winner, a few years earlier, of the 'Louis Diener Prize' for men only! My new award brought more exposure for me and I was invited to give many recitals. In my programmes I included French music as well as Classical and Romantic. Saint-Saëns, Debussy, Ravel, Fauré but also Casadesus compositions. I liked to present a balanced programme with a wide range of styles, from the *clavecinistes*, through Classical and Romantic composers, to what we considered at the time 'modern'.

The type of 'specialised' programmes were not in fashion, although pianists like Risler dared present entire Beethoven evenings on the *integrale* of Chopin, while Perlemuter and Casadesus gave entire Ravel evenings

There were very exciting times for me as I was also invited to be the soloist with the established orchestras : *Pas de Loup, L'Amoureux, Colonne*, in concertos by French composers, Saint-Saëns and Ravel, the Fauré *Ballade*, occasionally asking me to play a Mozart concerto which I always loved playing.

I often think of my first rehearsal with the orchestra when I was surrounded by all those instruments and heard the 'real thing'. Until then Robert was playing the orchestral part on the second piano and I was so fascinated by those timbres which inspired me to respond in a totally different way.

Robert and I started to play a great deal together and our Duo was getting quite well known.Yet,I wanted to study and learn more about piano playing. Moskowsky was a celebrated pianist whose compositions I often included in my recital programmes and I had some lessons with him.

Then I decided to study with Edouard Risler who was a truly outstanding musician. He inspired me greatly and I gained a new insight into my playing of the great classics, although I also loved working with him on Chopin and other composers.

At that time there was another pianist who played an important role in my life. Cortot was conducting his famous classes at the *Ecole Normale* which attracted pianists from all over the world. Taking part in his masterclasses, when he discussed the technical aspects in the minutest details and listening to his magical performances, of Schumann, in particular, were unforgettable experiences. He was, I believe, the first great pedagogue to discuss the use of arm-weight and relaxation in piano playing. This was new to me – as in my previous training the accent was mainly on finger technique. Thanks to Cortot, my piano playing developed gained more ample sonorities and a wider tonal range.

You and Robert devoted much of your life to teaching – both privately and in Conservatories, principally at the American School at Fontainebleau, whose extraordinary reputation owed much to Robert's very popular masterclasses. How did you cope with so much teaching while carrying on with your concerts as well as having to look after your children?

I believe the attitude of French artists is different from that of colleagues in other countries. In France, most artists consider it an honour to be appointed professors at the Paris Conservatoire or at higher institutions like the *Ecole Normale*, Scuola Cantorum, or at National Conservatories. Combining the performing and pedagogical careers seems natural.

It is also true that we were not yet living in the 'jet era'. We travelled at leisure, we had time to rest between concerts and, although some distances took a long time to cover, there was not the stress of these days. We were also surrounded by people who helped us with the children, and the household duties, thus we could devote ourselves entirely to our music, more so in Robert's case, since he was travelling every-where in Europe and the States.

In my case, the situation changed when I started my family. I could not travel with Robert as easily as before, but we still managed to appear as a Duo which achieved quite a reputation.

I stayed at home more and more so I took a number of pupils and found teaching very stimulating. I tried to give my students a thorough foundation, just as I had received. I became very interested to find out which particular approach to teaching would have the best results.

Marguerite Long had a very systematic approach and I realised that a well-organised programme of studying was most effective. I then devised a set of daily exercises which I also practised myself and which my pupils actually enjoyed especially when they realised how much these helped them progress very fast. Although some of today's pedagogues do not believe in regular exercises and studies, I am convinced of their efficacy in building a thorough virtuoso technique.

In my whole artistic career I have met and heard many outstanding pianists and other instrumentalists and all of them, without exception, acknowledged that they had been brought up on similar ideas. Robert often said that the hand must be fully trained by the age of twelve to reach the highest degree of virtuosity. After this age it is difficult to obtain the same results as the bones and joints do not respond with the same flexibility.

While having to stay at home to look after the children, my first born, Jean, started to show great interest in playing the piano. We thought it best for me to teach him regularly, supervising his practice every day while Robert would give him a 'special' lesson once a month. We both believed that it was only right that a child should have lessons with his parents – just as we did. I was taught by my mother for several years, until I entered Marguerite Long Preparatory Class. She was a good pianist herself and taught at the Conservatoire in Algiers, where I had spent the first seven years of my life. Robert had been taught by an Aunt, also an accomplished pianist, who actually brought him up – as he never knew his mother. He grew up in a family of very fine musicians, and even after he got his *Premier Prix* he continued to have lessons with his aunt.

Our little Jean loved his lessons, and was a serious pupil. Once a month, Robert gave him a lesson and the boy looked forward to this special day with great excitement. At this early age he seemed to have realised that music was very important for his parents and he accepted this as a part of his life also. His progress was such that it prompted

Robert to remark one day, jokingly: 'It looks as if our Duo will soon become a Trio!' This actually did happen when, years later, we recorded the Mozart Triple Concerto.

The American School at Fontainebleau was by now an important centre of studies for pianists. Robert accepted the post of director, yet continued to hold his celebrated masterclasses devoted to a specific composer, or to just one work. He ended the class with a recital which included the works studied, a perfect illustration of how these should be played. I also managed to teach some of the students when I could get away from the family. The school continued to flourish, but this had to stop when the Second World War broke out.

What did you do when Paris fell under the Nazi occupation and the School had to be closed?

We were very fortunate to be on a tour of concerts in America and, when our friends heard what had happened in France, they urged us to stay. We could not attempt to cross the Atlantic with three children, thus the best solution was to start a new life over there. This was a sad decision, we missed France and our friends so much, but we thought that it was necessary. There were ample opportunities for both of us – Robert's reputation brought more and more engagements throughout the States. He gave many concerts and masterclasses in Music Faculties in which I often joined, as well as participating in Duo concerts.

We then had the idea to open the American Piano School of Fontainebleau over there, and, through a series of favourable circumstances, we arrived in Newport, Massachusetts, where we found suitable premises for our new venture. This did not take long to develop, many students coming from all over the USA and we adjusted well to our new situation. But, in our hearts we were longing for the end of that terrible war so that we could return to our beloved home in Paris.

We came back in 1946 and almost immediately we started our old way of life. We had only one goal – to reopen the school at Fontainebleau. In our excitement we thought that this could happen the next day, so to speak, but it was not that easy. However, gradually it got into shape and students began to cross the Atlantic, anxious to continue their studies with Robert. Other great musical personalities – Isidore Philipp and Nadia Boulanger among them – were invited to join us, maintaining the prestige of the school. Nadia stayed on until she died at the age of 92.

You and Robert have recorded solo works and concertos as well as a Duo. Do you think that recordings are necessary for artists?

I certainly do. In our case, recordings have been so much a part of our life togeth First, there were the 78s, then the LPs, and now, with the arrival of CDs, Classical music can reach more and more people – especially the young ones – in supermarkets or big stores. Thus artists get greater exposure, and their names are on everyone's lips. For me, Robert's recordings are more than simple discs. Each one marks a specific moment, a special time vividly imprinted on my mind. Especially precious to me is the recording of the Mozart Triple Concerto with our son Jean who was killed in an accident only a few months before Robert's death. Jean had grown into a very sensitive pianist and left a number of other recordings, including one of Chabrier's piano music. I have lost these two most wonderful people of my life and it is great for me to feel their presence when listening to these recordings.

They are also a solace for me, as music helps me to carry on with my busy life as, although advanced in age, I still do some teaching but only in masterclass situation and I am still sitting on juries in competitions. I find it very rewarding, especially when – on rare moments – I hear an original talent waiting to be discovered.

I am now devoting a lot of my time and energies to the Casadesus International Piano Competition in Cleveland, which I dedicate to Robert's teaching and his compositions. Hearing the many young competitors playing Robert's works makes me feel more in touch.

I felt the same when I had the urge to write the book *Mes Noces Musicales* – our book.

Piano Journal VOL 15 NO 43 1994

Menahem Pressler

We have read a great deal about the Beaux Arts Trio, especially in recent weeks, with the fortieth anniversary of the founding of this superb ensemble. You are the only founder-member still with the Trio, yet the most refined interpretations have been maintained in spite of the changes of string players. Surely you started your career as a solo pianist; in which case, how did you come to form the Trio?

Of course, I first studied the piano because I loved the instrument since I was a child. We were living in Magdeburg, in Germany, and, like all middle-class intelligentsia, there was a piano in the house. It was like another toy for me, so I spent a lot of time playing tunes, and soon I started to have proper lessons. I do not recall ever having been told to 'practise'. Playing the piano for me was very exciting – I was fascinated by the variety of sounds which I could produce, and I have retained this fascination all my life. The only difference is that now I know that it is my own search, my living with the piano for so many years, which result in creating these sounds. When I was thirteen, my family emigrated to Palestine (only later on it became Israel), having fled Nazi Germany. That was in 1936, and as soon as my parents settled in the new home, I resumed my piano lessons. We were recommended to a fine Russian teacher, llya Rudiakov, a very good pianist himself who had studied with Max Pauer, and later with Cortot in Paris. He was the right teacher for me at the time, as he encouraged me to listen to the quality of the tone which each composer demands. It is only through listening that one learns, and it is important for an interpreter to realise how the composer speaks to you and what his music means to you.

Later on I was introduced to Leo Kestenberg, one of the most outstanding musicians I had the fortune to come across. He was an extraordinary pianist – he had studied with Busoni – but he was also a musician of great stature. He became a sort of guru to all his students, and I revered him. I was avidly getting though all kind of studies, early keyboard music, and under my master's guidance I was able to study in depth most of the great works of the piano repertoire. I started on a career without even trying too hard. First, I found myself being asked to give some recitals, then, to my great satisfaction, I was invited to be the soloist in the Saint Saens Concerto with the recently founded Israel Philharmonic. Soon afterwards, I arrived in the USA, as everyone thought that this was the place where a young pianist should be heard. Indeed, I took part in the first Debussy Competition in California and I won! I was just seventeen and, here I was, taken on by the much-feared manager, Arthur Jackson, who arranged several impressive tours, to play with the greatest American orchestras – New York, Philadelphia, Chicago – under the most celebrated conductors – Mitropoulos, Szell, Stokowski, Enesco, among them. I never looked back. But it was very important for me to find time for study: I had to learn many new works for recitals, and prepare new concertos, which I performed both in Israel and in the States. There I attended Egon Petri's courses – a Busoni pupil like Kestenberg. Though very different, it was interesting to find how the same foundation, the same roots, produced such diverse personalities. I met another great artist, Robert Casadesus, who played a role in my search for greater refinement in my playing. Casadesus played French music like no one else and I was eager to acquire those subtle shades of tones. He also was one of the most memorable Mozart interpreters, which made such an impact on my own playing.

It was in the summer of 1955 that I was invited to play at the Tanglewood Music Campus, where some of the most talented young musicians gathered to work with the great luminaries of the musical profession. It so happened that a recording company, Parlophone, asked me if I could get some good players to form a trio. I got very excited, and I approached Daniel Guilet, a violinist who had already made a name in the profession, and Bernard Greenhaus, a cellist whose playing I greatly admired. Our first concert was scheduled for 13th July, to be followed by eight other concerts in the chamber music series. The recording company gave us a contract for nine concerts for that summer. Our ensemble was a tremendous success, almost overnight, and the nine concerts became seventy! The Trio, which we named the Beaux Arts, was invited to play literally throughout the States, in big halls, at Festivals, in Music Faculties, and it has continued like that for he past forty years.

Actually you are the only member of the Trio who is still in it! Bernard Greenhaus had to retire seven years ago because of advanced arthritis, then Peter Willey joined the ensemble. Daniel Guilet retired in 1970, after which Isidore Cohen stepped in his place. Then, only two years ago, Ida Kavafian became the violinist of the ensemble. Did these changes affect the way you worked together? Indeed, with each combination of players, how did all three of you respond to one another in their quest to find a common language?

These changes took place over long periods, when the Trio had already established its style. The recordings and many articles also helped us to realise which particular directions we should take. The audiences also played an enormous part in our development. Ultimately, it was our great desire to convey to those audiences our ideas. In an ensemble like this, the pianist plays a most important role, but it is always a question of balance, of listening to one another, of giving in to one another, as no one dares to impose any specific points of interpretation. We discuss, we may make suggestions, but, ultimately, it is our intense involvement in making music together that matters. It is so interesting to observe, while rehearsing, how much we agree about the different styles of each composer; the texture just changes when the music demands it, often quite spontaneously.

This year seems to be so much more crowded, with concerts, recordings, and special awards to you personally. The celebrations of your forty years are in full swing, and these put enormous pressure on you, and on the other members of the Trio. How can you cope with so much travelling, having to play in different parts of the world, completing the special recordings for this anniversary, as well as teaching the eighteen students at Indiana University at Bloomington? How do you keep smiling through all of this?

There is no secret; I just love everything I do. My main concern is how to maintain my technique so that I can give my best in performance. It is not enough to know the works inside out; I have to be at the piano and, yes, practise assiduously so that my fingers always obey me. We pianists are like athletes, and no great achiever dares to appear in a match without warming up his muscles. Why should we be expected to do otherwise? I am known in the profession as a compulsive rehearser, driving my partners to do the same. I know it is not always easy for them. Finding the time for everything is hard. I dare not look at my schedule for the rest of the year, with some hundred-and-twenty concerts for the Trio, apart from my solo appearances. One of the most exciting events will be the 40th Anniversary Concert on 13th July, in Tanglewood, the exact date of our very first concert in

1955. For my 'Services to Chamber Music' I received, last January, the 'Chamber Music America' award, one of the most coveted medals of the profession (Serkin and Horshowski, are among the past recipients). And only recently I was made an 'Honorary Citizen of Mainz', when the Guttenberg University conferred an Honorary Doctorate on me.

This year, Philips have produced a complete set of recordings covering the forty years of the Beaux Arts Trio to celebrate this anniversary; and those who acquire the set will have a special bonus, the recording issued by Parlophone of the first concert of the Trio. We find it surprisingly good! The playing sounds so fresh and exuberant.

As we are talking about the enormous number of recordings you have done and continue to do, what do you think of today's technology compared to the earlier recordings, when recording engineers did not expect note-perfect performances?

It was not quite so. We, the artists, demanded from ourselves the best we could do. We spent many hours in the studio together with the engineer trying again and again and, in the end, the decision to go ahead and issue the recording came quite simply by mutual agreement. It is very important to have a good rapport with the engineer, and the collaborations went quite smoothly. Today's recordings are, actually, too perfect, and the public expects the same perfection from our live performances. This is my answer when I am accused of 'over-rehearsing', 'over-practising'. I dare not appear in front of an audience if I know that I have not done my work of preparing for that performance. No matter how tired I am after a whole night's flight, I would get first to the hall, practise for two or three hours, grab a sandwich, and only then take a nap before starting the rehearsals with my partners. My fortune is that I can relax and even sleep when I have a pause, and I wake up completely refreshed, ready for the concert. As an artist, it is my goal to bring out the best in myself, always, and strive for more. It is no use sitting on one's laurels thinking that, well, the audience will accept what you are giving them anyway. No, this is not my philosophy. Especially now that I am appearing more and more as a solo pianist, in recitals and with orchestras. I cannot allow myself to become slack.

This year I still have several important commitments. I have been invited to give the Closure Recital of the Queen Elizabeth Competition in Brussels, in May. At this notorious competition, the organisers have included a series of masterclasses conducted by some of the members of the Jury, and I have to give the final recital. It is not easy to play for an audience consisting mostly of pianists, my colleagues on the Jury, and the young candidates, to whom I am supposed to set an example.

1996 is also getting crowded, with a recital at Carnegie Hall on 21st February in the series of 'Great Pianists', as well as playing concertos with several orchestras: Mozart with the Vienna Chamber Orchestra and with the Suisse Romande in Geneva, among others, as well as the many Trio engagements and recordings. In between all these I am greatly committed to my teaching. Sometimes, I have to fly to Bloomington just for two days from wherever I find myself performing, give my lessons, and return to complete the concerts or recordings. I agree with my wife and my friends who try to convince me to slow down. But how can I? Teaching is very important for me. I was awarded the special title of 'Distinguished Professor' in recognition of my many years of devoted work with students. Teaching, like performing, is 'giving'. In my teaching I try to give my students what I have received. An artist is the outcome of one's tradition and background, and I want to pass this on to younger musicians, to bring in them an awareness of what the instrument demands, how to develop an understanding of styles, as well as the skill to interpret what the composers mean to convey, and many other aspects of teaching.

Of course, fingers must be able to obey the orders from the brain. I may be old- fashioned, but I do think Czerny, Clementi, Crammer, were very clever, they knew how to develop agility and other technical skills. Above all, I try to inspire my students to make music. Skill does not mean playing fast notes as fast as possible, but to translate those fast notes into musical ideas. Then, they almost play themselves, and do not sound as 'technique'. What really moves the fingers is the ideas which you have created in the mind. Yet, I demand from my students to strive to achieve the most beautiful, refined tone, always. If one hears such a sound in the inner ear, all one has to do is to try to match that tone with the tone one produces. I believe that such a struggle is certainly worth pursuing. The reward is so satisfying, and I hope such work is of help to my students. It has worked for me, and I can't see why it should not bring results for those who attempt it.

You switch from playing in your ensemble to playing solo quite frequently. Do you find it difficult to switch from playing from the music to having to perform from memory?

I do not find it difficult, at least not at present, but there is a definite change in my attitude, in my behaviour. Fortunately, this does not affect my performances. This is probably due to the fact that every piece of music I play is very clearly 'recorded' in my mind. I am convinced that all of us, the three partners, could perform our repertoire without music, we know it so thoroughly. But when I have to play in a recital or with orchestra, my 'automatic pilot' takes over, and I am again the solo pianist, with my great experience of over forty years of uninterrupted playing. Then, my concern is only with the music I have to give to the audience, not whether I am able to play without music!

Some time ago I went to hear Sviatoslav Richter, who, in recent years, plays only with music. This does not take away from the greatness of his performances, although the audiences seem to wonder what has happened to such an artist. It was very interesting to hear him talk about this change of attitude. He believes that all artists should do the same, that by this visual contact with the music, one is capable of extraordinary heights of sensitivity and beauty. There must be something in Richter's philosophy.

Some very great artists have played with music, but only when they reached a certain age and began to worry about memory lapses. Pianists like Myra Hess or Clifford Curzon liked to have the score to rely on so that they could give of their best, instead of worrying unduly in case they forgot.

Yes, I know many more. It is actually quite common for pianists to play contemporary and avant-garde works from the music, although some choose to memorise everything.

Your many activities will surely take you into the next millennium. What plans have you for the more immediate future?

There is still so much to learn. We are constantly searching for new works for the Trio, although we have an enormous repertoire of over one hundred-and-twenty works! We love including a contemporary composer as often as we can in our programmes, when a concert is not devoted to one composer or to a special period. But what I really need is to be able to spread my engagements so that I do not have to fight for time to do everything. As you see, I am my own enemy in this respect, simply because everything I do is so important to me, for my well-being. This crazy rhythm seems to suit me and, yes, it is so rewarding. As my students know, as long as I have my ice-box well stocked with cold drinks in my Studio, everything is all right!

Barry Douglas

You are the fourth British winner of the Tchaikowsky International Piano Competition — a great achievement for British pianism. I had the pleasure to interview the previous three for the EPTA Piano Journal: John Ogdon, John Lill, and Peter Donohoe. When you were awarded the first prize, in 1989, Professor Lev Vlassenko, President of EPTA Russia, himself a second prize laureate of the very first competition and one of the permanent members of the jury, remarked: 'British pianists? They have done very well. Out of the eight competitions so far, four have been won by them!'

First of all I should like to say that I am really Irish, although from the British Isles. I mention this because, so often when I am abroad, I am introduced as an 'English pianist'!

To come back to the Tchaikowsky competition and what it meant for me. Indeed, my career simply took off afterwards. On a personal level, I became fascinated by the Russian people, by their warmth and their eagerness to meet musicians from other countries and I also loved to listen to the language. I thought then and there that, if I had the opportunity, I would want to learn Russian, to speak it and to read the literature in the original language.

I was very interested to know more about you when you decided, sometime in 1991 or 1992, to take a year off from your highly successful career to devote yourself to other studies and enrolled at Oxford University to read Russian and Philosophy. You took a great risk, because we do know how quickly agents and audiences tend to forget an artist who not appearing regularly on the musical scene. What encouraged you to take such a daring decision?

I wanted to have one year away from concerts to re-examine what it was that I had achieved, what I wanted to achieve, and to think for myself how best to proceed if I wanted to change my attitude to music, to my own playing or how I could generally change my way of playing for the better. I wanted to re-examine my repertoire, to find out what works I really should and wish to study in order to develop in more than one direction.

Also I needed to stop travelling throughout the world for one year as this is such an unnatural existence. I felt that I was losing my 'centre', and I had a great urge to regain it. This was very important for me. I also felt that it would be good to revert to being a 'human being' again, 'stationary', not a travelling one, at least for some time.

I think that is what it was and the only way to do it was to change direction. It was risky, but the urge was stronger than my fear. In the end, it worked out very well. All those who had helped me in the past are now very accommodating, and have been looking after my career with great enthusiasm since I came down from university in 1993.

I must say that I did admire your courage. It is true, though, that you had already achieved some fame by that time and that you could rest on your laurels. You did not withdraw because you were a failure, on the contrary. Did that experience, the search for your own truth, come up to your expectations?

Yes, and even more! Intellectually, I believe that I found some answers to my great interest in Russian language and literature. The fact that I could have the time to do this, in itself, was satisfying. I could also indulge in being retrospective without worrying about getting to my piano to prepare for the next concert. In a sense, I wanted to step back to learn to play the piano again, to re-examine my whole attitude to music in general. When I got to the end of my academic year, even the works I knew extremely well I saw in a new light. I became aware of new dimensions which were reflected in my interpretations and in my piano playing, which gained a new impetus. Also I learnt a lot of new music, as I had the time – and this was very valuable. Above all, I came to realise that although music is very important to me – the most important thing in my life next to my family – it is still only part of what life is and one has to see everything in the right perspective.

You are one of the few privileged artists who has been able to reshape your career, your whole life, as you wanted.

Yes, this is so. When I started my career, I had to fit in with whatever was demanded of me. As a young artist, I had to accept everything – although I must admit I had many and great satisfactions.

But now I have managed to grab hold of the reins. I am in control. More than this, I cannot say. I have succeeded in placing my music on such a level that I do not neglect my life, the life experiences such as love, drama, despair and other human emotions. If you do not recharge your batteries, how can you play the great works, since music is about life experiences?

On the other hand, I believe that it is necessary to replenish one's memory bank of emotions, which are stored inside anyway, because we live day after day, but often it becomes too much of a routine – and this is what I am trying to avoid at all costs.

At what point did you feel that you were ready to return to your so-called 'ordinary life' as a pianist?

I arranged with my agents to start again to play in October 1993. I have been away from the concert circuit for nearly two years, but I felt so refreshed and full of energy and excitement. I was actually eager to come back, but this time, as I said, I could make my own choices.

During the time you were away from concerts your name did circulate, as you had already made quite a few recordings. What do the recordings mean to you, to your life, apart from their usefulness for your career? At present, there is such a flood of CDs on the market, that I wonder if there will soon be a saturation point.

Recordings are a mixed blessing. For an artist it is good to be made to think carefully what you want to say, what your views of a particular work are, and how you can encapsulate them in one disc. All the different facets which come out in a live performance have all to be expressed in one single version. In my experience, a recording is just a document of a particular version at a particular time in your life. There is a positive aspect and a negative one. The positive one we have just talked about. The negative one is that recording is an unnatural activity because music is about feeling alive, it is about that spontaneous, instantaneous exchange in a concert hall or even in a room between the artist and his audience.

Although this is not my favourite activity, I have done and I continue making more recordings. But, of course, I much prefer live concerts with all their occasional imperfections.

I understand that the positive aspect is what the recordings do for an artist's career. There is now a trend among record companies to produce 'integrales' of one com-

poser, or, occasionally of all the works recorded by one artist, transferred now onto CD. Are you in favour of this type of marketing?

Frankly, I do not agree with this. I think that there are only a few musicians who can play complete versions of, let us say, all the Beethoven sonatas. There are, however, many musicians who can say that they have known all these works for many years, but this surely was as part of their studies. But this does not mean that they should actually attempt to record them. I often wonder about the people who buy the many records with all the Haydn's symphonies, all the Schubert's sonatas or now all the Bach's cantatas. Do they really listen to them?

I believe that they really do. I know quite a lot of people, great music lovers, not professional musicians, who prefer to listen to music in the quietness of their own home. They are keen to know more and to learn more and having complete sets of recordings of one composer, they are able to get a broader understanding of the different stages of his creation.

This may be so and it may be interesting if one listens to these recordings in a systematic way, but I defy anyone who has bought all the Haydn symphonies to have listened to all of them!

I am inclined to agree with you about the artists who record such complete works of one composer. Unless the artist can bring some new insight, there are not many who can sustain the same mastery throughout. However, I do think that albums of an artist's recordings, such as Pop and Jazz musicians do, should be launched and I think there should be a good public for such CDs.

This is a very good idea, and I am all for it. I would quite like to see something like 'Barry Douglas on a Liszt Recital Disc' or a recital programme of Bach, Chopin, Debussy and Prokofiev on another disc. In this case you have a record with a good selection of music which is enjoyable to listen to on an evening, relaxing with a glass of wine, which is how I think records should be listened to.

There is another new development among record companies, to bring out CDs of artists of the past. I personally find these a great joy as well as a great lesson on so many levels.

I also find this simply fabulous – especially since modern technology ensures that the old recordings can be heard, and even more clearly!

Can you tell us something about your early musical upbringing? Did you start having piano lessons as a child in Ireland?

Yes, I started to have lessons with a local teacher, but I was a rather ordinary pupil. No one thought of me as a potential musician. I later went to the Belfast Music School where I had some teachers who did not have any training or experience but there were a few who had vision and talent. Fortunately for me, they were supportive and they gave me a chance, they just let me go my own way. A very good pianist came then to Belfast Music School at that time, Felicitas Lewinter, a pupil of Emil Sauer, who had studied with Liszt and her lessons were like an incredible thunderbolt for me.

I was sixteen, and I did not know what I wanted to do or to be. I was playing the piano, tried to play other instruments, and did a bit of conducting. But then, she inspired me and made me realise that the piano could be a very wonderful thing.

I developed a real passion for it but my only worry was that I was a late developer and I was not really able to play anything well until I was twenty.

This is very interesting, because all the artists I have interviewed for the EPTA Piano Journal were child prodigies, who showed amazing abilities from an early age and their parents did everything to get them very good teachers.

No, I was not at all like that. But after meeting Felicitas Lewinter my life changed completely, I just wanted to find out how to play this 'damn piano'.

I was eighteen when I entered the Royal College of Music in London and that opened up a whole new world, not only the teaching but also great chamber music, interesting concerts and, above all, exchanges with other students.

I was fascinated by the tremendous concert life in London which was really incredible after Belfast, where the music that there was could not satisfy my hunger for great music. I went every night to a concert or the opera. That is where I got my main music education, listening to singers and trying hard to make the piano sing like that. John Barstow, my piano teacher, is a fabulous musician. He is a very good pianist and he was a very caring teacher for me. He encouraged me to listen to as many pianists, as many operas and symphonies as possible, but also to go to the theatre to get acquainted with the great plays and with great acting. I am grateful to him for stimulating me to learn as much as I could and this has broaden my outlook. Of course, he insisted on developing my technique and I spend hours and hours to get to play all the pieces I wanted to learn. I became very self-critical. I realised that if I wanted to achieve my goal, that was to reach my highest potential, I had to work very hard at everything – my technique and acquiring a wide repertoire – I had first and foremost learn to listen critically to my own playing.

Soon after you left the College you went to study with Maria Curcio, and while working with her you won the Tchaikowsky Competition, an event which made a great impact on the musical life in this country. The RCM must have basked in your glory, and it must have given great satisfaction to John Barstow, who really helped you to become a pianist.

Indeed, it was a wonderful moment to be there, in Moscow, at the Tchaikowsky Conservatory, and to be awarded the first prize at such an extraordinary competition.

I thought how privileged I was to have had two great teachers, although so different, realising how much I had gained through studying with them. I am afraid there don't seem to be new interesting teachers for our young pianists these days, although there are many who produce outstanding keyboard players. Working with Maria Curcio was an overwhelming experience. She is so very forceful. You have to be very careful not to be swallowed! She has very definite ideas about technique, and she demands that her approach to playing the piano must be accepted. She changed a few things in my playing, but what impressed me most is her dedication to an uncompromising attitude to music. You have to decide how not to compromise in your interpretations and to be as faithful to the music and to the composer as possible. Maria does not believe in short cuts nor in doing anything for effect. The performance must be the outcome of genuine feeling, and genuine technical attitude, and this was, indeed, very inspiring.

I have met a number of pianists who have studied with Maria, and they have all talked about her very definite ideas on the interpretation of repertoire. Did she try to impose her ideas on your performances?

She imposes her ideas on people who have no ideas themselves. She believes, as I do, that rather than have no ideas it is better to let them have someone else's. The danger is that to follow the teacher's guidance faithfully, the student may not develop any ideas for himself. Experience and dedication may bring some awareness. But, I believe that a teacher has another, and more important function: to draw out what is there. Of course, if there is nothing there, no teacher can do much. Yet, a great teacher can inspire the students to learn to listen, then hear what you did not hear before.

Competitions have done a great deal for you. Do you advise young pianists to participate in this type of contest?

As with recordings, there are positive and negative points, and if you realise what they are, there are no problems. Unfortunately, many young artists seem to get swallowed up by the philosophy of competitions – if there is any – and it is imperative that part of an artist should remain defiant and able to stand up to the pressure of conforming. Competitions have a tendency to make young artists compromise, they tend to adapt their playing to what they think the juries would like to hear. Their main goal is not to play wrong notes and most competitors play in a bland, safe way, which wins competitions. I am afraid, this has very little to do with great music. This is why in all the competitions that happen every year, it may be that every three years you may hear one pianist that is truly interesting. Sometimes the most original personalities get knocked out in the first round because they are more adventurous.

Of course, the advantages by far outweigh the disadvantages. It is very difficult to start a career and it is by winning a prize at one of the prestigious contests that a young artist can get launched as well as getting money and concerts as part of the prize. Some competitions offer grants for further studies with a great pedagogue ad there are other advantages: there are many useful contacts made at such gatherings And one meets other artists and learns from such exchanges.

You collaborated with the film director, John Schlessinger, in the making of the film Madame Souzatska, which depicted a rather hysterical piano teacher. I was also involved in the day to day planning of the film, as both the director and the actress Shirley MacLane, came to me for advice on how to teach.

In fact, the film was more a lesson on how not to teach! The teacher in the film was so worried herself, no wonder the young student was unable to perform in public just when he had his great chance.

Both Schlessinger and Shirley were very interested in my work on how to cope with unnecessary tensions and with performance anxiety. As we talk about this aspect in performance, how do you cope with the stress and tensions of such a demanding career?

For me, it is the music that matters. If I am involved in the performance with all my being, the music helps me to find the way to achieve this.

What are your plans for the immediate future?

I gave several performances in September of Brahms' Concerto No. 1 with the Hallé Orchestra under the baton of Kent Nagano in Manchester and with the London Symphony Orchestra in London with the conductor Stainslaw Skrowaczewski.

I am preparing a Wigmore Hall Recital for January 1996 when I shall give the first London performance of *Tenebrae*, a very fine work by John McCabe. He wrote this very moving piece for me and I gave the world premiere at the Harrogate Festival. *Tenebrae* makes a great impact on first hearing, a rare occurrence with contemporary piano music.

I am also planning to study new repertoire for future recitals here and overseas. There is still so much to learn.

Dominique Merlet

Dominique Merlet, one of the most important pianists and pedagogues of our time, has dominated the French piano scene for more than thirty years. After his early appearances, he was hailed by critics and audiences as a pianist of great stature, a virtuoso and a poet of rare sensitivity. He was also admired for his understanding of various different styles — not only for his interpretations of the Classical and Romantic repertoire, but particularly for the subtlety and clarity he brought to his performances of the French impressionists.

At the age of thirty-four, he was appointed Professor at the Paris Conservatoire — the youngest staff member of this prestigious institution at that time. He brought to his teaching the same dedication that he gave to his own studies, and during the eighteen years at the Conservatoire he has launched a whole generation of young artists, many of them winners of international piano competitions. For a French artist to be appointed Professor at such a venerable institution is considered an honour which enhances the reputation of an artist — unlike in other countries, where great performers only occasionally condescend to listen to a young aspiring pianist.

Dominique Merlet continues performing, as well as holding regular courses in both Geneva and Paris; he is also recording a series of CDs which include the complete works of Ravel, Debussy, and Chopin.

You are conducting Master Classes in many Conservatoires and Music Colleges. So-called 'Master Classes' are often given by mediocre musicians — an abuse of the term 'Master Class' which reduces the importance of an 'open class' conducted by a great 'Master'. What is expected, in your opinion, from a 'Master'?

I do think of the term 'Master' as we have been brought up to, as an artist we revere, a teacher who inspired us in our youth, who was a constant example, showing us how to approach the music we were studying and how to shape our whole attitude towards our aspirations, our hopes, striving to achieve the utmost, always. I would expect the same honest dedication from today's Master: a complete musician with profound knowledge of a broad repertoire, an understanding of what piano technique is about and, above all, an artist who has done a great deal of research into different editions and the latest publications. He must also be aware of the historical and social implications, as well as of the achievements in other fields – the Arts and literature. We must remember that each composer is the product of so many influences, not only of the teaching, and one must also have a good grasp of the composers' own growth through different periods of their lives.

In my own teaching, whether at the *Classes de Virtuosité et Perfectionnement* which I give regularly in Geneva and Paris, or when working with piano students in different countries, I try to analyse the performance from many aspects. With my experience I am able to assess immediately the player's understanding of the work and his ability to express musical intentions. Usually, I talk first about the music – its special place in a historical context, or in the composer's development – so that the player perceives the importance of a particular style to interpret that piece. I try to convey to the student what the composer wanted to say, as one cannot play only as one feels. I then help the student to realise what his or her technical limitations are, and how these can be overcome. An incorrect posture hinders technical freedom, and, as soon as I point this out, there is a noticeable improvement. But technique is only a minor aspect of a performance – we all know what damage wrong posture and excessive tensions in joints and muscles can do apart from hindering freedom of movements. What is so noticeable when posture is adjusted and arms and hands are relaxed is the quality of sound the player produces. Often the pianist is quite surprised to hear such sounds, perhaps these are the tones he intended to produce and did not know how to! I cannot understand why so many teachers allow their students to play with stiffness in the arms, and particularly the wrists.

In your work with young pianists who play at these Master Classes you have really very little time to discuss their technique in depth. How can you help them if their technique is inadequate?

Usually the participants are selected by the Keyboard Department of each Conservatoire or Faculty, therefore only the most advanced are taking part and these have a fairly good 'working technique'. I can only make some suggestions about what they should do to develop what they already possess – what type of exercises or études would be useful for each candidate, since each pianist presents specific problems. Yet, there are certain 'performance practices' which have to be respected by all – teachers and students – and these demand an understanding of the keyboard action, how to achieve a variety of tones through different touches, as well as a clear knowledge of how to use one's playing apparatus.

There are, of course, several pianistic approaches, all aiming to bring the same result: a good technical control in order to perform at one's best. I cannot change this in the short time I have, but I think it is very important for the student to realise what his technical limitations are and how to correct them, even though I know that not much can be done then and there.

With my own students it is different, as we have all the time ahead of us to work together on every aspect of performance. I do expect them to give a good part of their practising time to their technique, to analyse their movements, the different touches, so that they become aware of the sensations they experience when using the arm weight, so vital in piano playing; how to release it to produce the desired sonorities; what relaxed arms and wrists feel like both away from the instrument and when playing; or when to use forearm rotation consciously and when to 'allow' it for certain technical passages. We work intensively on developing finger control. I do not recommend high finger articulation, with fingers playing like little hammers, but to get a firm grip of the key, experiencing a close contact as if the key is an extension of the finger. Then we analyse the different touches which play such an important role in the interpretation of the different styles.

When the students have acquired the necessary control of their body and of the instrument, working on the repertoire is much more rewarding. We can concentrate on what the music demands, what the composer wants to say, what his message is. I am a great believer in respecting the text, especially now that Urtexts are accessible, most of them with highly interesting commentaries. Thus, the composer's phrasing and articulation can also be respected. We work a great deal on pedalling, and on quality of sound, from the subtlest *pianissimo* to most energetic *fortissimo*, always aiming at making music, never forcing the tone.

Moreover, I try to inspire my students to be creative, avoiding the constant imitation of performances which they hear on discs, even though given by their ideal performers. I do not wish to produce stereotypical players but young artists, able to develop their own personality and individuality.

I owe a great deal to my own teachers, to those who influenced me. As a young boy I obeyed my teacher who was the product of the French piano school, with emphasis on training fingers through endless exercises and etudes, using finger articulation. I must admit that this helped me to develop a clear, nimble finger technique which was a good basis on which to add any new ideas or approach. It was later on when I went to the Geneva Conservatoire in the *Classe de Virtuosité et Perfectionnement* of Louis Hildbrant that I realised what piano playing means and what piano playing demands.

When I won the Geneva International Competition in 1957 – the same year as Martha Argerich, when Pollini came second – I had to decide what to do about my career. I had many concerts both in France and in Switzerland, but I realised that I was not ready and I needed to learn so much more, as I was searching for different kinds of musical experiences. Hildbrant thought that I might benefit from working with a Russian émigré who was making quite a name with his 'new approach', so I knocked at the door of Monsieur Pierre Kostanoff. I was not disappointed. He had a broad knowledge of what he considered 'true piano playing', and his influence on my development was very intense. He had a scientific approach to every aspect of technique, and this was very important for me. I could not accept just to be told: 'do this like that', I had to understand why and how, and he always had a good, clear explanation. It was Kostanoff who showed me how to use the forearm rotation when needed, and this added extra dimension to my playing. It also brought new ideas to my teaching, as I already had a number of pupils, and when I was appointed professor at the Paris Conservatoire I felt that I was able to cope with young pianists at a high level, some preparing for 'Premier Prix'.

It must be difficult to find the time to keep up with your own playing and recording if you are involved with so much teaching, travelling, and sitting on juries. How do you combine all these activities?

I have devised a well-structured programme. The morning is always free for my own playing, thus I have several hours for good practice. The technique has to be maintained, and my repertoire needs to be revised constantly so that I am ready, at any time, to face the public or work with the engineers in the recording studio. I cannot allow any slackening of my standards. This is what I am expecting from my students, and when I illustrate any points of interpretation I cannot appear unprepared or unable to do so. Even when travelling, I try to find some time for practising before a recital, and this is one of the conditions I stipulate to agents. This I cannot do when I am on juries at international competitions, as we all have be on duty from early morning until late in the evening!

The International Competitions have become a sort of industry. They spread not only to many more countries, but also to different towns, usually naming them after a famous composer thus there are now the Safonov, Rachmaninov, Enescu, Lipatti, Horowitz competitions — to mention only a few beside the famous ones like Tchaikowsky, Liszt, Chopin, Bartok, Busoni, and so on. You often sit on juries, which surely means that you are in favour of young musicians appearing at such competitions.

I have to admit, like many of my colleagues, that there are arguments for and against, and all are valid.

On the positive side, I strongly believe that it is good for young musicians to have a goal, to prepare for some of the most prestigious competitions even if they perform only in the first stages. They have the opportunity to be heard by a discerning audience and, with some luck, by agents. Their names appear in programmes along with other interesting young pianists, they meet and hear the other candidates and this, in itself, is not only an eye-opener as to the high standard required, but also a valuable lesson.

On the negative side, it can be really depressing for these young pianists, some of them getting quite known in the areas where they have established the beginning of their career, if they are eliminated in the early stages. For us, on the jury, it is disappointing to hear these musicians, all with great potential, giving almost identical performances probably thinking that, unless they present 'correct' interpretations, they do not stand a chance. It is so seldom that one hears a pianist with an original personality; although quite a few present outstanding performances, unfortunately not sustained throughout the tests. Those who manage to cope with the ordeal of sitting through all the tests and reach the finals may be rewarded and, for the few who succeed, there cannot be a better training for the stamina needed to withstand the pressures of a career as a soloist.

We hear a great deal of criticism of how the marks are given by members of the jury, and stories of how occasional pressure exerted to favour certain candidates. Have you experienced such influences?

No, and I was not aware of any such influences in any competitions in which I took part. On the contrary. As often happens, some candidates have been students of certain jury members and, in these cases, one can recommend one's pupil but the vote does not count, while in other competitions the professor is not even allowed to vote for his student. It is seldom that there is a unanimous decision, since the judges have different artistic ideals and tastes but then, of course, the majority of votes gives the answer, and the final decision has to be accepted by all – jury and candidates.

We have already talked about the many recordings now on the market. There is a flood of CDs, and recording companies are competing with one another, trying to bring out complete sets to include all the works of various composers or whole volumes produced by one artist. What do you think of this expansion?

The fact that I participate in producing CDs shows what my attitude is. The discs are an essential complement to an artist's career, they reach listeners, potential audiences in many countries, and impresarios get to know of artists through the reviews in specialist magazines.

For us, artists, working with engineers in a studio is an essential part of our career. Although one thinks of recording techniques as the techniques of repair, since no flaws are permissible, the advances in this field are truly staggering. The quality of sound one can hear these days, with the finest nuances and dynamics, from the most subtle pianissimo to resounding fortissimo, is so impressive. One can actually *hear the silence!*

For myself, I shall always prefer a live audience. The close contact with the public is so fulfilling. Yet, it is very important to have these series of recordings. They will remain as a testimony of what I wanted to say, and I hope that I have succeeded.

Thanks for talking to us and I can assure you that your readers, many of them EPTA members in many European countries, will value the views of our Honorary European President on the various aspects of piano teaching and performance.

Piano Journal VOL 17 NO 49 1996

Martino Tirimo

1997 is the year of the Schubert bicentenary, and the whole world of music is preparing for this great event. *Concerts, competitions, and new recordings are taking place in every country to celebrate the achievements of this unique composer. You have been involved more than most in contributing to the many events leading up to this anniversary. In November and December 1996 you gave three Wigmore Hall recitals, all dedicated to the piano music of Schubert, a composer with whom you have developed an extraordinary rapport through your exhaustive research. This time you have included your latest ideas on phrasing, articulation, and stylistic completion in your new complete edition of Schubert's piano works, the first volume of which will be published in February 1997 by Wiener Urtext. You have also released the first two volumes of CD recordings of the 21 Sonatas on the EMI label in good time for the start of the celebrations, recordings which likewise embody your latest thinking on the subject. All devotees of Schubert, especially scholars, teachers, and performers, have anxiously awaited this publication of the complete piano works. Indeed, you were commissioned quite a few years ago by Chappell's to prepare the 'final and complete edition', but the project had to be abandoned. Refusing to be deterred, you have now busied yourself afresh with this project. Are you satisfied with the way your new edition has taken shape?*

1996 has been a most extraordinary year for me: I have been immersed in Schubert's piano music as well as in all his other works in order to reach the understanding I wanted. The experience I acquired previously, when I was commissioned to prepare a complete edition without, at that time, being able to carry it through to fruition, was, in fact, helpful for my main purpose. It gave me the needed time to revise my ideas and, for that matter, my goals. In a search lasting all these years, I did not try to look for authenticity (in the narrow sense) but sought rather to present the sort of information whereby performers and students of Schubert's music could then make their own decisions. It is common knowledge that there are many problems well nigh impossible to solve.

Even the most respected editions do not come up with final solutions. To take the D Major D850 Sonata as an example, the autograph edition and the first edition, published during his lifetime, present considerable differences. While one would think that the autograph edition should be more authentic, it is the first edition which must have the last word, as Schubert must have seen it before it was printed. At this point, the editor has to bring to bear his knowledge and discrimination, and ultimately take the necessary decisions. Sometimes there are obvious errors, and it is very difficult to decide whether the right choice is to correct them or not.

In the A Minor Sonata D845, the subsidiary theme presents four or five different types of articulation; some show staccato, others slurs. There must be a uniform way, and, although it may be difficult to arrive at a choice, it is the editor's job to correct such 'errors' in the edition. It is vital, too, that every sonata or other work should have an extensive introduction as to its background, dates of composition and publication, along with any other relevant information.

What do you consider innovative in your edition? The idea of 'Urtext' has been the topic of many discussions by musicians and musicologists, but the question still remains: 'Which Urtext'?

I consider my edition to be the first to present all the works in chronological order just as I have done in my CD recordings (of which the first two volumes have already been issued by EMI). This I consider of value for Schubert scholars, performers, and students. They can thus observe Schubert's development as a composer from the earliest stages, how his style evolved, and how he deployed his thematic material. My other decision was to include works left unfinished by Schubert and which I have completed. This was a major consideration, especially since, in my estimation, these works are 'deceptively' incomplete. Schubert was very careful to bring all these works to the point of recapitulation and, actually, in the case of the B Major Sonata D575, he completed the recapitulation at a later date. In my edition, I have included the piano pieces which were left incomplete, but which I have tried to bring to a conclusion, even writing a coda when I thought it necessary. Of course, Schubert was a great master, and it was not an easy decision for me to attempt this task, which I considered indispensable if I were to present a comprehensive edition of his piano music. In seeking to fulfil this aim, I went out of my way to keep to his own manner of working, judging by the way he treated his thematic material, modulations and the like; in other words, I tried my very best! I hope I have succeeded.

Your research into Schubert's music and the many performances you have given of it over the years – the first complete cycle at the South Bank goes back as far as 1975 – form only a part of your repertoire which encompasses a phenomenal range of composers and styles. Apart from your Schubert releases, you have recently recorded the complete piano works of Debussy, while concerto recordings include the EMI CDs of the Rachmaninov Second Concerto and Paganini Variations, which received the Gold Disc Award (1995); the re-released EMI recordings of both Brahms concertos with the London Philharmonic Orchestra under Kurt Sanderling and Yoel Levi were likewise rapturously received. Your concerto repertoire extends to some 60 concertos, among them the Michael Tippett Piano Concerto, which you performed with Sir Michael conducting the BBC Symphony Orchestra, a performance which was televised live from Coventry Cathedral on the occasion of the composer's 90th birthday. How did you come upon Tippett's music?

A friend of mine brought me the score, and it did not take me long to realise that here was a work of major importance, which had to be studied and performed. I first played it in Dresden when Tippett agreed to conduct it himself, and since then I have given several performances and have come to love it along with other music by Michael Tippett.

You mention the Dresden Symphony Orchestra. You have played and conducted from the keyboard all five Beethoven concertos with this orchestra. Do you find this twofold activity satisfying?

Directing from the keyboard can be most satisfying if one is fortunate enough to have an ensemble in harmony with your ideas and responsive to your musical intentions. I played the five concertos with them on several occasions, but it did not always come up to my expectations. For myself, I find being soloist and conductor at the same time a valid and valuable exercise on two counts: firstly, it enables me to stamp my interpretation on the whole of the work and, secondly, it represents the way that many of these classical concertos were performed in the first place.

Your career has encompssed many areas of musical life, from performer to researcher, teacher, and conductor. Who were your first teachers, and which of the musicians who crossed your path had the greatest influence on your studies and on your approach to music?

In first place, I owe a great debt to my father, having been born into a family of dedicated musicians in Cyprus. My father was a fine violinist who had studied abroad in Austria, Italy, and also in London. He played the piano quite well and he was keen on developing the musical life in Cyprus, where he put on opera performances, conducting them himself and bringing soloists from La Scala and other important opera houses. I don't even remember when I first started to play the piano; it was always there in our home, and I played on it everything I could lay my hands on. My father supervised my studies, and I absorbed everything at such a rate that he even entrusted me with conducting *La Traviata* when I was only nine. It is true that I knew the score inside out from assisting him, and could sing all the arias, but *La Traviata*! The first rehearsal was very scary but, since my father had told me to do it, I soldiered on. Soon, the rehearsals started going better until, in the end, I conducted all of seven performances. To my amazement, I was even offered to conduct a series of performances in Italy but my father, very wisely, said no. He believed in my musical abilities, but he didn't want to see me leading the life of a musical prodigy. Although he wanted me to learn as much about music as possible, he wanted me even more to enjoy a proper education and grow up as a normal boy. The whole family subsequently moved to London, and I received a scholarship to Bedales, a co-educational school run by an enlightened headmaster and great educationalist. New concepts in education were constantly being put into practice at this school, in which music played a leading role. Those years were the happiest of my life, when I found the freedom to develop in many new directions. The Director of Music at that time, who taught me the piano, was Ronald Biggs: he encouraged me to take part in all musical activities but, at the same time, there was no shirking the academic work.

After Bedales, I continued my studies at the Royal Academy, where my first piano professor was Franz Reizenstein. He was not only an outstanding pianist, but a distinguished composer and, since I was also studying composition, I learned to search into a work so as to find the inner meaning and understand what the composer was trying to convey. Meanwhile, my career was taking shape, and I started to give concerts and to conduct in Dresden as well as in England. It was then that I decided to study with Richard Hauser, one of the celebrated professors at the Vienna Hochschule. Vienna suited me and I was eager to learn as much as I could. This involved visiting libraries to consult valuable manuscripts, and I became fascinated with what I discovered! On my return to London, I met Gordon Green, who became the most important single influence on my piano playing. Working with him was a most wonderful experience in more than one sense, and we would spend much of our lesson-time talking about the many facets of a single work. As a pianist, I gained new dimensions in my search to create a wealth of sounds from the instrument and, in my teaching, I tried to emulate him, always stressing how valuable it is to search inside oneself to uncover more and more of one's own intrinsic musicianship – a real voyage of self discovery!

I consider myself doubly privileged in getting more from my students than they get from me! It is this constant exchange between teacher and student which makes the lessons so remarkable. My main concern is to instil in the student an interest in the totality of a composer's output. One does not study just one piano piece, one tries rather to grasp the whole creative process culminating in that particular work, going into it ever more deeply, searching, searching... To play Schubert on the piano one must know his songs, how he tried to get the piano itself to 'sing'. In a letter to his father dated July 25th 1835, Schubert writes how 'the keys become singing voices under my hands!' But in his sonatas, like those of Beethoven, it is a different story. There they both felt free to express themselves in an innovative way, sometimes requiring an orchestral, sometimes a vocal approach, but always introducing and exploring novel ideas. My students and I work first on the general structure before going into details; thus the musical and pianistic elements are thoroughly integrated. I firmly believe that a teacher's role is to encourage the student, above all, to learn to listen, to develop the inner ear as the only way to develop the quality of one's tone. We pianists have to express our musical and pianistic ideas entirely through the tones we produce from the instrument. Hence the need to listen more and more intently!

I would like to hear your view on the act of performing. You have played the piano all your life, well before your first recital which you gave when only six years old. You have done a fair bit of conducting either from the keyboard or from the podium, and you know by experience how to create a rapport with your audiences. I am very interested in a phenomenon in performance known as the 'peak experience' or 'flow', that magic moment that all performers experience at one time or another, when the music seems to take over and forms a circuit, flowing through and uniting performer, instrument, music, and public alike. Are you able to describe such moments?

I can't really single out just one moment. It takes a good many – the piano I play on, the hall, the people in the audience. I feel so wonderfully relaxed while playing, but at the same time all the intensity is there together with a state of excitement. My mind is unusually clear yet, in a strange way, as if with a double perspective. Yes, I am taking part and I know it is me playing yet, at the same time, I am also somewhere else, looking on and taking note. I so remember several such experiences as if they were yesterday, when I felt so light as if I were on drugs, although I have never taken drugs. But this is how I imagine it feels. Once I was playing on a wonderful piano, a Bösendorfer, in a small college in America. On this occasion, my playing became transfigured; there was such magic just in putting my fingers into the keys, feeling the sensation of the action and the beauty of the tones which emerged. The experience was so intense, so integrated, that my playing entered a state of total empathy. I can recall several other such experiences, but what is even more remarkable is when such moments occur when listening to young pianists in competitions. I have been on many juries and am always quick to feel the difference between 'ordinary' piano playing and the moment when the music starts to speak for itself – this is playing at its optimum. There is a moment of bliss, when artist and music become one, and you can feel that the audience shares in this unity – there is a complete hush, they just listen and are totally at peace. That is the moment when I know that a true artist is playing – one can always tell.

Your experience of international competitions cuts both ways, not only as a member of the jury but, when you were younger, as a contestant yourself in the Munich and Geneva Competitions. What advice would you give to aspiring young competitors?

Indeed I have taken part in competitions, sometimes acting on the advice of others, and sometimes of my own choice. My own impression of my playing did not always coincide with the jury's, but the experience was certainly worthwhile. I believe young pianists should decide for themselves whether or not they may benefit from such events. Of course, most of them attempt such ordeals in the hope that they may win a prize and thus launch, or at least enhance, their career prospects. But if anyone asks for my advice, I try to make him or her aware that the results should not be taken as the goal; they should be aware by now that not all winners have made it in the profession. Where are all the prize winners that one no longer hears of? And there are young pianists who are making a name for themselves without ever having taken part in any competition. We all know that this is a difficult profession, and that those able to stand the stress and exorbitant demands will make it anyway.

1997 promises to be something of an annus mirabilis for you, with the Schubert celebrations in full swing, with your long-awaited complete edition of his piano works soon to be available, and with other CD recordings on the way. Even more newsworthy is the fact that you are the first recipient of the Steinway & Sons Piano Professorship initiated this year at the London College of Music (Thames Valley University). This is an extremely exciting new development for the piano profession and for those young musicians in particular who will benefit from the masterclasses which you will be holding at the College.

Piano Journal VOL 18 NO 52 1997

Garrick Ohlsson

While still a student of Sacha Gorodnitzky at the Juilliard School, Garrick Ohisson was launched on an international concert career after becoming the first American to win First Prize at the Warsaw Chopin Competition in 1971. Chopin counted as only one facet of a prodigious repertoire which contains no fewer than 70 concertos. Yet he always found himself coming back to Chopin, as if to his first love, trying to grasp the composer's message at ever deeper levels. We met last October as Garrick Ohisson began his Chopin marathon at the Wigmore Hall, performing the composer's complete piano works in six recitals, a feat which had already earned him the acclaim of critics throughout the USA as one of the greatest Chopin interpreters of our time.

When did you first consider presenting the entire oeuvre of Chopin?

It came as a natural development of my constant searching to understand what Chopin had to say to our present generation, how he would have performed his own works, and what inspired him to conjure sounds from his piano never dreamt of until his arrival on the scene. To get anywhere near my goal meant studying every note he ever composed as well as everything his pupils, friends, and critics had to say about his playing, not forgetting the many letters he himself wrote and received. This exhaustive grounding, I believe, was what sparked my decision to present his piano music in a well-structured series. Planning the programme of each recital was another hurdle, given the constraint of having to condense everything into only six recitals. As a consequence, each of the six lasts between two and two-and-a-half hours – a supreme test of the audience's endurance. The only other alternative would have been to spread them over eight evenings, as unacceptable to the public as it most certainly was to my agents and the hall managers.

There was also another more practical reason for this plan of action. The record company, Arabesque, approached me one day with an irresistible offer to record the complete piano music of Chopin and I accepted without even considering what it would entail. It was what I had always hoped to do, and the opportunity came at the right time. In my ignorance, I thought that making recordings gave the artist the right to pick and choose between a variety of 'takes' before opting for the definitive version. I soon learned, through some none too pleasant experiences, that this was by no means quite so simple. Nevertheless, I established an excellent rapport with the engineers, and director of the company and we were all happy about carrying on with the project. The first eight CDs have already been completed, with another four still to go.

My total immersion in the Chopin project couldn't help but be reflected in this matching series of recitals, which began already in the United States in 1995, and which have since spread to several European capitals. Soon I shall be going back to Poland where, ever since my winning the Competition there, I have been received with open arms as a conquering hero, as a pop-star, and do I love it! Playing Chopin in Chopin's native country has always been a challenge. But I have made so many wonderful Polish friends that each time I go there I feel as if I were going home.

What surprised me most was hearing that, after you won such a coveted award and with your career at such a turning-point, you then decided to return to study in New York with Irma Wolpe Rademacher, a rather controversial musical personality with some distinctly unorthodox ideas about how to approach both the music and the instrument. What led you to take such an unexpected step?

This was one of those strange happenings which can turn one's whole life around. After winning the Warsaw Competition, which followed other earlier successes in the Busoni International Competition in Bolzano and the Montreal Competition in Canada, I was literally overwhelmed with the number of concerts and Masterclasses I was asked to give. To be asked to teach advanced students in conservatoires, where only a short while ago I had been on the receiving end, was a major boost to my young ego. It was in the midst of one such Masterclass at the New England Conservatory in Boston that a slight middle-aged lady walked in. No sooner had I started to discuss with a student the work he had just played than she seized the music, strode to the piano, and proceeded to tell us, illustrating one point after another, how that particular piece should be approached, how to study the phrasing (which in her opinion was all wrong), the precise tone-quality for each modulation, each motive, how to pedal each chord, each progression – she just went on and on! So many finer points were revealed to me that I could only stand there enthralled, speechless. In any other situation I would have felt grossly insulted and upstaged by such an exhibition of bad manners, demonstrating as she did to my whole class that here was I, daring to teach others how to play a work which I had not understood myself! Instead of showing indignation, I heard myself asking – very humbly – when I might meet her again.

Soon afterwards I went to visit Irma Wolpe in New York, and thus began one of the most important and fulfilling periods of my life. It came at a time when I was consciously searching for new directions, to grasp the works I wanted to master in a new light, to make them altogether my own. Irma was the answer to all these quests. Going to play for her at regular intervals became a sort of pilgrimage, a purification of my attitudes to music-making. These were not lessons in the accepted sense, as when a master 'teaches' a student what to do and how and when to do it by matching up a certain movement with the expression of a musical idea. These were rather endless sessions, discussions, in which we delved into the complexities of a work which she was then able to dissect in its minutest details before, magically, bringing it together again in a sublime unity. At such moments, I had the feeling of having grasped the core of what she was trying to make me hear, so that whether I succeeded or not afterwards did not really matter. What mattered were those intimations of having reached a 'Truth' when interpreting a great work, which I found more and more fascinating. She recognised in me a most avid disciple, and must have relished being able to expound her ideas, philosophy, and immense knowledge to the full. For my part, this collaboration with Irma was utterly absorbing and inspiring.

Did Irma try to change your actual piano technique? Surely you must have reached a high degree of virtuosity and control of the keyboard to have been able to master all the works demanded of you in the various stages of the competitions from which you emerged the winner?

Yes, I thought I could play the piano – that is, until I met Irma! Not that she worked with me specifically on keyboard 'technique'. She opened my ears to new sounds, new shadings which she knew unerringly how to produce and which I learned to match. For the first time, I realised that the colour of a tone can be altered through certain pressures on the key or imperceptible hand or arm movements – enriching one's palette with the most subtle nuances and endless gradations of tone and dynamics. So invaluable did I find this approach that I arranged for a film company to make a short documentary of Irma demonstrating her approach to the instrument – what touch or touches were needed to produce her exquisite sounds, and many other aspects of piano playing, including pedalling. We laboured hard and long on this project, and I only hope that the film is now in some accessible archives where students and performers can benefit from it.

Indeed, Garrick, this is not the first time we have met. I actually 'met' you watching this very film! I first met Irma Wolpe in New York, when she was in the throes of making the film with you, while teaching at the New England Conservatory. I went to meet Leonard Shur, the well-known pianist and professor also at the New England Conservatory, who suggested that I should meet Irma, because she was, like me, of Romanian extraction. He also added that she was one of their most colourful personalities, with some highly original ideas as a pedagogue. After our first meeting, she used to come to EPTA Conferences in London, until her illness rendered her unable to travel. It was at one of the EPTA conferences that she showed the film which you just mentioned.

Your mentioning the film and Irma's last illness enables me to look back and appreciate that it was only after I was unable to see her any more that I could shake off any such influences and become my own man. She helped me to grow as a musician, to gain my full independence, and to rely only on myself, with a sure sense of where I was going.

You had other teachers, of course, and they must also have contributed to your development as a pianist. What of your beginnings at the piano?

I was no prodigy, able to rattle off everything by the age of four or five. Neither were my parents musical, but they did encourage me when I asked to learn the piano. I was eight years old when I heard some children playing in my school and made up my mind that this was what I too must do. My parents probably thought of this as just another part of my education. But I thought differently! Every piece I encountered held new thrills for me, and my teacher, Tom Lishman, was convinced of my talent and arranged for me to study at the Westchester Conservatory not far from my home. I must have done well there to be accepted at thirteen by the Juilliard, where I went on revering my professors and just played and played! Although I was quite good at maths and languages, it was music which always came first. My main professor at Juilliard was Sacha Gorodnitzky, but that didn't prevent me having occasional lessons with the legendary Rosinna Lhevinne who, although by then in her nineties, was still teaching. It was awe-inspiring to hear her talk about music, and how Josef Lhevinne, her husband, would approach certain works, and how often she would take issue with him. All the same, my main interest lay in enlarging my repertoire and in gaining experience of the concert platform whenever the opportunity occurred. Nothing else concerned me, and in this I was no different to the rest of my fellow-students in that giant incubator of budding talents which was the Juilliard.

At about this time I started to have pains in my hands and arms, mild aches at first but becoming ever more acute. Having such pains was simply considered a sign that 'you did your work thoroughly'. Soon there came a moment when I couldn't play at all. Suddenly I realised that my whole life, my career which was not yet started, was on the point of ruin. I fell into a deep depression which only a musician who finds himself in similar circumstances could understand.

One day I received an invitation through one of my colleagues from a lady who was anxious to discuss my condition, promising help. She was Olga Barabini, a fine pianist who had made quite a name for herself in Italy, but who had to abandon a promising career because of her horrendous panic attacks when on the platform. Subsequently, she had become a stunning society hostess with a salon where artists and authors mixed with bankers and financiers – a surefire combination! She explained that she had heard me play at some Juilliard concerts and thought I had real talent. When she was told about my plight, her only thought was to help me. At the time, 'relaxation' was the byword among piano pundits following on the discoveries earlier in the century on the part of Breithaupt and Matthay. Olga Barabini taught me to relax my arms, and the pains simply vanished! Only then did I realise how tense my muscles had been, and understood the connection between the stiffness and the pains I had experienced. Looking back, I often think how fortunate I was to have developed my arm injury when I did. Perhaps there is a predestined time for any happening in one's life. From then on, I learned from her to play with great freedom of movement, at the same time developing an awareness of how best to use my hands, arms, and whole body to serve the music to be played. Working with her was providential, and her trust in me and my abilities was to remain a lasting inspiration. It was she who encouraged me to enter the

Busoni and the Montreal Competitions and, when I came first in both, exclaimed exultantly: 'Right, next is the Chopin in Warsaw!'

So here I am able to do what I really want, to play the works I love most, to have the opportunities every artist dreams about, to appear in the most important world centres, with my only responsibility that of safeguarding this healthy approach to my music-making. I now look forward to completing the next four CDs for Arabesque, and continuing my Chopin cycle in London and in other European capitals.

You have made many recordings with other labels apart from Arabesque: Angel, Telarc, Delos, Nonesuch, Hänssler, and Virgin Classics. You are also a passionate chamber music player, having made recordings with the Cleveland, Tokyo, and Takacs string quartets. You have also recorded with the FOG Trio, which you founded with violinist Jorla Fleexanis and cellist Michael Grebaffier, the name presumably the acrostic of your three initials. Do you find these activities fulfilling?

Playing with other musicians remains always my ideal way of making music. I love the way we interact and respond to each other's phrasing, tone colours, spontaneous outbursts. We have tremendous fun and excitement when we are in agreement. But for that we must be prepared to give and take constantly. As to recordings, well, these are now a foregone part of our survival as artists. Nowadays, CDs do our travelling for us, reaching beyond the concert hall into the privacy of the home. It is good to feel that, wherever I go, my recordings will have been there before me. All the same, there is nothing to compare with a live concert, where one can interact directly with the listeners and be cocooned in their waves of warmth. After the two-and-a-half hours of my Chopin recitals, I feel drained of any energy, yet happy all the while to be in this state.

You are so involved in your life as a performer. How do you prepare for these feats of physical and artistic endurance?

Having performed since very young, I have developed a certain 'technique' but, primarily, it has always been a labour of love. I love my audience and I love my music: it is as simple as that! Nevertheless, it didn't come without a conscious search on my part into how one can sustain this ability to perform without wasting energy, and at an optimal level of self-realisation. With this in mind, I studied various disciplines such as Yoga and Transcendental Meditation of which the latter – the quiet withdrawal into oneself for certain periods of each day – established itself

as by far the best approach for me. Every time I stop working, I feel this renewal of my energies, a stillness in mind and body which launches me into a transcendental realm and fortifies me for taking up my task anew
.

I am glad to hear you broach such matters since I myself have made a special study of the 'phenomenon of peak performance', that moment when the playing lifts off, when the music flows through the artist into the audience and beyond. Psychologists call this phenomenon the flow, and it applies not only to musical performance, but also to athletics, theatre, ballet, in short, to all such moments of being carried away in pursuit of one's creative goal. I would be interested to hear of your experiences.

Ever since I started to appear in public I began asking myself why it was that sometimes everything seemed to fall into place, even in the midst of the most gruelling programmes, while at other times a gremlin seemed to get into the works. Before, I simply accepted it as part and parcel of an artist's life, but your mentioning it so pointedly gives me courage to delve deeper into some aspects of my platform behaviour.

When I walk onto the stage, I am already keyed up both in mind and body for whatever is to come. But on those occasions when I experience this magic state, which you describe so well as being like a vessel through which the music flows, there is no longer any difference between the music and myself – we are *one* and indivisible. This usually happens when I am immersed in music to which I feel very close emotionally. More often than not this will be a slow-moving piece – a nocturne or Adagio – never when I am involved in virtuoso passages. This magical moment may last only a few seconds or, conversely, a long time – I lose any notion of actual time as such. I hope that I do not sound arrogant when I say that at these moments 'I am it'. Having meditated for several years now, such a transcendent state is not unfamiliar to me, but there are some fundamental differences. When playing in this state, I have the uncanny sensation of being at once inside myself and outside my body, with my mind extraordinarily clear and able to follow every moment of my playing. I may be 'physically' performing but at the same time remain in close communion with my audience. At other times, though more rarely, I have had similar experiences while attending concerts. I remember one such moment when I was about 14 and Josef Krips was conducting the New York Philharmonic in Beethoven's Seventh Symphony, which I had never heard before, a whole new range of experiences to take in all at once. When the orchestra played the second movement it was almost more than I could bear. I felt myself completely transported, and realised that this is how one experiences music when the whole of one's being is involved. The intensity of that moment was unforgettable – it will always be with me! And this is what I always hope to recapture whenever I go to a concert and what I hope to communicate each time I give a concert myself.

You are living a very rich and rounded life as a musician what with performances, recordings and occasional masterclasses. Have you ever thought of doing some teaching in a conservatoire or music faculty?

Yes, I have often given this some thought. When I work with young students in a masterclass situation, I love the free exchange of views. The participants are usually well-prepared and perform as in a full-dress concert with the only difference that we discuss the work and the performance afterwards. But to teach on a regular basis, to take the responsibility of training such outstanding young talents for the profession – I don't think I'm ready for this as yet. I am still too bound up with my own music-making to be able to give to the next generation what they need, and what I would feel honour-bound to give them, especially following the shining example set me by my own teachers. No doubt a time will come when I shall feel moved to do this, but that time is not yet.

Piano Journal VOL 19 NO 55 1998

Peter Feuchtwanger
teacher of David Helfgott

The Film Shine – yet another film about playing the piano following in the wake of Madame Sousatska and The Piano – has been showing to capacity audiences throughout the English speaking world as well as Western Europe. It has made an immediate impact and provoked heated discussions among musicians on one side and critics, journalists, psychiatrists and psychologists on the other, not so much as to the actual quality of the film, but with regard to the pianist, David Helfgott, whose life it depicts.

How do you explain this unbelievable response from so many different walks of life to a film which has none of the usual ingredients for making an instant success – violence, drugs, sex – yet has managed to touch the innermost core of everyone's sensitivity and imagination?

I believe it is because of its seering humanity. The film is based on a true story, the plight of a young Australian prodigy of Polish-Jewish descent who suffered a total breakdown just when he reached the zenith of his ambitions – to perform Rachmaninov's Third Piano Concerto in London with the Orchestra of the Royal College of Music, where he had been studying. The next twelve years found him in a psychiatric hospital, in a world of shadows, withdrawn into a horrendous inner inferno. He then made a miraculous recovery which amazed all the doctors who had diagnosed his condition as 'irreversible'. Watching the scenes where David is shown sitting alone on a bench completely oblivious to anything going around him, even when one of his sisters tries to get a flicker of recognition from him, was almost unbearable. The first light in this dark night of the soul, only came when he walked in while a Music Therapy session was in progress. Like an automaton he was drawn to the piano sitting down next to the therapist and starting timidly to touch the keys. Minutes later he had joined in, improvising with the therapist and playing with more and more excitement, as if he had never been parted from the piano in all those long years of despair.

271

Such moments in the film are unforgettable and bring out an emotional response in each one of us. From then on the film shows how he succeeds in conquering his fear of facing people. Plucking up courage to enter a café, he sees a piano in the corner, goes straight to it and starts to play. Thenceforward he is there every night, playing for hours to an ever-growing audience enthralled by his total identification with the piano – his only means of communication.

One evening, Gillian, an astrologer happened to drop in. She was so moved by David and his extraordinary abandon while playing such a wide range of repertoire that she decided then and there to devote her life and all her energies to help him develop his musical potential to the utmost. Soon they became man and wife, since when there has been constant spiritual growth for them both – he finding love and inspiration for which he craved, she being rewarded by watching him get ever stronger physically as well as artistically so as to be able to cope with his newfound career. The immense success of the film may be also due to the fact that in each of us there is still that little child who believes in fairy stories, with the prince (or, in this case princess) arriving at the crucial moment, whereupon they fall in love, marry and live happily ever after.

There is another side to the story, though. David Helfgott has become a household name, thanks to Shine, like The Piano, having received an Oscar for the superb performance of the actor who impersonated him. Along with the film, David was swept into the glare of the cameras, with all the ensuing razzmatazz and commercialisation, out of which he emerged as a pop-star of Classical music! This created a rather unfavourable reaction, with Gillian and his agents being accused of abusing his new celebrity status to organise appearances everywhere and also for charging exorbitant fees! While audiences, many of whom have never entered a concert hall before in their lives, crowd in from all sides to give him standing ovations, musicians and critics are divided into 'pro' and 'con', some praising his performances as unique events, others writing derogatory, and sometimes insulting, articles. In the midst of all the hue and cry is David, sublimely unaware, playing his heart out with so much love and goodness that one cannot help being touched by it. To me and to many of us, he represents a triumph over adversity – a genuine success story.

I recently had the opportunity to hear him at his first London appearance in the Royal Festival Hall where his charismatic personality, coupled with some truly exquisite moments in his playing, conquered his listeners. Of course, there are aspects of his performance which do not satisfy those whose ears are accustomed to Horowitz or who expect to hear Beethoven's Appassionata sonata as interpreted by Pollini or a Barenboim.

He plays more for himself and his constant singing along with the music or beating time with one hand whenever there is a rest in the music, can become irritating. But when he comes into his own in encore pieces such as Flight of the Bumble Bee, La Campanella or Liszt's Sixth Hungarian Rhapsody, one can expect memorable experiences.

In the course of an Australian documentary, I was very impressed to observe him having a piano lesson with his teacher over there, Alice Garrard, who studied with Bartok in Budapest. How serious and intent is he, listening to her comments and trying to apply them in his playing.

Peter, you first met David in 1986, when Gillian brought him to London to study with you. No wonder that his agent at the time and Gillian thought that you would be the right person for David. Not only are you a great pedagogue but your Feuchtwanger Exercises: From relaxation to virtuosity have been used by a great number of outstanding young pianists, some of them first-prize winners at international piano competitions who follow you wherever you conduct your masterclasses, whether in European capitals or in Korea, Japan, Israel, America.

Pianists like Martha Argerich and Shura Cherkassky have always acknowledged your contribution to piano teaching and performance. Thus I believe you were better suited to helping David than anyone else through an approach which frees the whole body, and by extension, the mind, of unnecessary tensions. This is what David needed if he were to ever think of undertaking such exhausting concert tours from one continent to another. How did you get on with him on his first visit to London?

Early in 1986, I received a letter from David's agent enquiring if I would accept him to study with me. He told me the whole story and enclosed a cassette of him playing the Chopin Ballade in G minor. David had only recently started to play again and was in great demand for concerts throughout Australia, appearing on radio and television but Gillian wanted him to go back to his studies that had been so abruptly brought to a close. Listening to the cassette, I realised that here was a pianist of immense gifts but one who badly needed disciplining if his performances were not to become blurred by his enormous outpouring of emotion. I accepted the challenge gladly, especially since, as a young man in London, I had become interested in Music Therapy, which was only then being developed, and worked with a friend who was a music therapist in a psychiatric hospital. I found the experience very rewarding and my new understanding of the human psyche became reflected in my teaching so that my attitude to my students gained new dimensions. Soon after the initial contact had been made, I received a television documentary which I studied carefully, observing how David sat at the piano, his appalling posture and his way of using his hands and arms. I was also able to note how he behaved away from the keyboard – in so 'physical' a state of constant movement that any stillness eluded him. It was fascinating to watch him talk, the words tumbling over one another – quite unable to stop once he gets going. David and Gillian arrived in London as soon as they received my answer and we established a good rapport from the outset. There was an immediate trust, with David sitting at the piano and starting to play without the least hesitation – enjoying himself hugely!

Meanwhile I was watching his hands and fingers which achieved naturally, of their own accord, everything one tries to teach other pianists. The keyboard seemed to be an extension of his whole being and he showed an incredible and quite intuitive musical intelligence, being totally absorbed in what he was doing. But I was distressed by the way he sits, stooped over the keyboard, making a lot of unnecessary body movements which interfere with technical skill and accuracy. He also sings loudly while playing – which may help his breathing with the music, but does distract the audience from listening and may become quite irritating. My task was a difficult one. Here was a pianist whom I consider to be an unfulfilled musical genius, who has only recently come back to life as a performer. Hence my greatest concern was not to destroy his newly found joy and elation at being able to share his gifts with his audiences. I had to be extremely careful as to how to approach him, how to point out what I expected him to do. I did not intimate that intuition is not always reliable and that what he really needed was to discipline himself to study thoroughly the whole structure of a work along with the motivic connections which make it coherent. All the same I was worried how to bring some organization into his studies without destroying any of the magic. Nevertheless he proved a most diligent student, anxious to please me and, of course, to win Gillian's approval. Our work together became tremendous fun – we laughed a lot, and I had to devise ways to keep his concentration alert when he was not actually playing so as to get him to pay attention to what I was trying to convey. It was so much easier for him to follow the line of least resistance and simply get involved in his own playing, although he accepted my views that what he had been doing on an intuitive level now had to be thought out.

David and Gillian continued to come to London whenever I was there or otherwise would attend my masterclasses in Bonn, Vienna, Sion or Copenhagen. Playing for knowledgeable musicians was a new experience for him. He made an immediate impact on the other young pianists and, in his turn, revelled as being accepted as a serious musician by his colleagues. Every one was enthralled by his total commitment and the ease with which he could play the most difficult passages, trying hard at the same time to incorporate my ideas. Sometimes he responded immediately, with a childlike delight that he could do what I expected. In Copenhagen, one of my students was so moved by his playing and personality that he decided on the spot to give up his own prospects to devote his entire energies to helping David's career. Since then he has done splendid work as David's 'personal agent' and launched the first CDs which are now in such great demand everywhere. For myself, I was discovering every day various aspects of David's personality such as his uncanny memory. Whatever work you mention he can play it instantly, without the slightest hesitation and his memory is not only confined to music. He needs to read a name or sentence only once to remember it ever after. When he first met me, he asked if Leon Feuchtwanger – the well-known German author – was my father (actually he was cousin of my father!) Our friendship has grown over the years, nurtured my mutual trust and love. My dearest wish is that I may have succeeded in some measure to strike a balance between his amazing potential and an organised attitude to his playing. I do know that every time we had the opportunity to work together he gained confidence, so that both Gillian and himself felt stronger and better able to face the difficulties ahead.

More than ten years have passed since he first came to study with you. Surely, during your many encounters you talked about other things than music and the piano. With your insight into the psychology of young musicians, most of them on threshold of their careers or already launched, you must have asked yourself many times what really triggered his collapse. I saw both the film and the documentary and it was so interesting to observe the 'real' David, not the actor. There is enormous tension in the way he talks incessantly, the words pouring out before he has even had a moment to sift his thoughts. Yet when he plays – as you already pointed out – his arms and hands move in complete co-ordination with the music, his fingers caressing the keys and coaxing exquisite sounds from them. As you know, his teacher at the Royal College of Music was Cyril Smith, one of the most brilliant of British pianists, but his playing could not have been more different from David's. He belonged to the school of 'high finger articulation' which created a lot of muscular tension so that he himself was extremely tense in his performance. In the end he had a stroke, which left him paralysed on one side and I can't help wondering whether, in studying with him, David might have been affected, even unconsciously, by his teacher's tensions. Did he ever mention his time in College?

We talked about everything. The more he trusted me, the more open he became. Often it was about his childhood home in Perth or about his father, who was depicted in the film as an intolerant, often violent man. Leaving home to go to London in open defiance of his father's orders has left a deep scar, which together with the terrible scenes and beatings he received, obviously created a constant conflict in his mind. He also told me about a disastrous relationship he had had with a young woman whom he went so far as to marry – he only referred to her as Clara – who cared neither for his music nor his playing – she actually sold his piano which he had received as a prize! The utter despair which this produced might well have contributed to his breakdown. There must have been many reasons, some of them deep-rooted while others may just have triggered the final blow. Who can know the real causes of such mysterious and serious mental illnesses? What really matters is his amazing well-being, his *joie de vivre*, which gives such tremendous satisfaction to Gillian, his many friends and which excites his audiences.

David's case poses so many questions of concern to musicians, psychologists, medical practitioners and all those involved in the field of Performing Arts Medicine. Both you and I have been working for quite a few years with pianists' physical and psychological problems and have succeeded in curing many who would otherwise have had to stop playing altogether because of pain, injuries or depression. In my work at the International Society for the Study of Tension in Performance (ISSTIP) Performing Arts Clinic I have helped several hundred musicians come back to their studies or careers, sometimes after years of being able to play their instruments. We know only too well that all these injuries are caused by excessive tension and have witnessed repeatedly the psychological trauma which ensues then these musicians are not only in physical pain but are cut off from their instruments and everything they have striven for years to achieve. Their existence appears futile: a deep depression sets in and they are left dependent on drugs which may relieve their mental state for a while but can never cure it. Perhaps the impact of the film may have something to do with the fact that many musicians either identify their situation with David's or they know someone who has been through a similar ordeal.

I can only say that being in a position to help pianists who might otherwise have had to abandon their careers gives me immense satisfaction. How well I understand Gillian and her feelings have brought so much happiness to David. Yet she is also receiving so much from and through him in return.

Another opportunity arose for you to work with David when he went on his American tour. As I understand it, you were brought over by plane to give David some refresher lessons before his controversial debut in Boston and before he went on to tour Canada where, actually, he had rave reviews. Do you think he has grown as a pianist?

I was very glad when I received the call to go to Boston to help him. I found the same never-ending state of joy, of excitement and the same childish impatience to go to the piano as soon as possible. Perhaps the keyboard is the place where he feels most secure. I was wondering whether he might have been affected by Gillian's apprehension, the agent's bustling around, no matter how hard they tried to keep David out of it. It is difficult to say whether his playing has grown or not. He certainly was doing his best to take in my comments and suggestions and he managed to apply everything during the concert. But I was very careful not to disturb him just before his performance. He shows the same extraordinary qualities as ever, certain favourite pieces he does like no one else but, again, there are technical flaws and he cannot help getting over-emotional in his interpretations. Does this matter? Even if some critics are too insensitive to celebrate this man's triumphs against all obstacles, there are many who respond to his playing, not so much with their intellect as with their heart. So much goodness and love pours out of him when he plays that I am convinced that we cannot but become better and more human beings from having heard him and from having known him.

Piano Journal VOL 18 NO 53 1997

Nancy Lee Harper

Nancy Lee Harper became President of EPTA Portugal in 1998 and has developed music at the University of Aveiro into a truly international centre of pianism and scholarship. She has introduced courses at Master's and Doctoral levels, and her students have unique opportunities to work with some of the leading pianists of our time who take part in the annual Festival 'Celebrating Great Pianists' which she organises. Nancy has greatly contributed to EPTA during these past seven years, having taken part in the Annual European Conferences of EPTA Associations with illustrated lecture recitals introducing Portuguese music and other topics of unusual interest to our members. Since then Nancy has visited many EPTA countries to perform, to conduct seminars and masterclasses, or to sit on the juries of piano competitions.

A pianist of stature, Nancy studied first in the USA, then for a while in London with Denise Lasimonne, the adopted daughter of Tobias Matthay, who introduced her to his teaching method using arm-weight and relaxation as fundamental aspects of a piano technique. On her return to the USA she completed her Doctorate at North Texas University. Her latest book on de Falla is due to be published by Scarecrow Press in 2005.

Most pianists I have interviewed have been prodigies, of whom either one or both parents were musicians; they would turn to the piano as to another toy or in order to pick out actual tunes. Were you such a child?

One of my earliest memories is of the piano. I adored its sound, identified with it from the start and cried to be allowed to play it. Nevertheless, I had a very hard time convincing my parents that this was to be my destiny, in spite of the fact that my mother saw it coming when she observed me beating time to the music with my hands at just two months old. My father was a medical doctor and my mother an occupational therapist who had studied the piano when she was a child. She was extremely musical and I can still hear her beautiful singing voice in my ears today. We had no piano at home. However, during the Sunday dinners at my paternal grandparents' home, I would go to their piano and pretend I could play and read the hymnbook. This was the only contact I had with the instrument until just before my tenth birthday when, after I had given up all hope of ever having the opportunity to learn to play, fate intervened.

My grandmother died during our time in Miami, Florida where my father had been posted as an Army doctor and where I studied ballet. She left me her piano and when we returned to our native Arkansas I began piano lessons. What a thrill that was! I studied with the local teacher for three years until I had learned all she could teach me. Then I became a pupil of Nena Plant Wideman in Shreveport, Louisiana where I remained for four years. She had a tremendous influence on me. After only four years of study at the age of 14, I made my debut in the Schumann Piano Concerto with the Shreveport Symphony under Rudolf Ganz. The following year I played the Tchaikovsky First Concerto with several orchestras including the New Orleans Philharmonic, the North Texas State University Orchestra and the Shreveport Symphony under Jens Nygaard, a conductor from New York. Most of the performances were a result of having won piano competitions, but once or twice John Shenaut, the conductor of the Shreveport Symphony, would invite me to play when they needed a soloist or when they had a young people's concert. This, of course, constituted heaven-sent experience. At 16 during my final year in high school, I played the Franck *Symphonic Variations* with the Shreveport Symphony under Harry John Brown.

So you were something of a prodigy after all, playing with the great conductor and pianist Rudolf Ganz, himself a student of Busoni. Surely such achievements must have encouraged you to continue studying towards a career.

Yes, of course, even though I was not a child prodigy. I learned very quickly and worked very hard, arising at 5.30 am in order to practise before school and afterwards practised another three hours. So, while the days were long, I was in my element! I did a lot of accompanying for the band members or at church and became a good sight-reader. I also played French horn, but gave it up at 14 or 15 because I simply had no time for both, in spite of having placed first chair in the All-State Band.

Everyone thought that I would have a big career as a concert pianist. After graduation, I was invited to play in St. Moritz, Switzerland, as the

USA representative in a Summer Festival.

As there was little subsidy, my parents felt they could not afford for me to go if I were to attend university the following autumn. For personal reasons and because of my young age, I was not allowed to attend the Juilliard School or Florida State University. So I went to study with Dalies Frantz, a former student of Artur Schnabel at the University of Texas at Austin. Little did I know how this event would change my entire life! Not only had Dalies had a brilliant career for ten years but, because of his good looks and talent, he was often hired by MGM to make movies of great pianists' lives, if I remember correctly. When World War II broke out, his film career came to an untimely end. His wife committed suicide. His personal life was in shambles. At the time I knew him, he was very ill. Nevertheless, he had a most interesting class in which I was his youngest pupil. James Dick, his star student, entered the Tchaikovsky Competition in Moscow that year, placing in the upper echelons. Dalies's teaching approach could be diabolically sadistic at times – either you were on Cloud 9 or you were devastated! On 1 December 1965 he died. I had been with him less than three months, yet I was completely traumatised by his personality and by this experience. I became psychologically blocked and couldn't play any more. It was like being in a severe car accident and having to learn how to walk again. I became ill and had to leave for six months, yet I was determined to conquer this problem. So I went back but opted not to study with Charles Rosen, who was then substituting for Dalies, and decided instead to pursue Piano Pedagogy with a most remarkable lady, Verna Harder. She had one of the first Piano Pedagogy courses in America and was an absolutely fantastic teacher. It was wonderful to observe her work with children. In spite of this turn of events, it took me a long time to recover from the experience with Dalies Frantz. I had psychosomatic illnesses that led to major surgery while I was at the university. There was no one to talk to about my emotional pain. In those days, if you went to a psychiatrist you were considered crazy, and I was not – only very depressed. I was still searching for 'me'. It was during this time that I became attracted to the Bahá'í Faith with its wide-ranging teachings, which to this day continue to influence the pattern of my life.

Fortunately you survived your traumatic experiences at University long enough to take on new challenges although not, as had been expected originally, to join the international circuit. Instead, you chose to enrol in courses on Piano Pedagogy which gave you a broader insight into what was to be your future development as teacher, performer and, later on, as organiser of international seminars and conferences. Tell me, when did you first come to Europe?

At the end of my university studies, on the advice of the wonderful Frank Mannheimer, with whom I had studied for two summers, I decided that I would come to England to study piano with Denise Lasimonne, Tobias Matthay's adopted daughter. I studied many things with her: Bach's *Italian Concerto*, Mozart and Schubert sonatas, Chopin's B Minor Sonata and ballades, some chamber music of Brahms and Beethoven with cellist Rohan de Saram amongst other things. She was born in France and we spent six months in Paris where she taught. During my studies with her an amazing break-through occurred. With good reason we used to call her 'the liberator'! I began to feel as if a dam were about to burst in my head. The music started to flow again and I began to find my voice. One day she said to me, 'Nancy, I did not know you had so much talent.' Really, it was such a freeing experience. I am eternally grateful for that time. I stayed on with Denise another year and simultaneously entered the Royal Academy of Music in post-graduate studies, studying Accompanying and Chamber Music with Geoffrey Pratley, Composition with Patrick Savill and Harpsichord with Geraint Jones. I also taught privately in Reading and London. I remember playing in some competition at the Wigmore Hall.

Did you stay on in Europe after your studies?

No, I was not sure that I would have a career as a concert pianist and did not pursue the international competition circuit. So I returned to the USA in 1972 where I married my husband and began a family – this is now almost 33 years ago. I began teaching when I was 19 years old and particularly love working with children, love their imagination, and find it gratifying to be able to mould their musical awareness. I think that it is very important to continue to perform while maintaining a teaching career. How easy it is to forget the challenges of playing a new work, for example! When my own children were very young, I not only taught them but also taught in a preparatory department of a junior college in Texas. Later I was a teaching assistant at the University of North Texas during my doctoral studies in Piano Performance. And I taught in Argentina where we lived during the '70s: those horrifying years of the *desaparecidos*. I also had performing opportunities there and loved the warm Argentine people.

When did you seriously come back to the idea of a career in music?

The opportunities for renewed concertising occurred after my doctoral studies when we moved to Santa Fe, New Mexico – an unusually active musical community. There I was engaged as the principal keyboardist with the Orchestra of Santa Fe and its chamber music subsidiary, the Ensemble of Santa Fe. I also taught at the College of Santa Fe. I went through an experimental stage of playing the harpsichord and the fortepiano, even having my own instruments made for me, so as the better to understand Baroque and Classical performance practice. While there, I performed with some excellent musicians such as Nicholas McGeegan, James Oliver Buswell III, Jurgen Hübscher and opera singers from Santa Fe and New York. But in spite of all the performing opportunities, I soon reached a plateau and longed for more stimuli. Within a short time, Portugal opened to us.

Portugal gave you the best opportunity to develop your teaching programme at all levels – first at the University do Minho in Braga for two years and subsequently for the past ten years at the University of Aveiro, where you founded EPTA Portugal. I was particularly grateful to Graziela Cintra of the Portuguese Music Education Association for recommending you as the best potential organiser of EPTA Portugal, despite her reservations about your being American. Thus it was that EPTA Portugal became a reality! Thanks to your combined commitment to your teaching, to your students and to EPTA, it has become one of the strongest and most active of our National Associations.

Yes, Graziela certainly knew how difficult it would be in Portugal. And if it's difficult for a Portuguese, then how much more so for a foreigner! However, I have had marvellous help and support, and now EPTA Portugal has acquired some truly outstanding members. The Portuguese are such creative and caring people – forever enthusiastic to learn new things while preserving their national heritage!

You first became interested in the music of Spanish composers through your Doctoral thesis on the Piano Sonatas of Rodolfo Hälffter, a contemporary of Manuel de Falla.

Yes, I've always loved Spanish music, especially that of the 20th century. I came to Falla through Hälffter, a great man whom I visited three times in Mexico City where he lived after being exiled from his native Madrid during the Spanish Civil War. He presented me with a limited-edition Falla document entitled *Superposiciones* and it was this composer's sketchbook that really piqued my curiosity about Falla – friend to Stravinsky, Debussy, Ravel, Viñes, Picasso and so many other important artists of the first half of the twentieth century. Falla seriously considered becoming a piano teacher even after his public adherence to composition. His pianistic heritage can be traced back to Bach, through his teachers José Tragó, Georges Mathias (a pupil of Chopin), etc. Being in Portugal has made it possible to know other noteworthy Iberian composers. The Iberian influence in the sonatas of Domenico Scarlatti, whose Portuguese manuscripts are being currently studied by an Italian doctoral student of mine, fascinate me. I enjoy playing works of little-known composers or little-known works of important composers. I've made a world-première recording of Portuguese contemporary solo piano works on the *Numérica* label and am doing several other projects including Hälffter's complete solo piano works.

So your own book on de Falla will come out soon?

Scarecrow Press will be publishing it at the end of February 2005. This is my second Falla book, the first being a bio-bibliography published by Greenwood Press in 1998. Already I am planning a third one – this time about Falla and the piano. People forget that he was an excellent pianist in his own right and won an important national competition against Frank Marshall in 1905, the same year that he won the San Fernando Fine Arts composition competition for his opera, *La Vida Breve*. He just didn't have the nervous constitution to be a concert career. That was before you invented your technique, Carola!

Competitions at every level, from early to advanced or professional stages, have become very much a part of the piano profession and continue to multiply like mushrooms. They are justified as keeping teachers, parents and pupils motivated, and there is no denying that students work better when there is a goal in view. What are your views?

I love competitions, both from a personal standpoint as well as a professional one. Winning or losing, there is much to be learned from competing. After all, we are born into this world competing – competing with siblings, with friends, with colleagues. Competitions are a great stimulus and catalyst for young people, as well as a measure of growth. One learns so much from hearing peers perform and from going through the challenges of a competition. As you remember,

Paul Pollei said at the EPTA conference in Budapest that he believed the future of piano playing is in competitions. In 2004, I founded an International Piano Competition in honour of one of Portugal's great pianists and EPTA Portugal honorary member, Helena Sá e Costa, and plan to propose a national piano competition to EPTA Portugal because I think it will stimulate piano playing and raise the level of awareness there.

Your work in Aveiro with the many young pianists who take part in your Annual International Course and Festival 'Celebrating Great Pianists' has given you an overview of the serious physical and psychological problems which can confront young performers at the beginning of their careers if not while still studying. You have taken these problems to heart and have since undergone training as a Music Medicine Practitioner at the Courses set up by the International Society for the Study of Tension in Performance (ISSTIP) in London in 2003/2004. Thus you are now in a position to be able to offer lasting help to your students and colleagues in need of advice or actual therapy. I had the pleasure of coming to your second Festival in 2001 when I worked with the pianists — most of them affected by stiffness in joints and muscles produced by tension. It was then that you decided to pursue these studies and, hopefully, to set up your own Centre of Research at the University of Aveiro. Your dissertation, Zoning into Piano Performance: The Peak Experience, which earned you a distinction on graduation, has embraced the subject of my own research over many years (cf. The Phenomenon of 'Peak Experience' or 'The Flow' in Musical Performance, Piano Journal No.65). My article was based on some 50 interviews with great pianists of our time who were asked to comment on their own experiences of 'the flow'. You have developed these studies further and we hope that your dissertation will soon be published. When you played as a child, do you remember such 'peak' moments?

Absolutely! From a very early age, I knew I was going to be a pianist. I cannot tell you what happens when I go to the piano short of being convinced that it is possible to understand all of humanity from the piano bench. At other times, solutions to pressing problems will immediately present themselves. Often I am transported to worlds beyond when at the piano. Of course, working out fingering and technical problems can comstitute a rude return to reality so that the 'Peak Experience' doesn't usually happen during those times. Deliberate practice is very necessary, yet practice and the 'Peak' are not synonymous.

While you may not have had great technical training as a child, your musicality guided your fingers to do what they should. As a teenager, when you were playing those concerti, did you experience that magic moment whilst performing?

I remember so well being nervous at my first performance of the Schumann Concerto, but something wonderful happened and I became 'hooked'. It was magic! It was the excitement of the moment and the thrill of communicating with the audience. The Peak Experience (P.E.) far transcends the nervous condition present during performance, even though nerves can destroy everything if we let them. One of the interesting things – and perhaps unique, as there probably have been no cross-cultural studies done on this subject so far – is that P.E. is not exclusive to any race or culture. There are no boundaries, no borders. It is part of the human experience. Having interviewed Portuguese as well as Brazilian pianists about their experiences while performing, I am led to believe that anyone can experience it. The results were all very similar indeed. I believe P.E. is a birthright common to our human condition in general.

One writer whom I interviewed described how, in the middle of the night, her typewriter would take over as if with a life of its own. This would be even more attention-provoking if it weren't so uncanny. I have talked to many creative artists who, when they try to describe their experience all say the same thing: a cold, sweaty, trembling sensation – strange and mysterious – about which you never know when it starts and when it finishes.

You seem to be inferring that supernatural forces may be at work in the operation of P.E. For me, P.E. involves a very high state of awareness in which total concentration is present. When performing, we are not only in touch with ourselves but also with an infinite source of energy or life-force. I think that anyone can achieve this experience. It may take a lifetime for one person or it may happen more often than not with another. Some of the pianists whom I interviewed didn't wish for P.E. to occur every time they performed, preferring the experience to remain apart from their normal state during performance. For instance, P.E. may occur perfectly naturally and spontaneously with children when they are completely absorbed in their playing. I well remember my oldest child, aged three or four, taking bits of wood and nails and building his toy cars in Argentina, working outside for hours, totally absorbed in his 'work' with utter joy in his creation. Ironically, this same child was diagnosed with hyperactivity and attention-deficit disorder years later in the traditional school setting, not being able to sit still and 'learn'. Such a contradiction! P.E., I believe, also engenders a very high state of happiness. P.E. surely must be a condition of the higher self, although if it ever became a common, everyday occurrence, there would probably be yet other experiences lurking beyond it. If you have ever done meditation, then you know that you are able to go to different levels. Music can be a kind of meditation conducive to P.E. As has been said, 'Music is a ladder by which the souls may ascend to the realm on high'.

When you perform, what happens? Are you aware of your state of mind and body?

Yes, indeed, the level of awareness is usually greatly enhanced, especially with the audience. There is a high level of excitement and great joy and I think my performance ability has grown. When I was younger, P.E. just happened, not always, but freely and spontaneously when it did. Later, when I underwent those years of psychological blockage, I was absolutely miserable and uncomfortable performing in front of audiences for a very long time. I was really hung up on getting things right – playing the right notes, getting the 'right' expression, using the 'right' amount of pedal, etc. Life's experiences helped to overcome some of these phobias. When I went through the period of raising children, of teaching, of getting my doctorate, I had to perform a lot – often accompanying and playing chamber music with little rehearsal or practice. There is nothing like lots of experience to give one confidence and comfort on the stage. Adjusting to different acoustical situations, different pianos, different audiences – all these things contribute to an artist's maturity. Because of the big detour I made at 17, my life certainly didn't follow the normal path.

One thing is sure: you have put Aveiro on the map! Your International Piano Festival, 'Celebrating the Great Pianists', has been a signal success and you have introduced new master's and doctor's courses at the university. But what interests me particularly, both for EPTA and for ISSTIP, is the fact that you are now planning a very important Centre of Music Medicine which will bring together musicians and medical specialists in the field, psychologists, physiologists, physiotherapists as well as complementary medicine practitioners. Such a centre at Aveiro, under your direction, will ensure that Portugal carries on with the work initiated by ISSTIP in the training of music medicine practitioners. The needs are still great but let us hope that prevention of future problems and injuries will bring the desired results, prevention being better than cure.

Certainly there is an urgent need for it! I envision a Performance Studies Centre with a strong emphasis on music medicine. There is nothing like that in all of Portugal. In fact, there is only one music therapy course in the country and, as you know, that is not at all what music medicine is about. Recently, I received the first post-doctoral proposal in music medicine at our university – a brilliant young Portuguese woman returning from England who wants to continue her studies on the effect of hormones on the singing voice. I am very excited about this proposal, which should give the impetus for the creation of such a centre and help to find the necessary funding for it.

Piano Journal VOL 25 NO 76 2005

Diane Andersen

'Die Grande Dame des belgischen Klavier' *is how the Lübecker Nach-richten described Diane Andersen.*

Her career has been influenced by personal contacts and artistic collabora-tions with some of the most important musical personalities of the twentieth century. She played Mozart with Sawallisch conducting (Orchestre de la Suisse Romande), Berg with Boulez and Maderna (Brussels and Rai Roma), piano duo pieces by Tansman with Tansman himself (Belgian Radio and Television Orchestra). Add to that her personal contacts with Kodaly and his wife Emma Gruber, Igor Markevitch, Alexandre Tansman and Madeleine Milhaud.

Denijs Dille, founder of the Bartok Archivum Budapest, a personal friend and biographer of Bartok, wrote about Andersen's solo Bartok CD that '. . . this being really the interpretation of Bartok that agrees with the spirit and technique of Bartok himself.'

Diane Andersen has played in famous venues such as Victoria Hall (Ge-neva), Palais des Beaux-Arts (Brussels), Liszt Ferenc Zeneakademia (Bu-dapest), Concertgebouw (Amsterdam), Teatro della Fenice (Venice), Ru-dolfinum (Prague), Carnegie Hall (New York). Her London appearance last March under the auspices of ILAMS was hailed as a 'triumphant . . . and memorable event!'

Among her recent CD's is a first-ever recording of the Cello and Piano Sonata and Piano Quintet by Adolphe Biarent, a composer whom she single-handedly rescued from undeserved oblivion, which won the International Classical Music Award in Cannes (2003).

After a career as a very sought-after professor at the Conservatoire Royal de Musique de Bruxelles, she is constantly in demand as a judge of interna-tional piano competitions and for masterclasses the world over.

Diane, we met a long time ago, in 1987, when you came to Graz Hoch Schule fur Musik, at the European Conference of the EPTA Associations organised by

Professor Sebastian Benda, President EPTA Austria.

You were invited to present your views on setting up the French section of EPTA Belgium, which, at the time, addressed only the Flemmish pianists and teachers, with Louise Hesbain, Piano professor at the Antwerpen Music Academy, as President. She was a remarkable organiser, did very good work and she actually organised a European Conference when EPTA had only 3 European associations. Sebastian Benda proposed to you 'Why not start a French branch in Belgium?' You came to Graz and the problem then was not so much whether EPTA would support this proposal as whether Louise and her committee would even countenance it since it had been tried before without success.

This time, with 21 countries participating in the European Conference, the pressure to keep politics out of music had the right response and Louise Hesbain was unable to exert her veto. Thus EPTA Belgium (Wallonie Bruxelles) was set up with Diane Andersen as President, while Louis Hesbain continued as President of EPTA Belgium (Flanders Brussels) to everyone's satisfaction!

You have now been President of EPTA Belgium (Walloni-Bruxelles) for 15 years and since then, both EPTA and Diane have grown from strength to strength. You have been a sort of EPTA ambassador: wherever you travel through the many European countries giving concerts and master classes, you also talk about EPTA, the Piano Journal and how beneficial it is for pianists and particularly for teachers to be part of a world organisation such as this. Indeed, this is how new EPTA Associations sprang up, such as EPTA Turkey and EPTA Serbia/Voyvodina. Needless to add that EPTA is grateful to Diane for her continuous support.

It is not difficult to do all this when you believe in what you are doing. But however important EPTA – your great idea, Carola – has now become, you need the right people to work to realize this ideal. I can add that I am a very happy to be the president of EPTA Belgium (Wallonie/Bruxelles) in which our team of Jean-Luc Balthazar, François Thiry, Dominique Cornil and myself have been working together since the very beginning, some 15 years ago. This is quite an achievement, don't you think?

To come back to your own life and career: you came to London many years ago as a successful young pianist, having been awarded the Harriet Cohen Bach Medal and having given recitals and made many recordings with your first husband, Andre Gertler. You played in London as a soloist with orchestra conducted by Constantin Silvestri. It was rather amusing that when you became President of EPTA Belgium (Wallonie/Bruxelles), my late husband, Miron Grindea, who was responsible for arranging Silversti's concerts at the time, asked: 'I wonder if Diane Andersen is the same beautiful young pianist who played with Silvestri?' Indeed, you were the one!

·I guess it was in 1962, quite a long time ago. The Harriet Cohen Bach Medal for my 'outstanding performances' was awarded to me at a special ceremony in Brussels in a very beautiful apartment at the Grand Place, particularly impressive for someone as young as I then was to be meeting the famous members of the Jury, which included Zoltan Kodaly and Darius Milhaud.

You showed unusual abilities from a very early age and started to perform and win competitions even as a child. Tell us about your first years at the piano.

My first years at the piano were rather chaotic because my parents kept on moving from one place and also from one country to another. When I was two years old, we lived in England, at Clitheroe, and I do remember spending time at the piano, playing tunes I heard on the radio or that my mother sang to me.

We then moved to Maison Lafitte near Paris where there was a piano which I played by ear. I was 4 by then and I tried to teach myself to read by cutting letters from newspapers so as to form them into words and thought it would be easy to learn to read music in the same way.

At this point my mother decided that it was time to get a piano teacher, so a nice young teacher who studied at the Paris Conservatoire arrived.

I loved having lessons with her, because after the lesson she allowed me to ride on her bicycle which I greatly enjoyed! She gave me the *Methode Rose*, most of the pieces of which I went through very quickly, and she was amazed when I pointed out some misprints in what would have been a dominant chord of G major whereupon she took me to her own teacher for advice on 'how to teach such a child'!

Soon afterwards we moved again following my father's new post, so I had a new teacher who was no good for me and who just let me play everything as I felt, never correcting nor helping me in any way. Fortunately, when I was seven we moved to Copenhagen where I started to learn with yet another, but I was not happy with the many exercises she tried to make me practise when I was craving to play pieces by great composers.

My parents were not musical but my mother did her best to support me, particularly when I won an important competition and, at last, I was taken to the teacher who knew how to treat young pianists. She was an old lady from a very musical family (grand-daughter of the Danish composer and conductor H.C. Lumbye) who opened my mind to the great music of the piano repertoire. Thanks to her constant support and enthusiasm, I won many competitions; by now, she had convinced my parents that I should follow a career as a pianist.

She remained my beloved teacher until I was 13, when we had to leave Copenhagen for Brussels where my father got an important job and where I was accepted at the Conservatoire Royal de Musique, first to study with an assistant of the Professor who had to make sure that my technique was up to the required standard. For the first time I realised how important it was to learn how to practise, how to hold the hand or how to move the fingers to acquire agility, in fact, I was learning how to play the piano!

I soon started to have lessons with Stefan Askenase, the great Polish pianist and professor at the Conservatoire, a pupil of Sauer, himself pupil of Liszt. He never talked about technique, expecting me to play all the great works of the repertoire. He was most inspiring and I learnt a great deal by listening to him and observing how he played.

It took me years before finding my own way of playing the piano, in which I felt comfortable and believed to be right. By then I was a mature pianist.

In my many years of experience as a pedagogue, I came to the conclusion that there is such a thing as a good or bad method of teaching the piano. The more I searched, the more I became convinced that the most important thing is to be conscious of how your own body functions, and from there go on to find the most effective and comfortable way to play, whatever the situation. I believe that we have to solve our pianistic problems in our own individual fashion and, when working with a student, my first task is to find out how he/she respond to the music and, particularly, how he/she relates to the instrument. In this way, I try to help my students by giving them the right tools which should then become their own, thus avoiding the difficulties I have experienced myself.

One important conclusion which I reached was that the musical language is the unique guideline for developing a piano technique able to express the most varied and subtle tones and nuances demanded by the music one studies. Technique alone, far from being the ideal approach, should be only the means to achieve one's ideal of interpreting the music.

You continued your studies at the Brussels Royal Conservatoire while at the same time already giving concerts.

I studied with Askenase for several years while I attended master classes given by great artists (master classes being nowhere as many and frequent as now) – among them was the wonderful pianist Lili Krauss who actually was a colleague of my first husband at the Liszt Music Academy in Budapest. She had made a name in Budapest as well as in Vienna as a uniquely sensitive pianist; her Mozart-playing was greatly admired not only by the public but also by her peers. She was also exquisitely beautiful, my father in law who knew Lily form her childhood in Budapest, used to tell me: 'You know, Lili Kraus ... that was something incredible!'

I remember first meeting Lili Kraus in Vienna, when my husband and I arrived there in 1939, just before the war, on a tour of European music festivals. She gave a Mozart Duo recital with the violinist Simon Goldberg – an unforgettable evening. Later on we corresponded when she was in her final years, still teaching at North Texas University where her students simply worshipped her. EPTA had only started and she was too ill to travel to Europe but she was greatly interested in the new organisation and its ideals. Our colleague in Holland, Frans Schreuder, has known her since the war years when they were both interned in a Japanese Prisoners of War Camp. He was only eight or nine years old while Lili was already an established pianist who, thanks to her playing, was given preferential treatment by a music-loving camp official.

I was very young when I attended her master classes in the sixties, at the Eduard van Beinum Stichting in Breukelen, a beautiful place near Amsterdam. While in Budapest, I was fortunate enough to study with Annie Fisher, who was a friend of André since their student days at the Franz Liszt Academy.

You played for several years with your husband, Andre Gertler, and made many recordings of violin and piano sonatas as well as trios and other chamber music.

Indeed I had splendid opportunities. André (who was a friend of Bartok and who had also often given concerts with him) and I performed and recorded for Supraphon the three Bartok Sonatas, the Contrasts as well as other Bartok's works for violin and piano, which were awarded the Prix de l'Académie Charles Cros in Paris. At that time there were only LP records but these recordings have been transcribed on CDs, on the Baltic label thanks to the old Supraphon company having leased them to Baltic.

Not only I had these splendid opportunities but I also had the privilege to play with great conductors like Boulez, Maderna and Sawallisch.

You have made a 'world' career, touring throughout Europe and recently giving recitals and master classes in USA from coast to coast. Many are the juries of international competitions to which you have been invited. What do you think of today's young pianists and their chances to make a career?

We all know the difficulties which confront young pianists on the threshold of their careers. We in EPTA try to help them by giving them opportunities to appear on Young Artists platforms at EPTA National or international conferences. It is important for them to be heard by musical audiences and also by concert agents who attend such gatherings. In addition many young pianists take part in international competitions and some of them do the circuit of such competitions as an outlet for their need to perform and be heard. Unfortunately, these competitions can only award one First Prize, and even these are not always the answer. Many such prize-winners have not made a name and are now forgotten by the public.

EPTA Belgium (Wallonie Bruxelles) organises annual competitions for young pianists up to 18 years old – now international – and I am always impressed with the very high standard of piano playing of these youngsters.

It is true that many young pianists have to earn their living by teaching, either privately or in music schools or other institutions. Teaching can be a rewarding experience and our responsibility as teachers is to stimulate our students and young pupils to be motivated in their studies. That is why it is important to arrange regular performances and prepare them for competitions within their age groups and standards.

To quote Professor Paul Pollei (at the EPTA Conference in Norway in 2000) 'we have to maintain the continuous interest in piano teaching and only through competitions can we involve everyone – pupils, teachers and parents'. This is, indeed, greatly needed and indispensable for the piano-teaching profession.

You have done pioneering work in discovering, performing, recording on CDs and generally making known the music of Belgian composers for piano and chamber music. To give one example, you recorded the complete works of Joseph Jongen, a marathon achievement, and now you have embarked on a new project, having discovered the lost music of an unknown composer, Adolphe Biarent. Tell us about your search and the thrill that comes with such a discovery.

The Jongen music is not really a discovery but I loved it and wanted to make it more known and performed. I have recorded the first two CDs of his piano music but there are 3 more CDs which will include his complete works for piano and piano duet.

It was a few years ago on discovering a cello sonata by the late 19th century French/Belgian composer Adolphe Biarent that I began to search for more works by this extraordinary composer who died in 1917. He probably committed suicide as a result of the war.

I first discovered his Cello Sonata by an extraordinary coincidence. I was given the music which had been printed printed privately by the Institute for Belgian Wallonian Culture – *L'Institut Jule Destrée* – a Belgian politician who was very devoted to the culture of Wallonie, the French speaking part of Belgium. The Institute was founded later on, after he had already died, as a homage to him and his work.

When I started to work in depth on Biarent Cello Sonata I became fascinated by its originality and richness of texture, that I decided to explore and find other works by this truly great composer. My search brought me into contact with the former secretary of the Institute. At the time this was being closed down, the Concierge put out lots of boxes with papers and manuscripts for collection by the dustmen, unless someone should take pity on them. The Secretary kept several boxes but just stocked them in chicken-coop. There I found them and had to spend days picking through and drying the messy contents, and trying to organise what had once been the manuscripts of orchestral and chamber works. Among them, I found a most moving Quintet which is still in manuscript but which we recorded on CD, together with the Cello Sonata. The recording was awarded the Cannes International Classical Music Award in 2003.

The Cello Sonata is a truly great work containing very powerful music which alternates with more subtle sounds; there is imagination of the highest order in the 'ethereal' ending of the sonata, as if everything were about to melt into thin air. When Mark Drobinsky and I first performed the Sonata we were thrilled to get the same rapt response from the audience.

You show great interest in fin-de-siecle and early 20th century composers – like Vincent d'Indy (who's Piano sonata you have recorded), Darius Milhaud and Ernst Toch.

I spend a lot of time in libraries and, it is true, find some treasures along the way. Like Biarent, Vincent d'Indy was fascinated by the 'ethereal' atmosphere, which they both created in their music. D'Indy ends his sonata in the same way as Biarent ended his cello sonata – creating this magical aura of sound in the final moments.Other composers have explored the same idea: Chopin in the extraordinary *Finale* of his tragic Sonata in Bb Minor, which heralds the later Impressionists in music and in art.

My latest recordings, still to be released, will include the Second Piano concerto by Ernst Toch, a neglected genius, better-known in the United States than in Europe, followed by the Piano concerto by Dianne Goolkasian-Rahbee (which she dedicated to me) and her Fourth Piano Sonata, along with other solo pieces.

Irina Osipova

You have been President of EPTA Russia since 1996 and you have managed to develop the organisation throughout the Russian continent while at the same continuing with your own career as pianist and Piano Professor at the Tchaikowsky Conservatory where you are also in charge of the Accompaniment class.

You have inherited EPTA Russia, which was already quite well established although this was during the Soviet era. When Professor Lev Vlasenko set up EPTA Soviet Russia in 1988 he was not allowed to do as much as he wanted. In Soviet Russia only one organisation was allowed to function with membership, the Artists Union, with several millions members as they were compelled to register. It was fortunate that when I went to Moscow trying to arrange with Professor Vlassenko the possibility of setting up EPTA Soviet Russia, I was supported by Serge Usanov, the Secretary of the Union and soon afterwards, both, Lev Vlasenko and Serge Usanov came to London for the launching of EPTA Soviet Russia at Steinway Hall, which was an extraordinary event at the time.

In 1989 EPTA Soviet Russia managed to organise the European Conference of all EPTA Associations at the Tchaikowsky Conservatory in Moscow, which made an enormous impact on the piano teaching profession throughout the Soviet Russia and in the whole of Europe. Pianists and teachers travelled for nights from far away places in Russia to arrive at the Conservatory for this great event. It was the first time that teachers and pianists were permitted to meet in great number in one place, in Moscow. EPTA members also came in great numbers as this was the first time that they could attend such a conference. Pianists from the Baltic countries were present when a miracle happened.

Then Soviet Russia became simply Russia and the three Baltic countries: Lithuania, Latvia and Estonia got their independence and, at that moment, not only EPTA Soviet Russia became EPTA Russia, but EPTA Lithuania, EPTA Latvia and EPTA Estonia were born. The three new Presidents had all been students of Lev Vlasenko at the Tchaikowky Conservatory. Glasnost had arrived. There was a euphoric atmosphere, everyone dancing and singing, the excitement went on and on.

Sadly, Vlasenko died a few years later and EPTA Russia had to find another

President. That was not easy until I met you in London when you came to give classes at the North London Piano School and we were introduced by Dr. Michael Schreider. You had the courage to take this difficult task over and accepted the challenge of re-organising EPTA Russia.

When you proposed to me to revive EPTA Russia I was immediately very interested but I knew I would be confronted by enormous hurdles from many quarters, politically and professionally, not to mention the financial difficulties. It was not a question of 're-organising' as there has not been any official organisation so I really had to start from scratch.

It was at the European Conference of EPTA Associations in Rome when the situation was clarified. As you may remember, a Russian piano teacher from Saratov tried to set up EPTA Russia with another President and arrived in Rome with a group of friends hoping to scuttle our arrangements. I had been worried that such an intrigue could happen and I brought with me two letters from the greatest pianists and professors from the Tchaikowsky Conservatory, Evgheni Malinin and Viktor Merzansky, who supported me fully. The EPTA Council appointed me officially as President of EPTA Russia and from then on the rest is known, as our activities are published regularly in the Piano Journal.

What difficulties did you encounter when you tried to organise EPTA Russia as an Association with members or when you tried to organise the first meeting of teachers?

Indeed I met with enormous difficulties, nothing ran smoothly. To register the Association on a legal basis took a long time; we had to pay a large sum to a solicitor and to the State, but I was determined to succeed. Finally, EPTA Russia was officially registers in 1997 under the title of 'Society of Piano Education in Russia'. I managed to include also ISSTIP – International Society for the Study of Tension in Performance – in the same Society.

Since then we have organised many meetings of teachers in Moscow and in the other Centres which have sprung up in other parts of Russia. There are now 9 EPTA Russia Centres (see *Piano Journal*). We have also organised many National Piano Competitions in these Centres and the Annual Rachmaninov International Competition takes place in Tambov in August. We also organise an Annual National Competition for Young Pianists up to 18 in Moscow.

You have brought into EPTA your expertise, your enthusiasm and your unbelievable capacity to develop EPTA Russia to what it is today. You have managed to bring almost the whole country into EPTA Russia. How many branches are there?

There are 9 branches, each one with its own Chairman. Some of them are more active than others; they organise meetings of teachers and competitions – at national and also on international levels. These branches are part of EPTA Russia but they are completely independent, they have total freedom to organise their events as suits their group of teachers. This is also important for EPTA as more and more teachers are joining their own association, thus the membership grows constantly.

It is impressive to see that EPTA Russia publishes its own Journal, Pianoforte. This is a great achievement as we know very well how costly such an exercise is and how time consuming this is for the editor. Are you editing Pianoforte or do you have some assistants?

We publish *Pianoforte* Magazine four times a year and we have reached number 29. Yes, I have to do all the work, gathering material, arranging the printing, correcting proofs, send the magazine to members both in Russia and abroad, then to the authorities and to other institutions. This is not a commercial magazine, it is only for EPTA members and, of course, it is part of the educational programme of the Society.

Let me congratulate you most warmly, from one editor to another, on the success you have made of your own magazine Pianoforte. However, it is very frustrating for us to look at the journal and not be able to read the articles, as they are in Russian. It would be of very great interest for our members to know more about piano teaching in Russia, from very beginning to advanced levels and about many other aspects such as memorising, practising, technical training, psychology of teaching and performance and many other topics.

Our piano students at the Conservatory levels or in other Institutions or Arts Faculties receive not only training in instrumental performance but all of them have to study 'Methodics of Teaching' – what in the West is known as Instrumental Pedagogy. I think that Piano Pedagogy should be given more emphasis in every country and piano teachers should get thorough training courses, particularly teachers specialising in working with children from their first piano lessons.

In the Music Schools, all children learn first *Solfège* – sight singing – before starting their instrumental lessons. The teaching of beginners is in the hands of specialised teachers, well trained; thus the pupils' first lessons are not given by 'any one who can play the piano'. (The 'lady next door' as it is known in EPTA). This explains the very high standard of playing of Russian children at international competitions.

Piano teaching in Russia seems to be at a mega-level, considering the enormous number of pupils in Music Schools and in Higher Education Institutions, before reaching the Music Academies, such as Tchaikowsky Conservatoire in Moscow or those in other main cities. What is the status of teachers?

Piano teachers encounter more and more difficulties throughout Russia due to the economic conditions. Music Schools, where most children from the age of 6 receive their musical education, are getting less funding than they had in the past, thus parents are expected now to contribute to their children's tuition.

The fact that parents are supporting their children's studies means that they are also following closely their development. All this is very welcome as long that they do not put too much pressure on the child to 'achieve'. The Music Schools keep a sharp eye on such parents, but a close collaboration between teacher and parents is recommended for the child's benefit.

Competitions seem to be the goal of teachers, pupils and parents. What are your views on having so many competitions at all levels, in every country?

I do not think that competitions are good for very young children. I do agree that it is important for them to learn to perform from the very beginning, playing the pieces they learn first in the class, in front of the other pupils. They also have to perform at assessments, examinations, in public concerts when parents and friends are invited, thus they get used from the very early stages to play in front of an audience. This should be a good training for future public concerts, and, eventually, by the time they are selected to take part in national or international competitions they have gained the necessary experience and their confidence had been built up in the right direction.

By that time, they have developed their technique, their musicianship, and they are ready to face audiences and juries without the stress which would otherwise affect their lives.

When I said that I do not think competitions are good for very young children if their teachers are too anxious to push a talented pupil, to show his or her standing in the profession as a teacher. We then have those ambitious parents who put a lot of pressure on their children expecting them to win every time they sit for such contests, which can be so damaging to the pupils. I often remark that competitions are more for the parents or for the teachers than for the children!

Every teacher has to give a lot of attention to their pupils preparing them for their examinations and other assessments and for other concerts or festivals. Moreover, if students are preparing for a career, competitions become part of their training. This seems to be the only way they can get the right exposure, to be heard by the right audiences and sometimes they may appear on television or radio even if they do not win a prize.

We talked about teaching in Russia and about the role of teachers. What is the status of students and how do they manage to continue their studies when the economic condition affects the Ministry of Culture and Education grants ?

These precarious conditions seem to be everywhere, not only in Russia, although we were privileged for many years under the Soviet regime and afterwards, when music and arts were at the top of the priorities for grants and sponsorship from the government. Music schools flourished and more and more children were encouraged to study music from a very early age, thus piano playing also flourished throughout the country.

The Music schools are still continuing as before; the teachers work just as hard, but these days, the grants are not sufficient and parents have to contribute to their children's music education . Perhaps this is not a bad thing as they do take greater interest and they make sure that the practising is done regularly. The main concern and worry is that the government might decide to cut the number of Music Schools, which means that many teachers may become redundant. In the past, all students who finished the college or conservatoire were assured of a job in a Music School, although it may be in a remote part of the country.

This is not possible now; there are more potential teachers than jobs. Yet I understand that in the Western countries the situation is worse and most young teachers have to start somewhere, they have to teach privately, and that is if they can get pupils.

In spite of all these difficulties ahead, the number of students applying to study at Higher Education establishments is considerable. Only at the Tchaikowsky Conservatoire several hundreds sat for the entrance examination. We have a very high level of competition to enter in the Moscow Conservatoire. There are bursaries for those who satisfy the jury and this year 38 students were admitted as scholars. These students will have regular lessons with a professor and will continue their studies for five years to obtain the Diploma. They are the elite of Russian performers and are helped to take part in the important competitions and eventually this will help them to start their career. Those who obtain lower marks are allowed to take courses at the Moscow Conservatoire but they have to pay for their tuition.

Does this mean that the Tchaikowsky Conservatoire has two tiers of students?

It is not really so, it only means that the outstanding pianists are already giving concerts, they are really professionals and they embark on their career while still students in the Conservatoire, as it often happens when they win a prestigious competition like the Tchaikowsky, Van Cliburn, Leeds, or others. Their successes reflect the high level of Russian piano school. But, as in so many institutions, there are quite a few good pianists although not of the same calibre as the scholars, and these are also given the opportunity to study at the Moscow Conservatoire, but they have to pay for their tuition. I understand that this is the norm in most European countries and in USA, where students have to take a loan.

What is it expected of the students to obtain their diploma?

To obtain the diploma after five years of studies, the students have to sit for their annual examinations abiding by the rules of the Conservatoire with regard to the repertoire, although they have the liberty to choose the works of the composers they perform. After all, the piano repertoire is vast and there are many works they can select to suit their personalities or their abilities.

There is a curriculum which gives guidance as to what technical studies are to be included in every year's examinations and what styles – such as Bach, the classics and romantic composers and, in final years, 20th century and *avant garde* music, but the choice of programme for examinations or recitals is left to the students and their professors to decide. For the final year, all students have to present one or two recitals and perform a Concerto with the Orchestra .

You have told us about teaching in Russia and the training of piano teachers . What about your own first years at the piano?

My first years at the piano were rather unusual. At the age of 6 I entered the Music School where I met the most wonderful teacher, Tamara Rogal-Levitskaya, a very good pianist, student of the great pianist and professor, Lev Oborin. I was so thrilled to have lessons with her and I must have progressed very fast trying to please her. She was very encouraging and all I wanted at that time was 'to be like my teacher'. But then the saddest thing happened. My father was sent to USA, at the Soviet Embassy, so the whole family followed. I just cried and cried and asked to be allowed to stay in Moscow to study music.

In the end my parents agreed and I then went to Moscow with my brother who had to continue his education at the State School – so there I was, aged just 7, having to do everything, practising the piano, doing my school work, as well as cleaning the house and cooking for the two of us! I was so happy studying with my beloved teacher, learning many pieces and progressing very fast under her guidance that I did not mind any difficulties.

You have a young daughter who loves the piano and she is now at the Music School of the Tchaikowsky Conservatory. Would you allow your daughter to go through such an experience?

Certainly not. The situation is so very different these days. No parent would be allowed, by law, to leave two young children alone in a house for several months! Perhaps these days we are more protective of our children than our parents were during the Soviet era. All I know is that it did not harm us, on the contrary. My brother was a little older than me and the two of us grew very close, we actually looked after one another. We really benefited from such an experience, it made us feel independent and able to cope with difficulties we met later on life.

I had to leave the Music School and Tamara who actually encouraged me. She thought that I have learnt enough from her and it was time to move on to the Music College where I met another highly interesting young teacher, Dmitry Blagoy, a student of Alexandr Goldweizer. I learnt a lot from him and my technique and my piano playing developed and I started to win the college competitions as well as national ones. Afterwards I was accepted at the Moscow Conservatory where I studied with Professor Eugene Malinin, a student of Heinrich Neuhaus – thus, during my studies I have received both the Russian and the German approach to piano technique.

After two years as a student of Professor Malinin, he took me as his assistant and at the same time I was asked to teach in the Accompaniment class, where I still teach, as well as teaching piano. That was in 1982.

You excelled in your studies and you won several important international Piano competitions, among them the Geneva; and you made history by winning the first Rachmaninov Competition in Soviet Russia. You have succeeded in developing your own career as a pianist, teacher and in recent years, since you have become President of EPTA Russia , you have made new contacts both for you and for the Russian pianists and your fame has spread throughout the European EPTA countries and beyond Europe.

Indeed I have made so many new contacts professionally, thanks to EPTA, that I am now invited to give concerts and master classes, or sit on juries not only at EPTA conferences but throughout the year in different countries. Although I have to work very hard to keep EPTA Russia going, every effort has been very worth while. It has brought me enormous satisfaction both artistically and personally. The new friends I have met through EPTA have been a great source of inspiration as we, performers or teachers, learn constantly and meeting such outstanding artists and pedagogues has taught me great lessons. And for this I am very grateful.

What do you think about the future of piano teaching?

I think it will go on as it is now for quite some time in spite of the difficulties encountered and, particularly of the changes in the structure of the society in general. Yet, I cannot believe that piano teaching will ever die, there will always be dedicated teachers who will continue to teach for the love of it, even without any payment, and as long as pianos and pupils exist, piano teaching will also go on.

And as long as EPTA continues its work bringing all of us together, pianists and teachers from many parts of the world, encouraging us to play and to teach, there is no danger that the piano teaching profession may disappear. And certainly, not in the 21st Century.

Piano Journal VOL 25 NO 78 2005

The Glasnost Experience
Tatiana Nikolaeva, Lev Vlasenko, Alexander Satz, Boris Berezovsky, Eugheni Kisin, Ana Kantor

To be in the USSR now is, I believe, every musician's wish and I consider myself privileged to have recently spent two most revealing weeks in Moscow and Leningrad. Sadly, lack of time and the very cold weather that interrupted many internal flights stopped me from visiting other places.

As this was my first visit to the USSR I wanted to make use of every moment to get acquainted with the artistic and cultural wealth of the two cities. Thus I managed to spend some time in the Hermitage Museum in Leningrad, with its extraordinary collection of works of Art, superbly displayed in the old palaces of the Tzars, the Dostoevsky and Pushkin Houses with most valuable documents relating to their life and creative output, and the Pushkin Museum in Moscow, the Lenin Museum, the Tolstoy Literary Museum where I had the greatest surprise: photos of great pianists Rachmaninov, and Wanda Landowska, playing duets with the great writer. I saw the great 'tourist' sites like the Kremlin, Red Square with its never-ending crocodile of pilgrims passing through the Lenin Mausoleum. What I really loved was walking through the Moscow streets, travelling on the Metro and going to the gigantic store 'Gum', mixing with the crowds.

My main objective, though, was to meet as many musicians as possible – professors, teachers, students – to watch some classes at the conservatories and to have the opportunity to talk about mutual problems concerning our profession. Yet, my everyday experiences went much further, having met people from various walks of life, from the humble chambermaid of the hotel of the people in the street always ready to help me if they thought I had lost my way, to the highly acclaimed 'People's artists' – musicians and actors. The reaction to a 'foreign' guest was the same: great warmth, a broad smile and an immense eagerness to communicate. If this is *glasnost* or the result of *glasnost*, then we should be grateful that it has happened and that it is still happening. There were some exciting coincidences. I did not have a pre-arranged appointment to visit the Tchaikovsky Conservatory in Moscow but, as I was passing by with my guide, she very kindly stopped the driver and we walked inside the majestic building. The porter did not really understand what we wanted, but as luck would have it just at that moment one of the professors came down the stairs and, being told about my coming from London, offered to take me to see one of the professors who spoke English. He was none other than **Professor Lev Vlassenko**, the very man I hoped to meet while in Moscow! (He is known in this country as he has several times been on the jury of the Leeds International Piano competition). He invited me to his studio – an impressive room with four grand pianos and the walls covered with portraits of the famous pianists and composers who have used this studio since the Conservatory's beginnings. Three of the pianos are in constant use (Professor Vlassenko is proud to have pianos of such quality) but the fourth one is only played on rare occasions – it is a finer instrument bought as a memorial to his professor, Jakob Flier, whose successor he is at present.

We were both very excited about our meeting, trying to talk about so many things at the same time, while the poor student who came for his lesson was almost forgotten. He went on practising, oblivious of what was going on around him. Lev Vlassenko was very enthusiastic about EPTA and about my proposal to get together with colleagues from various conservatories in the USSR to try to establish EPTA USSR. He promised to get immediately in touch with the right cultural departments which could be of some assistance, to discuss also with the Dean of the Conservatory how the Institution could be associated with such a project.

We arranged to meet as soon as I returned from Leningrad, where an appointment with the Deputy Director of the Rimsky-Korsakov Conservatory had been arranged for the next day. To reach Leningrad, most people travel by the night-sleeper, very comfortable trains, so that one arrives next morning rested, ready to get on with whatever jobs have been arranged. Arriving early morning in Leningrad, I was struck by the beauty of the superbly planned city (Peter the Great designed all the plans) enhanced by the glowing white snow. My visit to the Conservatory, a fine building with many large halls and corridors, reminding us of its great musical and historical tradition, was another important event for me. The Deputy Director (Pro-Rektor), Professor Genausti Napoleonovici Jalvis, received me in his office, to-

305

gether with the Head of Keyboard, Professor Igor Lebedev. Both expressed great interest in my proposal – to work towards establishing EPTA USSR – and Professor Jalvis, himself a pianist, is most anxious that Leningrad should play an important role in the founding of EPTA USSR as he believes, as we do, that representatives of all areas should be included. He is very proud to be at the helm of this famous institution with whom some of the greatest Russian musicians have been associated: Tchaikovsky, Rimsky-Korsakov, Glazounov, the great violinist and pedagogue Leopold Auer – who gave the world violinist like Heifetz, Milstein, Oistrach, Lasserson, to mention only a few. He took me on a conducted tour of the Conservatory, which recently had been visited by Leonard Bernstein and the Rt. Hon. Edward Heath, who conducted the Conservatory Orchestra, and afterwards he introduced me to **Professor Leonid Simtsev's** piano class. The lesson was conducted as a masterclass, one student performing while the others listened, taking notes of what the professor said, marking everything on their music. The student – in her first year at the Conservatory – played Brahms' *Paganini Variations* (Book 1)with great aplomb and impressive technique. I liked that Professor Simtsev allowed her to perform the whole work and only afterwards made some comments, illustrating them – admirably – on the second piano. Both Professor Simtsev and his students showed interest in my studies in how to cope with physical and psychological tensions in performance. I was allowed to work with the young pianist, who admitted that she experienced tiredness and discomfort while playing the technically demanding passages and that she could not really project her playing as she would have wanted to because she was rather anxious to do her best. This did not help! I showed her my simple technique on how to liberate the wrists and arm when playing, how to bring the body into a state of balance and, particularly, how to release tension around the mouth and the jaws, playing with lips slightly parted so that she could 'breathe with the music', not against it. In no time everything seemed easy and her physical comfort as well as her anxiety disappeared. Professor Simtsev then showed us how he copes with the physical 'tensions' when playing chords demanding great sonority, and we all had a very interesting exchange.

Returning to Moscow, I arrived punctually at the Conservatory at the appointed time with Lev Vlassenko. He was working with three students who were preparing for one of the important recitals as part of their curriculum. They had to play one of the obligatory pieces, Tchaikovsky's *The Seasons* and it was interesting for me to hear three different interpretations, each one with its particular qualities, yet convincingly performed. They also played some Classical works, Mozart's C major sonata K.330 and A minor K.310, as well as some Russian composers – Scriabin, Prokofiev, Rachmaninov.

It was interesting to watch Professor Vlassenko working with his students. As at the Leningrad Conservatory, the students played their programmes without being stopped. Only afterwards did he discuss various points, illustrating them at the other piano while the student was trying to do as the master told him. I was surprised that Lev Vlassenko did not try to impose any views on the interpretation.

In Mozart's A minor sonata the student took a very slow tempo in the Finale, which is marked *Presto* in every edition. When I commented on it Lev just smiled: 'You see, we do not aim at imposing a certain interpretation. If this young pianist likes this tempo, well, he must be free to experiment. You must agree that this was, after all, a highly musical performance.' He also explained that the pianists accepted to continue their training in the Conservatory had many years of professional teaching, from the age of six or even five, in the specialist Music School and afterwards, from the age of fourteen or fifteen in the Vocational Schools, where they are taught by very experienced teachers. To be accepted into the Conservatory they must possess a highly developed technique and a broad repertoire within their own 'Vocational Schools' or at National and International competitions. Those who enter this highest institution are going in the profession as performers and/or teachers in other conservatories or music schools throughout the country. In fact, what he was trying to say was that here are young musicians who are trained to perform at a high artistic level, so that they can be selected to participate in prestigious international competitions. All three students he considered 'competition material'.

What impressed me most was not the very high standard of technical achievement of each one of these pianists – this I expected – but the very relaxed atmosphere, the friendliness that existed between student and teacher. This I did not expect. I imagined the students treating their master with such awe, never daring to utter a word or question what was said, the teacher exerting his authority all through the lesson and not always in a very gentle manner.

Professor Vlassenko emphasised that unless there is mutual respect and understanding between teacher and student, there cannot be any successful relationship, and above all the student must trust his teacher.

In the Tchaikovsky Conservatoire there are at present four Chairs with the four main professors, apart from the other approximately fifty piano teachers. Professor Vlassenko himself has four assistants. One of them is pianist Vladimir Ovchinnikov, first prize-winner at the Leeds International Piano Competition. The other three are Eliza Virsaladze, who has succeeded the famous Heinrich Neuhaus, Tatiana Nikolaeva, who followed in Professor Goldenweiser's Chair and who teaches in the same studio in which she came as a pupil of Goldenweiser at the age of thirteen, and Victor Merzanov, who is quite well-known in Britain after his memorable masterclasses last year. I could not see Professors Merzanov and Virsaladze – they were out of town – but I had long talks with Lev Vlassenko and Tatiana Nikolaeva about their careers and about their responsibilities as professors as such an institution.

Lev Vlassenko comes from Georgia. As a child he showed great ability and he was accepted at the Central Music School where he first studied with Anastasia Virsaladze and later on, until the age of 18, at the Vocational School, with Bashkirov. His teachers suggested that he should continue his training at the Tchaikovsky Conservatory in Moscow, where he was accepted into Jakob Flier's class. While still a student he also attended classes at the Institute of Foreign Languages where he graduated as an interpreter in three languages: English, Spanish and French. Music was what he really wanted to do and after winning some important international prizes (1st Prize at the Liszt competition in Budapest, 2nd prize at the Tchaikovsky Competition, another prize at the Van Cliburn Competition) his career took an impressive turn. He was appointed Jakob Flier's assistant and got many engagements both in the USSR and abroad.

He often travels abroad giving concerts and masterclasses or being on juries at international competitions, but he believes that he must give a great deal of his attention and his energy to his students. At present he has fifteen students in the Conservatory and also he teaches several youngsters from the Central Music School which is attached to the Conservatory. The very talented pupils have the best opportunities, studying with some of the most outstanding pedagogues as well as being able to perform not only in the Music School but also in the Conservatory. Thus new generations of pianists are thoroughly prepared for the profession.

When I asked how the selection of pianists is done for international competitions Professor Vlassenko explained how the system works. First, each professor recommends the pianists which he would like to present at the Conservatory auditions when all the professors are judging. Only a small number are then selected among the winners to be sent to a further stage: a national competition, where candidates from all Soviet Conservatories are heard by a jury composed of a number of personalities of the world of music who decide which pianists should be sent to which competition. This explains why sometimes there are several Soviet candidates and, in Professor Vlassenko's words – 'At this stage we look for personality, as the majority of performers are experienced players, with fine pianistic qualities. What matters is how they project, how they communicate to and with the audience.'

I then went to meet **Tatiana Nikolaeva** and I had the pleasure of spending part of an afternoon with her in the studio not unlike Vlassenko's, with two grand pianos and with many historical portraits on the wall. The largest, in the middle in an impressive gilt frame, was that of her professor, Goldenweiser. Professor Nikolaeva had only arrived the previous evening from a series of concerts in France and was leaving next day for Berlin where she was going to perform the '32' Beethoven Sonatas. Yet she found time to do a day's teaching and to talk to me! There were only two students when I arrived. A pianist on the 'advanced course' played the Schumann *Toccata* in C and Mendelssohn *Scherzo* no. 2 in E minor (from *Fantasies* or *Caprices* op. 16). Tatiana listened with real enjoyment and praised the student for her exciting performance. Here again, the lesson took the form of a 'concert performance' as if a student never dares to appear in front of the master with a piece in the process of learning. I would have loved to hear how the teacher guides such an advanced student when a work has not been fully mastered. Or perhaps this does not happen at the Tchaikovsky Conservatory.

The next student was a 16-year old pupil from the Central Music School who had been accepted by Nikolaeva only from the beginning of the academic year. She considers him a highly talented youngster and is very interested in helping him develop a technique that could serve his innate musicality. She insists that a diet of studies is absolutely vital (Czerny, Cramer, Pishna etc.), but she also thinks that this young student will greatly benefit from learning Chopin *Etudes*. He played op. 10 No. 5 in G flat and op. 25 no. 1 in A flat and this time I had a glimpse of Tatiana's approach. She made him play slowly, emphasising the need to listen, always striving to produce beautiful sounds. She did not explain how he should practice to achieve fluency but made him hear the music, that all-important music. It became clear to me that once a student is accepted into Tatiana's class, the emphasis is on making music of a high calibre and that music and technique are one.

Professor Nikolaeva talked about her early studies as a child, with her mother who was a concert pianist, also a pupil of Goldenweiser. When her mother brought Tatiana to Goldenweiser at the age of 13, he must have been very impressed with her playing and he accepted her as a student, but the Second World War broke out and both mother and daughter had a very rough time. Yet, in spite of the hardships, she managed to play occasionally and even do some teaching. Only when the war ended could she resume her studies and her professor took her as his assistant. She always found teaching a rewarding experience, but now she would like to use all her energies to perform. 'Yet how can one not be happy when teaching such sensitive, dedicated youngsters?' said Tatiana, almost apologising that a moment earlier she talked only about her concert career. Like many other artists, she seems to manage doing both, and very successfully! She has been associated with the Mozarteum in Salzburg for the past 15 years in both capacities, as performer and teacher, and wherever she goes now in the West she conducts masterclasses in music colleges as well as giving recitals.

Tatiana Nikolaeva talks about her professor with deep respect and admiration – he has published many editions of all the classical sonatas which are still in use by the students in the USSR, where it almost impossible to get Urtext editions – and she likes to emphasise that all through her studies she had only one teacher, Goldenweiser. Although she herself conducts many masterclasses, she does not believe that musicians should go from one teacher to another in search of their 'identity'. I expressed my opinion that it is important for young performers to be exposed to other views, not only the ones of their teacher, and she agreed that it is vital that they should listen to many other artists and to different interpretations, but ultimately they must decide for themselves. We also talked about the problems confronting the students in conservatories in the USSR. Most of them are very ambitious and hope to make a name in the profession as performers and the stress is sometimes damaging.

Stage-fright seems to be the greatest concern among these young musicians as so much depends on each audition or public concert. On the other hand, there are jobs waiting for all those accepted to train in conservatories. Teachers retire much earlier (men at 60 or even 55 and women at 55) to make room for new generations but, some of the jobs are in remote places which do not give them enough scope to develop as performers or to be heard by important critics or international impresarios. After all, this is every young artist's dream, to make a name in the profession.

Tatiana Nikolaeva then talked about the glasnost and what it has brought to artists and intellectuals. She herself had been one of the privileged musicians who have been allowed to travel extensively and had been in contact with many other artists in other countries, but now this will be possible for many more. EPTA is the right organisation to offer these opportunities and she would very much hope to be part of EPTA USSR and work towards its realisation.

My next appointment was at the Gnessin Institute, another high academic institute in Moscow which enjoys great prestige both in the USSR and abroad, having well-known artists on the staff, among them, the violinist Vladimir Spivakov and the pianist **Alexander Sats**.

Boris Berezovsky, the winner of the fourth prize at the Leeds Competition took me to Professor Sats, with whom he had studied before entering the Tchaikovsky Conservatory, where he is now a second year student in Professor Eliza Virsaladze's class. Boris wanted to rehearse his programme for a duet recital with his friend Misha, a student at the Gnessin Institute, and Professor Sats very kindly allowed them to play in his class. When I arrived, the small studio was full, crammed with five or six ladies following the lesson with scores in their hands, whila a young girl played Beethoven Sonata op. 110 in A flat. I did not have the chance to hear him teach as, after only a few phrases he asked the student to postpone her lesson as he had promised to listen to the Duo. I was introduced to the group of listeners, five piano teachers from Novo-Sibirsk Music Schools, who had travelled for a whole week to come to Moscow to listen to some classes. They explained that this is often done; teachers are encouraged to watch lessons at important conservatories while professors from main colleges are sent to remote music schools to give masterclasses; thus a high standard of teaching is maintained throughout the Union. This time they were in for a treat as Boris and Misha were rehearsing for an important concert on which their participation in the Belgrade Piano Duet Competition depended. They had prepared a varied programme which included Mozart's Sonata in B flat (four hands, one piano) which they played with verve and charm, although the tempi were rather on the fast side. Professor Sats remarked on the need to maintain a steady tempo emphasising the importance of listening to one another to play melodic lines with the same quality of tone and expressing the same mood or character in imitative passages. I also heard them in Rachmaninov Suite op.5 for two pianos, a work which suited the duo splendidly and which they played with great panache and the right feeling.

Professor Sats jokingly remarked that when two such artists play he can relax in his chair, and just enjoy the performance. But this did not last long. As soon as he began to discuss the work, he got up, illustrated some new phrasing, suggesting different fingering in some passages, or pointed out how to achieve a better balance between the two instruments. I, for one, was amazed to see that whatever passage he mentioned, he illustrated from memory, whether there were a few bars from piano one part, or from piano two. Was this only a short term memory, having just heard the passages played, or had he really such an extraordinary knowledge of the repertoire?

Here again I found a very enthusiastic response to my proposal regarding EPTA USSR and Professor Sats, as well as the teachers from Siberia, stressed the need for such an organisation within the Soviet Union which will give them the possibility to travel abroad to meet colleagues from other countries. In answer, I stated the importance for European teachers of watching classes in Soviet Music Schools from early beginnings to intermediate standards, to learn something from these highly experienced trainers of virtuoso performers. Of course only very talented children get into Music Schools, yet unless the teaching is of a high level even great talents may get lost on the way.

This was a happy meeting and we parted on a note of hope that this was perhaps only the first of many more such encounters.

From Gnessin Institute – which also trains class music teachers as well as instrumental teachers – Boris took me to the Gnessin School of Music where children of all ages are admitted. I was fortunate to meet the now famous teacher, **Ana Kantor**, and observe her giving a lesson to her prodigy student, **Evgheni Kissin**, who has already performed with conductors like Karajan and others in most European cities. He is now seventeen and this is his last year at the Gnessin School. The lesson was a revelation. Evgheni played Liszt's *Spanish Rhapsody* with great virtuosity and at the same time with poetry and fire but Ana Kantor was not satisfied. She worked with him on that majestic opening until he understood that the intensity of the emotion had to be matched by the right gesture, a free swing of the arms from the top register, followed by a controlled fall playing the chords in the low register with firm hands and fingers, clearly voicing each note of the chord, each finger producing a different sound. He repeated this several times, until both were satisfied, although Evgheni remarked that there was a pause between the two chords. 'There is pause and pause' – answered Ana Kantor – 'but the music must be continuous even though a pause is respected.' She did not want a chopped sound and she made this clear to her pupil. From time to time she would comment on his posture, reminding him to hold the head up, with no tension at the shoulders or the sternum area, with arms extended, well balanced over the keyboard and to play without watching his hands or the keys. His hands changed their shape depending on what he was playing. The hand was almost flat, yet the 'bridge' was noticeable, with elongated fingers when playing a cantilena, and gripping the keys in depth in such a way that one could almost feel the strings vibrate; or, when playing chords, the fingers looked almost vertical, firm and strong, superbly controlled by this fine musical mind. Evgheni listened to his teacher as if every word was unravelling the mystery of a great interpretation and although his first performance was absolutely amazing, one could notice how it grew in depth and intensity while they were working together. It was interesting to observe that the teacher hardly ever illustrated on the piano, but, very often she would choreograph the gesture, in a broad arch, playing on the closed lid, making clear what sort of touch was demanded.

I wanted to know more about this prodigy pianist and Ana Kantor told me that he only started to have lessons at the age of seven. His ten years old sister was a pupil of Ana at the Gnessin School and the boy played all her pieces by ear. He said that 'he couldn't help learning them as she played them so many times'. The main problem was to teach him to read music and to realise that the written music had to be learnt. Within three or four years his progress was so amazing that he was invited to give many concerts, to play with most orchestras in the USSR, and to make a number of recordings. Soon his fame spread outside Russia and he had been in great demand ever since.

Once again I was struck by the beautiful relationship between teacher and pupil. Although Ana Kantor talked with authority, she did everything with such warmth and care as if all she wanted was to help him achieve his own desire to play as well as he could. I could not help remarking that, after hearing so much about this prodigy and seeing photos and his name on dozens of records, I expected to meet an arrogant little boy, full of his own importance. In one of his interviews I even read that 'he was not interested in competitions as he had managed to build a career 'without having to get a first prize!'

I was profoundly moved to meet a humble musician, working hard to improve his performance and particularly to hear him say: 'Everything I know and everything I do I owe to my teacher and I know that I can learn so much more from her.' Indeed, wherever Evgheni goes, his teacher goes with him, not to supervise his practising or go through the music again and again, but simply because he loves having her next to him when the audiences applaud him or when he relaxes between concerts.

We talked about his future studies after leaving the Gnessin School of Music. He had been accepted in the first year at the Tchaikovsky

Conservatory where he will be working side by side with other students. I was wondering how he will conform for another four or five years, respecting this well-established tradition, where geniuses like Richter, Gilels must have listened in awe to their professor Heinrich Neuhaus and many others before them when they were working with previous generations of masters. Perhaps this is what makes the Russian School of Piano what is it.

When I took my leave from Ana Kantor I asked her if she would like to address EPTA members when in London with Evgheni. 'I don't think I am able to talk about my work which I have done for so many years and I am still doing day after day. This is the only thing I can do and I would not know what to say about it', was her answer. Indeed this is a work of great dedication, as she said, 'day after day', each lesson adding something new and valuable and she could not talk about it in a nutshell, in just one hour or so.

How I wished I could see her working with other students! However, this was a very worthwhile experience, one of the highlights of my visit to the USSR.

Boris Berezovsky, who has been my chaperone through Moscow's music schools, invited me to visit his home to meet his parents, both musicians. At first I was a little apprehensive and even worried in case it was not good for them to associate too closely with a foreign visitor. But, to my great joy and pleasant surprise, I found that anyone can invite foreign visitors to their home and telephoning is now an easy way of communication, no one being afraid of being 'overheard'. Russians, like most people in Eastern or Central Europe, are very hospitable and I was received with great warmth and friendliness. Boris' mother had prepared a delicious meal and although we could not understand one another's language, the conversation flowed, thanks to Boris' interpreting. The parents have every reason to be proud of their young son's achievements so far and they would do everything possible to further his career. Fortunately, having won such a prize at the Leeds Competition, he was offered a number of concerts in the U.K. where he will come again for a concert tour in October this year.

His main concern is that he still has so much to learn and, as a second year student at the Conservatory, he has a few more years of study. He loves working with his teacher but he also realises that he needs to be exposed to other experiences and influences. He admits that he is one of the privileged young musicians in the USSR, having been able to travel and perform (in Yugoslavia where we first met and in the UK) as well as having been with other young pianists during the competition with whom he had some valuable exchanges and discussions. I stayed until late at Boris' house; we talked about many other topics and he was greatly interested in my studies of many years. I gave him some articles which I had brought with me and he was eager to learn more about the work of ISSTIP, and he would like to see such studies initiated in the Tchaikovsky Conservatory and in other music schools to give students the opportunity to learn how to cope with their problems before it is too late. However, these students are exposed to the public from a very early age and they know, somehow, what to expect from their performances. It is the strain of continually competing that is putting so much pressure on their stamina and if there is a way to combat this, why not learn about it? He then played for me the first movement of the Tchaikovsky Sonata. A fine majestic performance, not by a nineteen year old student with an inquisitive mind, but by a mature artist, intently involved in the music which he communicated with his whole being.

Through Boris I met an English pianist James Kirkby, a student at the Tchaikovsky Conservatory in his second year. It was most interesting to see how a foreign student fits into this stressful milieu, with hundreds of musicians, all very ambitious and having one goal – to achieve fame. James – a former Royal Academy Student in Hamish Milne's class – is a British Council scholar and this gives him a splendid opportunity to study in Moscow. He lives in the students hostel, having to share a room with a Russian student, a very good arrangement so they get to know each other and learn about their different ways of life. I wanted to know more about his studies and whether he found that his standard of virtuosity was not as high as that of colleagues. This was not his main concern. While he admitted that there are a number of fine, sensitive pianists in the Conservatory, there are also quite a few who managed to get in although they do not possess outstanding qualities. His first year in the Conservatory was not a very happy one. His knowledge of Russian was too rudimentary so he could hardly communicate with colleagues or with his professor. He also could not conform to the system of bringing a new piece to every lesson. He would have liked to be taught how to work, how to approach his studies, but this was not done. He had to summon up his courage and ask to study with another teacher, who would not be so demanding in 'quantity', building up a large repertoire, but who would like to work with the student on several works in depth. Working with Elisa Virsaladze is more suitable to his temperament and he is much happier. He has made many friends and he will be sad to leave Moscow at the end of the academic year, particularly now after witnessing so many important changes. We sat for quite some time talking over a coffee in the Conservatory canteen, a small but charming place where students and professors mingle and queue together for strong Russian tea, coffee and sandwiches – red Manchurian fish roe seems to be cheap – served by smiling girls at the counters.

We walked out together into the Moscow streets covered in soft, deep snow, still talking, both feeling that we were part of great, important times.

CAROLA GRINDEA
Piano Journal NO 28 1998